The Imagined Past

Also by Alan Holder:

Three Voyagers in Search of Europe: A Study of Henry James, Ezra Pound, and T. S. Eliot
A. R. Ammons

The Imagined Past

Portrayals
of Our History
in Modern American Literature

Alan Holder

Lewisburg
BUCKNELL UNIVERSITY PRESS
London and Toronto: Associated University Presses

© 1980 by Associated University Presses, Inc.

PS

Associated University Presses, Inc.   228
Cranbury, New Jersey 08512

H57

Associated University Presses
69 Fleet Street
London EC4Y 1EU, England   H6

Associated University Presses
Toronto M5E 1A7, Canada

Library of Congress Cataloging in Publication Data

Holder, Alan, 1932-
  The imagined past.

  Bibliography: p.
  Includes index.
  1. American literature—20th century—History and
criticism. 2. History in literature. 3. United
States in literature. I. Title.
PS228.H57H6   810'.9'358   78-75202
ISBN 0-8387-2319-5

Printed in the United States of America

for Deborah, David, *and* Nancy
part of the imagined future

Contents

Acknowledgments

Most of this book was written over a long series of summer "vacations." The work of the first summer was aided by a research grant from Williams College. Two other summer research grants were awarded to me by the City University of New York. I am grateful to these institutions for their support.

I wish to thank the Columbia University Library and the New York Public Library for the use of their resources.

Several of the book's chapters have appeared—in somewhat different form—as articles in various journals, and are being reprinted with their kind permission. Chapters 1 and 8 appeared in *American Quarterly,* copyright 1967 (and 1968), Trustees of the University of Pennsylvania; Chapter 7 in *South Atlantic Quarterly,* copyright 1969 by Duke University Press; Chapter 9 in *Concerning Poetry* (1969); Chapter 11 in *The New England Quarterly* (1971).

I also wish to thank the following publishers for having given me permission to quote from published works: New Directions and Hart-David, MacGibbon for William Carlos Williams, *In the American Grain,* copyright 1925 by James Laughlin; Random House, Inc. for William Faulkner, *Absalom, Absalom!* and *The Unvanquished,* Robert Penn Warren, *Brother to Dragons,* William Styron, *The Confessions of Nat Turner;* Swallow Press for Allen Tate, *The Fathers* and *Poems;* Harcourt Brace Jovanovich, Inc. for Eudora Welty, *The Robber Bridegroom,* "The Burning," and *The Wide Net and Other Stories,* Robert Lowell, *Lord*

9

Introduction

When he was in his early twenties, Ezra Pound apparently received a suggestion from his mother that he write an epic of the West, i.e., of America. From London, at the start of what was to become his long expatriation, the young poet replied: "Mrs. Columbia has no mysterious & shadowy past to make her interesting. . . . Epic of the West. It is as if I asked some one to write my biography. It is more as if I had asked them to do it 12 years ago." Whether he knew it or not, Pound, in this comment of 1908, was carrying into the twentieth century an observation about the relative thinness of American history that had been made by a number of earlier literary compatriots, including Washington Irving, James Fenimore Cooper, Nathaniel Hawthorne, and Henry James.

Despite the alleged blankness that confronted them when looking backward, these particular writers, with the exception of James, managed to create works that did draw (or at least appeared to) on the native past. Many other nineteenth-century American writers, largely under the influence of Sir Walter Scott, employed American historical themes (chiefly involving the Indians or the Revolution) in what may be seen as an expression of literary nationalism. The works that resulted from such appropriations of the American past partook heavily of legend, myth, romance, and melodrama. Only in a few instances did the use of these modes result in significant historical re-creation or illumination.

Irving's *A History of New York by Diedrich Knicker-*

11

bocker can be seen as a wry response to the antiquarianism of his day, the interest in local histories. Aware of the paucity of authentic native traditions, Irving offered comic, worked-up legendary material in his descriptions of the early Dutch settlers of America. We sometimes laugh with his narrator, Knickerbocker, but also at him, as he laments the passing of a golden age and calls his own times degenerate. His celebration of the past is hardly consistent with the pictures of it that he himself provides, which give us a decidedly unheroic view of the early days of our country. Irving's attitude toward the past here is satirical, but basically humorous and affectionate. He said he was interested in investing local scenes "with those imaginative and whimsical associations so seldom met with in our new country." Later in his career, Irving endowed other native scenes with a past conceived of as comic and picturesque. Both "Rip Van Winkle" and "The Legend of Sleepy Hollow" are set in "the past." But the story of Rip, in which Irving has domesticated a piece of European folklore, seems to partake of a certain timelessness (the changes wrought by the Revolution Rip has slept through are minimal), and the "Legend," as Daniel Hoffman has argued in *Form and Fable in American Fiction,* is really a portrayal of *"current* native character projected backwards in time. . . . " The pastness of "Legend" is mocked by Irving himself, who says that the story takes place "in a remote period of American history, that is to say, some thirty years since. . . . " In Irving, then, a concern with the American past manifests itself in terms of a playful imagination purveying comic fables of the picturesque. For one who had little quarrel with his present, there was no need to do more with the past.

The comic was not one of Cooper's strong points, and his treatment of American history, unlike Knickerbocker's humorous yearning for an earlier time, was informed by a serious, elegiac mood, a sense that real and often lamentable changes had taken place or were taking place in America.

Though he complained in *Notions of the Americans,* that there were "no annals for the historian" in our country, and "no obscure fictions for the writer of romance," he attempted to create significant images of the American past. In his Littlepage trilogy, he presented the case for having aristocratic families continue to exist in a democracy, celebrating them as they had lived in the middle of the eighteenth century, and seeing them threatened by the agitations of his own times.

Standing in paradoxical relation to the settled social order admired by Cooper in the Littlepage novels, is the hero of the Leather-Stocking tales, his more important rendering of the native past. Here, the source of values is not a society, mainly taken over from England, but Nature, embodied in the person of Natty Bumppo, Cooper's frontier hero. As Richard Chase observes, in *The American Novel and its Tradition,* Natty evolves from a real man, whose conception was influenced in part by stories that had sprung up about Daniel Boone, into "a general myth." He appears to embody for Cooper the best of early American possibilities, in his courage, stoicism, piety, and oneness with Nature. He partakes, in Chase's words, of "the abstract and ideal." But he is a doomed figure, disappearing before the onslaught of the American present, with its substitution of "civilization" for the wilderness and the culture of the Indian (whom Cooper views with ambivalence). Natty sees white society as superior to the ways of the Indian, but cannot be a part of it; he is, in effect, sacrificed to it. Cooper, then, while subscribing at one level to the dominant notion of history in nineteenth-century America, the idea of progress, presents in his Leather-Stocking tales an American past which offers a precious and heroic model incompatible with the inexorable development of his country. He gives us not so much a historical view as a dream of the country's past embodied in an isolated individual.

Henry Wadsworth Longfellow attempted, like Cooper, to

create a figure out of the American past who was larger than life, though his Hiawatha has not demonstrated anything like the staying power of Natty in the national imagination. Longfellow went much further than Cooper in removing his protagonist from history and setting him in a mythological context. A great number of works about the Indian had appeared before *Hiawatha,* but Longfellow was a pioneer in tapping the traditional stories of the American natives themselves, presenting a culture hero who, amid anthropomorphized settings, performed legendary exploits. For Longfellow, the American past, in the form of Indian folklore, provided a background of the picturesque, the "poetic," for an otherwise prosaic culture. Hiawatha is an idealized figure, the Indian, in Newton Arvin's words, as "Gentle Savage." Like Cooper's Natty, Hiawatha gives way before the westward movement of white civilization. He has a melancholy vision in which he sees his people scattered, warring with each other. But just as history proper enters the poem, with the coming of the white man, Longfellow ends his work, providing Hiawatha with a lovely exit. He does not die, but beautifully fades out of sight, becoming encased in the amber of legend. The nasty aspects of the Indian-white confrontation are avoided.

Besides the frontier and the Indian (as well as the American Revolution), the early days of New England constituted a major source of subject matter for nineteenth-century literature turned toward our past. Longfellow utilized this material in two very different ways. In "The Courtship of Miles Standish," more a contribution to schoolroom mythology than anything else, he drew on the Puritans for a story which is primarily a private drama of love and friendship, rather than the re-creation of another time and another place. Its focus is psychological rather than historical. It constitutes a pleasant tale, moving toward a pretty version of the timeless. When John Alden and Priscilla go off to their new home, Longfellow compares the scene to a picture of "the primitive, pastoral ages. . . ." He regards the couple as lovers in "the endless succession of lovers. . . ."

Something much more serious , indeed monumental, was in Longfellow's mind when he composed *The New England Tragedies*. This work (undoubtedly even less read today than *Hiawatha*), was supposedly meant to constitute the last part of a trilogy, *Christus,* a dramatization of the history of mankind's religious development. This final section was intended in some way to represent Charity (with the two preceding sections representing Faith and Hope, respectively). Leaving behind the legendary and pastoral modes of Longfellow's earlier treatments of the past, *John Endicott,* the first part of *The New England Tragedies,* tells of the Puritans' persecution of the Quakers. The second part, *Giles Corey of the Salem Farms,* deals with the witchcraft hysteria of 1692. All in all, neither of these two works possesses any distinction, but they do constitute a serious effort to portray some of the harsh facts of the American past, rather than simply looking to that past as a source of the picturesque, the charming, or the patriotic-heroic, qualities that were dominant in Longfellow's previous works (and in the historical pieces of his contemporary, John Greenleaf Whittier).

If Longfellow's *New England Tragedies* attempted to confront some of the uglier episodes of early America, they did so within his century's assumption that the principle of progress was operating in the unfolding of history (a doctrine subscribed to by such prominent historians as Prescott, Motley, and Parkman). Nathaniel Hawthorne addressed himself to the same manifestations of persecution in colonial New England that Longfellow dramatized, but without that comforting assumption, and with a more complex sensibility than the poet's (as evidenced, for example, if we compare Longfellow's idealized Quakers with Hawthorne's depiction of that sect in "The Gentle Boy"). And while Hawthorne's treatment of the New England past has its own elements of the picturesque, in the form of Gothic atmospherics and of romance, he brings to his fiction a critical consciousness that produced the most important examples of historical literature in nineteenth-century America. Rather than seeing the past as something simply left behind, which is a corollary of the idea of progress, Hawthorne viewed its events as having their consequences for the present, or as embodying elements which are recurring or ongoing in human existence, though his contemporaries might not have regarded them as such.

One of the great features of the American past, perhaps its greatest feature in Hawthorne's fiction, is our country's emergence as a separate cultural entity through its rejection of the Old World. This figures in one way or another in the tales "Endicott and the Red Cross," "The Gray Champion," "The Maypole of Merrymount," and "My Kinsman, Major Molineux," along with *The Scarlet Letter*. As Q. D. Leavis has pointed out in her essay "Hawthorne as Poet," Hawthorne finds early New England repressing or rejecting the folk and pagan components of European culture. (Interestingly enough, Hawthorne saw Europe as closer to Nature than was America, a notion that clearly set him apart from his American contemporaries, as well as from Cooper.) Through this rejection of Europe, in Hawthorne's view, America gained a greater rectitude, sense of reality, and self-reliance. It acquired a character that was finer but thinner than that of the Old World, this thinness manifesting itself to Hawthorne's eye in his own era. He shows an ambivalent response to this development, seeing in it both a great gain and a great loss for his country. (Michael Bell, in his *Hawthorne and the Historical Romance of New England,* finds him in his late works trying to overcome the consequences of an Endicott or Gray Champion, men who helped sever America's ties to Europe.)

Hawthorne's approach to the past, then, was partly a

matter of trying to define the nature of American culture by going back to its origins, its early differentiation from Europe. Included in these origins were instances of injustice, cruelty and violence, so that the birth of America was not for Hawthorne, as it was for his age, a comforting spectacle of liberty triumphing over tyranny. The evils committed by early Americans, both during the Puritan era and in the course of the Revolution, undercut the assumption that this country was to be a Utopia, in which the evils of Europe would simply be sloughed off. What the past testified to, and what it transmitted to the present, was human limitation, the inevitable conflict between the individual and society (as in *The Scarlet Letter*), or man's capacity for error or wrong-doing. In *The House of the Seven Gables,* the legacy of the past includes the consequences of an evil deed compounded by other such deeds in succeeding generations. As it unfolds, the book promises a very rich treatment of the past, con-ceiving of it in several ways: as a precious repository of human experience, as the source of paralysis and preten-tiousness in the present, as a series of recurring wrongs amounting to a hideous burden that needs to be cast off by enlightened people. But Hawthorne ultimately retreats from both his strong sense of the past and his radical questioning of the present, giving us a trivial happy ending. Neverthe-less, in his work taken as a whole, he exhibits an intense and consequential sense of the past.

Besides the early New England that engaged Hawthorne as well as others, the South figured prominently in the literature of the past produced by Americans of the nineteenth century. But there is little of interest to be found in the works centered on that region. William Gilmore Simms, who was influenced by Cooper, might be seen as having some historical importance because of his sense of the South as a distinct region which was evolving towards an ideal society. As such, he prefigures the Southern Agrarians of our own century. Also, his portrayal of certain Southern types might have helped establish them in that region's consciousness, to be more powerfully depicted by Faulkner. His works are heavily infused with elements of romance and melodrama that have not worn well.

In the years after the Civil War, the Old South appeared frequently in popular American literature as an idealized region. Note, for example, the works of Thomas Nelson Page and Joel Chandler Harris. Through the later nineteenth century and on into our own, readers were offered images of a charming and glamorous plantation society.

A writer who did not confine himself to such nostalgic images was George Washington Cable. Along with other local colorists of the post–Civil War period, Cable could paint pretty pictures of bygone days. But his novel *The Grandissimes* incorporates, besides its affection for the New Orleans of the early 1800s, a strong consciousness of the costs and injustices of a society marked by slavery. Showing a gift for social realism (though *The Grandissimes* is not devoid of sentimentality), Cable dramatizes the tangled and tortured relations between whites and blacks. Rather than presenting an idealized Southern aristocracy of the kind that figured prominently in lesser works, he looks at the irrationality, destructive pride, and violence that the upper class, for all its charm, was capable of. He shows an acute historical consciousness, focusing on the displacement of one social class by another during a particular period, and at the same time generates a sense of connection between the Old South and the region of his own day.

As with Hawthorne, it is a *critical* consciousness of the past that informs *The Grandissimes,* one aware of an earlier era's faults and weaknesses as well as of its virtues and attractions, capable of seeing the past as something other than a source of the picturesque or a dream region. To such a consciousness the past has been generated by the actions of flesh-and-blood human beings, and those actions have had consequences or implications for the American present, or for mankind in general.

In the course of the present century, a significant number of serious American literary artists have addressed themselves to our past. Unlike most of their well-known nineteenth-century predecessors, they have generally been able to take such a past for granted. (Pound is a kind of transitional figure here—initially echoing earlier laments about the paucity of American history, he came in time to draw on it.) This easy assumption of a history may be accounted for not only by our having, naturally, grown a century older, but by the accumulation of public events and the pace of cultural transformation having been so rapid as to further elongate our sense of time, seeming to place the earlier periods of our national existence at a distinct remove from our own, without necessarily obliterating all continuities.

The serious American writers of the earlier years of this century who were concerned with our past displayed a narrower version of the "critical consciousness" I have ascribed to Hawthorne and Cable; it was one specialized for attack. If they were able to assume that a substantial national record did indeed exist, it was for them largely a sorry one. Such a conviction manifested itself not so much in works of historical fiction or poetry, as in essays or books of cultural criticism. The chief figures here are Randolph Bourne, H. L. Mencken, Waldo Frank, and, perhaps most central, Van Wyck Brooks. Brooks's early works, beginning with *The Wine of the Puritans* (1908) and on through *The Ordeal of Mark Twain* (1920), depicted a culture blighted by Puritan and pioneer, a history exhibiting the triumph of materialism. Along with the other cultural critics, Brooks helped shape the rebellious, irreverent energies of the 1920s into an attack on the persisting "Puritanism" of America. Brooks's attention to the past came out of a concern for his present. His approach to American history may be seen as a searching out of the sources of the country's defects, the origins of those things that made for a fragmented culture which failed its people in general and its literary artists in particular.

In this book I endeavor to comment upon a substantial sampling of the noteworthy historical literature that has appeared in this century between World War I and the present, and that has focused on the American past. The works examined have been created by some of our most accomplished or ambitious figures—William Carlos Williams, William Faulkner, Allen Tate, Endora Welty, Robert Penn Warren, William Styron, John Barth, John Berryman, Charles Olson, and Robert Lowell. The sampling of writings discussed suggests the range, achievements, and failures of the native literature drawn from our history.

As with Hawthorne, the literary artists I deal with are often troubled by what their backward gaze reveals. Much in their works has sustained the spirit of attack that figured so prominently in the early Brooks and his contemporaries, though they have not necessarily concentrated on the same issues. Their imaginations are engaged by matters that have assumed particular weight in the contemporary apprehension of our past: the responses to the American wilderness, the displacement of the Indians, the relations between blacks and whites, the repeated eruption of violence, the conception and / or achievement of high possibilities in this land, and the fall from those possibilities. To a nation that has so persistently thought of itself as God's country, these writers and poets point out the part the Devil has had in its making.

But if they present us with a past that is considerably less than noble, if they derogate personages or events that have often been glorified, they produce an opposing effect as well. Even though they often attempt to debunk our past, they also aggrandize it, charging characters and actions drawn from our history with a special potency. Faulkner and Welty, who can mock such aggrandizing, themselves contribute to it.

Williams, Tate, Warren, and Barth, while sometimes intent on cutting the past down to size, allow room for the heroic, or at least for grand energies, though they may locate these in obscure places or perverse doings. Styron's and Berryman's protagonists are permitted to rise above their dubious surroundings. Olson and Lowell can find cause for pride in the very New England past that also pains them. Manifesting a desire to take a hard look at our history, these writers and poets are not totally immune to entrancement by it. What emerges from the works examined here, then, is a past that has been both deflated and made glamorous. All in all, it is larger than the present. For these literary artists, the need for something vital, vivid, resonant, something greater than their present seems able to afford, is ministered to by the historic.

With the exception of Williams's *In the American Grain,* which tends to think in terms of the American continent, the works I have chosen to discuss display a regional focus. The South in particular (though it is not a single South) figures again and again in the historical re-creations examined. The pull of the Southern past on the literary imagination reflects the distinctiveness of a region which has had, as pointed out in C. Vann Woodward's *The Burden of Southern History,* intense experiences with poverty, failure, defeat, and guilt. It retains, more than other sections of America, physical, social, and psychological remnants of the past, as well as an oral tradition that has helped keep that past alive. Thus, we find Allen Tate speaking, in one of his essays, of the "peculiarly historical consciousness" of the Southern writer. That consciousness can take a number of clearly different forms, as can be seen in the chapters on Faulkner, Tate, Welty, Warren, Styron, and Barth.

The other region that figures prominently in the works studied in this book, though to a lesser extent than the South, is New England. As the site of the Puritan experiment, of early conflicts between the individual and the state, as well as between whites and Indians, as the source of habits of mind that can still be seen operating in our country, New England attracts the interest of Berryman, Olson, and Lowell, in addition to Williams.

While each of the writers and poets discussed in this book has his particular way of imagining the past, they all attempt, at least in part, to convey a sense of the way it was in some bygone era, or to give us the significance or meaning of historical events and personages. Too often critics hasten to dismiss the question of historical accuracy with respect to literary works dealing with the past, treating a concern with such accuracy as an encroachment upon the privileges of the literary artifact, which they wish to see as autonomous. While the question of accuracy is certainly not the only one to be considered in the study of historical literature, to dismiss it out of hand is to ignore the intentions of such writers as are treated here (the matter of accuracy will be raised at several points in this book). This is not to claim that these writers necessarily feel bound to maintain a one-to-one correspondence between their presentations and the historical facts, but they do show at least some interest in conveying the spirit of the past, if not its letter.

As such, their works may be taken as complementary to (though one might see them as subversive of) the productions of historians, offering the textures of individual experience, and an emotional rendering of their materials, in place of the relatively panoramic or detached writing of the official recorders and interpreters of our past. Mighty and scrupulous as the labors of the historians might be, what comes to mind as we think of that past is often the episode, the memorable character or atmosphere or pronouncement created by our novelists and poets. It can be very difficult, if not impossible, to separate their imagined pasts from our sense of the way it was, nor would they wish us to.

The composers of historical literature help to keep the matter of the past alive, not only through their concern with the individual and the particular, but by their own involvement with their materials, an involvement that often manifests itself, as will be shown, in ambivalence, uncertainty, a particular preoccupation or prejudice. Such effects may result in deep flaws, in incoherence or unpersuasiveness, but they remind us of the difficulties and pitfalls in judging even what seems to be finished, and help us remember that the past is an ongoing invention, conditioned by the contours of the individual sensibility as well as by the interests and conceptions of a particular present, our history being not a given, but, rightfully, a matter for visions and revisions.

The Imagined Past

1

Puritan and Redskin:
William Carlos Williams's *In the American Grain*

While en route to Europe from America in 1924, William Carlos Williams occupied himself with a treatment of the most famous voyage ever made in the opposite direction.[1] His version of Columbus's discovery of the New World was eventually to become the second chapter of *In the American Grain* (1925). Touring a Europe that drew so many of our literati abroad in the 1920s, Williams kept part of his attention reserved for the land left temporarily behind, by continuing to work on that book. In maintaining this counterpoint to his foreign sojourning, he was, in effect, declaring his distance from the expatriate temper of the period.

One of the chapters of *In the American Grain* opens with a sketch of the Paris of the time, a Paris that had collected Pablo Picasso, Gertrude Stein, James Joyce, and Ezra Pound, among others. It is in this same chapter that Williams declares:

> what we [Americans] are has its origin in what *the nation* in the past has been . . . there is a source IN AMERICA for everything we think or do. . . . unless everything that is, proclaim a ground on which it stand, it has no worth . . . what has been morally, aesthetically worth while in America has rested upon peculiar and discoverable ground.[2]

Williams's shifting away from the exiles gathered in a foreign

27

capital to the "peculiar" ground of America nicely dramatized his belief that art must grow out of "local conditions."[3] During a career pursued in conscious opposition to the expatriate path taken by Ezra Pound and T.S. Eliot, he repeatedly asserted that the artist must steep himself in the multiple particulars of his native milieu.[4] A culture, Williams claimed,

> has to be where it arises, or everything related to the life there ceases. . . . It is the realization of the qualities of a place in relation to the life which occupies it; embracing everything involved, climate, geographic position, relative size, history, other cultures. . . .[5]

In the American Grain may be said to represent Williams's attempt to embrace the history of the place in which he found himself.

> Of mixed ancestry, I felt from earliest childhood that America was the only home I could ever possibly call my own. I felt that it was expressly founded for me, personally, and that it must be my first business in life to possess it; that only by making it my own from the beginning to my own day, in detail, should I ever have a basis for knowing where I stood.[6]

The work resulting from his ambition to "possess" his country, make its history a portable acquisition of his mind, turned out to be at once wider and narrower in scope than this statement would suggest. The "America" of *In the American Grain* came to include both Canada and Mexico; however, Williams's treatment of history per se ultimately got no closer to his "own day" than the period of the Civil War.[7]

He conceived of his task not merely as an artist's private act of self-education, but as a public enterprise, one which would break through the insulation from the native past that America, in his view, had built up. Accusing our historians of misperceptions and distortions (pp. 179, 188–90),[8] he adopted the strategy of going directly to the primary documents themselves (e.g., the journal of Columbus, the dispatches of Cortez). But what he produced is not a sourcebook; it is, rather, a highly selective, impressionistic account of our history, the product of his imagination playing over the documents.[9] Several central concerns emerge: a stressing of the place of the tragic in human endeavor, as opposed to our country's tendency to deny it; a displaying of heroes from out of the past as models to be used by the present; an attack on the persistence of Puritanism in our culture; and a celebration of the Indian, linking him to the spirit of the American earth.

In part, Williams's study of the past resulted, at least implicitly, in the desire to fill a large gap in the usual American conception of life's possibilities. At one point in the book he complains: "We have no feeling for the tragic. Let the sucker who fails get his. What's tragic in that? That's funny! To hell with him. He didn't make good, that's all" (p. 180). Whether or not Williams *consciously* intended to demonstrate the inadequacy of this characteristic American response, his selection and treatment of a number of figures out of the past reveal a strain in our history that might be called the American failure story. It is hard to believe that he did not have the dramatization of such a strain in mind when he chose to open his book by focusing on Eric the Red rather than Eric's son, Leif Erickson, who is more closely associated with the discovery of the American continent, and who would therefore seem a more appropriate figure with which to begin. (Leif plays only a secondary role in the "Red Eric" chapter.) But Leif was fortune's darling; indeed, he was called Leif the Lucky. This appellation only heightens, by contrast, the sense of frustration and defeat that is evoked in Williams's treatment of Red Eric, who feels displaced by the coming of Christianity to Greenland. Eric's unhappiness over the appearance of Christian priests, his sense of homelessness in the Greenland he discovered, is further heightened by Williams's having converted the neutral, third-person narrative of the original sagas into a brooding dramatic monologue, giving much more space than do the sources to Eric's rejection of Christianity.[10] Thus, the first personage to greet us in Williams's re-creation of the American past is one isolated and embittered, defiant, but hopelessly so.

The succeeding figure in the book, Columbus, would appear to be a supreme instance of magnificent success, not only in American history, but in the history of the world. Yet, in noting the marvelous feat of his first voyage to America, Williams says "it is as the achievement of a flower, pure, white, waxlike and fragrant, that Columbus' infatuated course must be depicted, especially when compared with the acrid and poisonous apple which was later by him to be proved" (p. 7). So Williams has no sooner recognized Columbus's achievement than he leaps forward in time, anticipating at the start the difficulties and ingratitude that Columbus will encounter despite his success. While the Columbus section ends on a triumphant note, with the text reverting to the first days of discovery (even fitting the events of several days into two, presumably to intensify the sense of Columbus's pleasure at what he saw), much of the chapter's materials have been chosen in such a way as to give us not a triumphant voyager so much as a terribly put-upon man, intrigued against, vilified, ruined. Williams calls him America's "first victim" (p. 10).

The next four chapters extend the portrait gallery of defeat and failure. While Prescott's *History of the Conquest of Mexico* focuses on Cortéz's triumph, it is Montezuma, as head of the doomed Aztec civilization, who is the central presence of Williams's "The Destruction of Tenochtitlan." In the next chapter Ponce de Leon, old, sorrowing over the death of his beloved dog, meets an abrupt, mocking end to his quest for the Fountain of Youth: "the Yamasses put an arrow into his thigh at the first landing—and let out his fountain. They flocked to the beach, jeered him as he was lifted to the shoulders of his men and carried away. Dead" (p. 44). We find a similar note in the next chapter. De Soto, moving through Indian territories, falls ill and dies without having discovered the gold he sought. Williams incorporates that portion of his source which says of De Soto "He was advanced by fortune, in the way she is wont to lead others, that he might fall the greater depth" (p. 57)—the path of the tragic hero. His property, Williams's version of the account tells us, was found to consist of "two male and three female slaves, three horses and seven hundred swine. From that time forward most of the people owned and raised hogs" (p. 58). In the original source, we are at least informed what each slave, horse, and hog was sold for. Williams's omitting of this information produces a compression that comments sardonically on the close of a great conquistador's career.[11]

As we move, in the next chapter, from the Spanish to the English, the pattern of failure or incompletion persists. Sir Walter Raleigh is presented as an instance of many-sided defeat. Williams calls him "that lost man: seer who failed, planter who never planted, poet whose works are questioned, leader without command, favorite deposed . . ." (p. 62). Among other things, Williams was undoubtedly thinking of Raleigh's difficult and fruitless expeditions to Guiana in search of El Dorado.

In presenting these figures (as well as Aaron Burr), Williams is trying to make his fellow Americans perceive that failure is as much a part of existence as success, trying to rid them of the innocence that proclaims otherwise (in varying ways, such of his contemporaries as Frost, Hemingway, Fitzgerald, and Faulkner also made this attempt). He describes the America Columbus was to discover as "a predestined and bitter fruit" (p. 7), Columbus's enemies as "natural and as much a part of the scheme as any other" (p. 10).

Williams's concern with examples from our history that do not fit into the American success pattern may derive not only from his "feeling for the tragic," but from his apparent belief that failure, or nonachievement, can breed valuable characteristics. It is such characteristics that the American Negro embodies according to the presentation of him in the short chapter "Advent of the Slaves." The Negro, "NOBODY" in America, is possessed of a poise "in a world where [he has] no authority . . ." (p. 209). Paradoxically, Williams seems to see the Negroes' lack of status as the source of tenderness *and* ferocity in them, both of which he finds attractive. Rather than responding to the Negro as an example of victimization, Williams regards him as adding a "delightful" quality to the American scene. This celebration of blacks in the book, along with Williams's praise of Indians and Catholics, can be seen as a refusal to accept White Anglo-Saxon Protestantism as the rightful basis of our culture, and as an attempt to advance characteristics embodied in these minority groups as the truly valuable components of America.

Complementing his depiction of the Negro as the American nobody is Williams's handling of such prominent success stories as those of Washington and Franklin. He suggests in both cases that success came at too high a cost, the repression of a valuable inner, anarchic passion in the case of Washington, the shutting out of the wild spirit of the American continent in the case of Franklin.[12] One use of the past for Williams, then, would appear to be the undermining of characteristic American assumptions about success and failure, the enlarging and complicating of our notions of life's possibilities and values.

A further examination of Williams's attempts to bring the past to bear on the present reveals in him two opposing conceptions of our history. In the first of these, he regards the American past as a repository of heroes,[13] men who can serve as models or inspiration for those living in the present.

It is his job to serve as a medium for putting us in contact with those heroes, who survive in distorted images, or hardly at all; through such contact their exemplary force will be released. His heroes include so well-known a figure as Daniel Boone, and the relatively obscure French Jesuit, Père Sebastian Rasles. Boone, we are told is "far from dead . . . but full of a rich regenerative violence he remains, when his history will be carefully reported, for us who have come after to call upon him" (p. 130). His life remains "still loaded with power . . ." (p. 136). Père Rasles, in his dealings with the Indians, displayed a generosity of spirit that is a "moral source . . . one of the sources that has shaped America and must be recognized" (p. 122). Rejecting the widely held notion of Aaron Burr as an unscrupulous adventurer, Williams finds in him, among other things, an admirable love of freedom and a disregard for public opinion. Such historical figures exist for Williams in a state of potential resurrection, our secular saviors if we would only recognize them as such.

But if the American past is capable of kindling in him a passionate admiration and a desire to see it embodied in the life of the present, it can just as frequently provoke him to radical rejection and rage. The prime villain is the spirit of Puritanism, which Williams sees as a force of the greatest importance both in its impact on early America, and in its effect on his own time as well. (The intense hostility of *In the American Grain* toward Puritanism makes it very much a book of the 1920s.) He finds that this spirit has manifested itself not only in Franklin's fear of the wilderness but also in our laws (he may have had Prohibition in mind) and in the shame our women are made to feel about their sexual desires. The Puritan temper has become "a malfeasant ghost that dominates us all" (p. 65). While Cotton Mather's books are not read, "what is in them lives and there hides, as in a lair from whence it sallies now and then to strike terror through the land" (p. 115). Williams's language here may strike us as extravagant, but it is appropriate to the intensity of his hatred. His preoccupation with the Puritans is evidenced by his giving more space to a selection from Mather on witches than to any other document that he uses in the book.[14]

In presenting the Puritans, he would appear to assume the role of psychiatrist to a culture, his patient the American mind, its malady a crippling inhibition that affects our sexuality, makes us avoid real relationships with others, and prevents us from opening ourselves to the spirit of the American earth. Operating on an assumption parallel to that once made by actual psychoanalysis, namely, that bringing to consciousness the source of a mental disorder will automatically result in the purgation of that disorder, Williams speaks of his wish "to drag this THING [Puritanism] out by itself to annihilate it" (p. 114). He says: "I wish only to disentangle the obscurities that oppress me, to track them to the root and to uproot them—" (p. 116).

Thus, the American past can draw forth both love and hatred from Williams. The two responses are closely related to each other in that at least some of his heroes, men he loves, possess in common a quality that sets them against the Puritanism he detests. In one instance, he makes this crucial antagonism explicit when he says "All that will be new in America will be anti-Puritan. It will be of another root. It will be more from the heart of Rasles, in the north [i.e., Canada]" (p. 120). "Puritan" in this context means a blindness to the American earth, the wilderness, the Indian, a blindness bred out of fear of the new and the vast. (The section from Mather that Williams reproduces refers to the "squallid, horrid American Desart" [p. 82].) His eye cocked on eternity, the Puritan had "nothing of curiosity, no wonder, for the new World. . ." (p. 112). He "was precluded from SEEING the Indian. They never realized the Indian in the least save as an unformed PURITAN" (p. 113). Such inability or unwillingness to apprehend the newness of the New World persists. "Our resistance to the wilderness has been too strong. . . .

As a violent 'puritanism' it breathes still" (pp. 115–16). Rasles, on the other hand, applied himself diligently to studying the language of the Indians, saying that it had "de vrayes beautés, & je ne sais quois d'énergique dans le tour & la maniere dont ils s'expriment."[15] His capacity for appreciation, exemplified in this statement, his knowledge of the habits and mentality of the Indians, his living among them, eating what they ate, sharing their strenuous life—all these greatly endear Rasles to Williams.[16]

Openness to the Indian, a readiness to regard him as companion or model, is the link connecting Rasles to other figures in the book who are treated by Williams with obvious affection. There is Thomas Morton, who consorted with the Massachusetts Indians, his establishment at Merrymount an affront to the Puritans of the Plymouth colony. Helping him erect the famous Maypole, the Indians were present at the ensuing revels. (Cf. Hawthorne's "The Maypole of Merrymount.") Williams thinks of Morton laying his hands "roughly perhaps but lovingly, upon the flesh of his Indian consorts. . ." (p. 80). To Daniel Boone, "the Indian was his greatest master" (p. 137). He chose an Indian for companion "even out of preference to his own sons. . ." (p. 139). Sam Houston ran away to live with the Indians when still very young, returned to them after the breakup of his first marriage, and took an Indian woman for his wife.

It is these facts that Williams chooses to focus on in his chapter about Houston, treating his famous victory at San Jacinto and all his ensuing career in less than a paragraph. That this emphasis on Houston's relationship with the Indians may be in part misleading, even when he is considered as a private man rather than a public figure, is indicated by Robert Penn Warren's remarks on him. Warren points out that Houston is not to be thought of "as a simple hunter and woodsman, a white runaway gone Indian. His head was full of the ambition to read Homer. He carried into the wilderness a copy of Pope's translation of the *Iliad*." During his retreat in the Texas campaign, he read Caesar's *Commentaries* and *Gulliver's Travels*.[17] Houston himself said he read the Pope translation so consistently he could "repeat it almost entire from beginning to end."[18] Williams never points to this appearance of European culture in Houston's life. He gives us a Houston who is a Redskin, purged of that which made him a Paleface as well. This concern with Houston and the Indian can certainly be justified by the evidence (there is, in addition to the man's personal relationships with the Indians, his repeated attempts to defend their rights against the greed and dishonesty of the whites), but its one-sidedness can also be taken as an expression of Williams's own preoccupations in *In the American Grain*.

Set against these men who reached out to the Indian—Rasles, Morton, Boone, Houston—there stands, at least by implication, Benjamin Franklin. At the end of his hostile chapter on the creator of Poor Richard, Williams speaks bitterly of "the suppression of the superb corn dance of the Chippewas. . ." (p. 157). Earlier in the chapter, he says "There has not yet appeared in the New World any one with sufficient strength for the open assertion. . . . Nowhere the open, free assertion save in the Indian. . . . Franklin is the full development of the timidity. . . . He was the dike keeper, keeping out the wilderness with his wits" (pp. 154–55). It can be seen, then, that the response made to the Indian serves Williams as a touchstone in his judgments on the men of the American past.

Several of the "original records" Williams consulted could have contributed to his sense of the Indians as a precious product of the New World, maligned by the reports of the early New England settlers. Thomas Morton spoke of the Massachusetts Indians as being "more full of humanity then [sic] the Christians."[19] Père Rasles noted both the Indian's skill as a warrior, and his tenderness toward children. Boone also spoke of these qualities, as well as of the Indian's " 'attachment for that land to which [he] belong[s],

unknown to the inhabitants of any other country.' '' The
hunter did not hesitate to declare to the day of his death that
the manners and habits of the Indians were ''far more
agreeable to him than those of a more civilized and refined
race.''[20] Houston, telling of his sojourn among the Indians as
a boy, said he had preferred ''the wild liberty of the Redmen
. . . [to] the tyranny of my own brothers.''[21]

But in Williams' sources there are materials that convey a
very different response to the American native. Champlain,
who is the subject of Williams' eighth chapter, was of the
opinion that the Indians ''are all in fact of no great worth.''[22]
Perhaps this was not a significant evaluation to Williams,
who describes Champlain as failing to perceive the essential
otherness of the wilderness, believing that it could be turned
into an extension of French civilization. But even in Boone,
whose attraction to the Indian Williams so stresses, we can
find the description of an occasion on which the Indians,
conducting a forced march of captives, tomahawked those
who were weak and faint, including women and children.[23]

Turning to the dispatches of Cortez (which Williams used
as the basis for his chapter on that explorer), we find awful
accounts of human sacrifices by the Indians of Mexico.
According to Cortez, the victims, sometimes children, had
their breasts cut open while still alive, their hearts and
entrails removed and offered to the idols. ''It is the most
terrible and frightful thing that has ever been seen.''[24]
Indians who had allied themselves with Cortez against
Montezuma showed the inhabitants of the beleagured
Tenochtitlan ''the bodies of their countrymen cut into
pieces, exclaiming. . . that they would have them for supper
that night and for breakfast the next day, as was in fact the
case.''[25] They rejoiced greatly at the Spaniard's decision to
level the city, and Cortez said: ''we had even more to do to
restrain our allies from the slaughter and the practice of
excessive cruelty, than to fight the enemy: the people of this
country being addicted to a cruelty exceeding what had ever

been known in any generation. . . ."[26] That a conquistador should have been provoked to such a comment is terrible tribute indeed to the Indian's capacity for cruelty.

Francis Parkman's *The Jesuits in North America in the Seventeenth Century* (a book Williams quotes from) made evident the hideous cruelty the North American Indian could display, not merely toward the white man but toward the members of other tribes. To spare our sensibilities, Parkman sometimes curtails his descriptions of Indian tortures, and most readers will rest content with the details he does give, of living victims having strips of flesh torn from them, fingers cut or bitten off, bodies burned piecemeal, their agonies protracted for hours.

Williams's Indians, Northern or Southern, are simply not portrayed in this way (though he cites Puritan torturing or killing of Quakers). When he mentions the practice of human sacrifice, he does so briefly or condoningly, his intention at one point being to condemn the white man's "sacrifices" of the witches at Salem rather than Indian behavior (p. 67). Following a long American literary tradition, Williams pictures the Indian as victim, the conquistador or colonist his oppressor. In so doing, he tends to convert people who were unjustly treated into total innocents. He is determined to have his savages noble, despite their ignoble savagery. Comparison with Parkman's account of the Indian immediately points up the lack of balance in Williams's book. Parkman is ready to admire the Indian's ability to face with courage and endurance the truly arduous circumstances of his life. But Parkman is also ready to exhibit his less attractive qualities.[27] (In all fairness it should be added that Parkman is *too* ready to do this.)

It is not, however, so much a question of one-sidedness in Williams's image of the Red Man that renders that image suspect. More crucial is the fact that a book making so much of the Indian, holding him up as a model of right, organic relationship to the New World, should be so unwilling (or unable) to portray him in any but the sketchiest manner. In the chapter on Rasles, cast in the form of a discussion between the author and Valery Larbaud,[28] Williams offers himself the opportunity to discourse on the Indian by having Larbaud ask him "Who were these Indians of whom you speak? What sort of men were they? What were their qualities?" (pp. 116–17). He responds by offering instances of victimization of the Indian by the white man, and the story of a Protestant minister refusing to allow Indians to touch him, in contrast with "the Catholic fathers in the north. . ." (p. 119). We then get some remarks on Puritan repressiveness, and praise of Rasles. Several pages go by before Williams offers a direct reply to Larbaud's questions, and then only a very short one. We are told that through Rasles, the Indian "stands out strangely revealed as a child, a passionate friend, a resourceful man and—a genius in attack, another music than the single horror of his war-whoop terrifying the invader" (p. 124). This minuscule description is simply not enough to sustain the burden of significance assigned to the Indian by the book. He ultimately figures in it only as a teasing presence, flitting through its pages, but staying just beyond our range of vision. Parkman, contemplating the disappearance of the Algonquin tribes, spoke of them as undergoing "that process of extermination, absorption, or expatriation, which, as there is reason to believe, had for many generations formed the gloomy and meaningless history of the greater part of this continent."[29] Williams does much too little to challenge this conception of the history of the Indian, whose near-disappearance he so laments.

The Indian is precious to Williams as "the flower of his world," a "natural expression" of the American continent (p. 137). The reaction to him by the French, Spanish, English, and their American-born descendants, is for Williams a synecdoche of the white man's response to the New World. To dramatize that response, Williams personifies the

American earth as a woman, linking this image to a recurrent metaphor of sexual union or marriage which represents the kind of love and acceptance of the New World that he constantly looks for in his exploration of our past.

The most explicit and extended occurrence of the earth-woman personification is to be found in the chapter on De Soto, where it takes the form of a series of speeches or responses by a "She," alternating with sections of narrative relating the exploits of the Spaniard. It is possible that Williams's use of this technique was inspired by his source, in which we find a series of messages or addresses composed by various Indian chieftains and directed to De Soto. These always begin in a most respectful way and might be thought of as feminine in their submissiveness. One was actually composed by a female chieftain. She, however, after being put under guard, tricked her captors and escaped. Williams's "She" combines in her being this same mixture of submissiveness and elusiveness, of yielding and defiance. "She" describes herself as beautiful, seductive, alternately victorious over and defeated by De Soto. Victory for her appears to consist of his turning "native," though the exact content of this is not clear. It may refer to De Soto's treachery in killing several natives (about which "She" says: "Well done, Spaniard! like an Indian"), or to his acceptance of two Indian wives, the gifts of a chief (pp. 45, 52, 53). Early in the chapter, "She" promises De Soto that he will receive nothing of her "save one long caress as of a great river passing forever upon your sweet corse" (p. 45). The meaning of this becomes clear only at the end of the section, when we are told of De Soto's corpse being consigned to the Mississippi river, and only if we have knowledge of Williams's *The Great American Novel* (1923). In that work, he says of De Soto:

The best he had done was to locate a river running across his path, the greatest he had ever seen or heard of, greater than the Nile, greater than the Euphrates, no less indeed than any. Here he had confronted the New World in all its mighty significance and something had penetrated his soul so that in the hour of need he had turned to this Mighty River rather than to any other thing. . . . Out of the tangle around him, out of the mess of his own past the river alone could give him rest. Should he die his body should be given to this last resting place. Into it Europe should pass as into a new world . . . . there at the edge of that mighty river he had seen those little fish who would soon be eating him, he, De Soto the mighty explorer—He smiled quietly to himself with a curious satisfaction.[30]

This passage provides a clue to what was in Williams's mind when, in his *American Grain* account of De Soto's river burial, he included a description of various kinds of fish. The description *is* found in his source, but there it occurs at a point prior to De Soto's death, and is given in reference to a *lake* rather than the Mississippi. In transposing the description, Williams apparently wished to suggest that only in death, eaten by fish of a great river in the New World, was De Soto's relationship to that world consummated (perhaps because only such consummation was possible to the essentially violent relationship of De Soto to America, though Williams appears to find De Soto's violence attracted to what it was directed against). Williams dramatizes that relationship largely in sexual terms, not only through his use of "She," who addresses De Soto as a lover, speaking of caresses (pp. 45, 48, 50), and of his having "straddled" her (p. 52), but through his reference to De Soto's descending corpse as a "solitary sperm . . ." (p. 58).

The beginning of the chapter that follows the one on De Soto, Williams's account of Sir Walter Raleigh, sustains the use of sexual metaphor, as it speaks of Raleigh "plunging his lust into the body of a new world . . ." (p. 59). According to Williams's image of him, Raleigh's interest in the Western Hemisphere appears as a release from or substitute for his unhappy, unstable relationship with Queen Elizabeth, though "it turned out to be a voyage on the body of his Queen: England, Elizabeth—Virginia" (p. 60). (The reference appears to be to Raleigh's having given the name Virginia to land discovered by an expedition to America that he had sent out.)[31] Williams's sexual language is in keeping with a metaphor Raleigh himself employed in his *Discovery of Guiana,* where he said "Guiana is a country that hath yet her maidenhead."[32] Perhaps because Raleigh never actually saw North America, and because his voyages to Guiana were unsuccessful, his relationship to the New World appears to figure in Williams's chapter as a kind of *coitus interruptus.* How greatly to be regretted, Williams seems to be saying, is the fact that Raleigh was never able to put his talents to work in America, not because he disdained or feared this continent, but only because of unfortunate circumstances.

In playing off Thomas Morton against the repressive Puritans, Williams employs no metaphor but he does present materials that are closely linked to the sexual imagery I have been noting. He offers Morton's "consorting with the Indian girls" as one cause for the "Puritan disgust" with him, considers the question of whether or not Indian women had a notion of chastity, and juxtaposes Morton's taking such women to bed with the Puritans' fear of touching the "bounties" of the New World (pp. 76, 80). A restrained sexuality is here equated to or at least connected with a refusal to accept the nature of the land. That Morton did accept it is attested to by his *New English Canaan,* where he repeatedly compares Old England to the New, favoring the latter.

Daniel Boone, sexless in the popular imagination, is introduced to us by Williams as "a great voluptuary . . ." (p. 130). The chapter in question proceeds to convert this unorthodox characterization into a metaphor, as we are told that "the beauty of a lavish, primitive embrace in savage, wild beast and forest . . . possessed him wholly," that

Boone "sought only with primal lust to grow close" to the New World's beauty (p. 136). He saw that "There must be a new wedding" (p. 137), i.e., of the self and the American earth, the prototype of such a wedding to be found in the Indian's continuity with his environment. Wedding and sexual (or at least generative) metaphors are also to be found in the chapter on Père Rasles, advanced in such a way as not to seem incongruous with a Jesuit's presumed celibacy. Of Rasles's interested, admiring response to Indian language, Williams says: "It is *this* to be *moral* . . . TO MARRY, to *touch*—to *give* . . . to create, to hybridize, to cross-pollenize . . ." (p. 121).

We are reminded of the chapter on Boone not only by the portrait of Rasles, but by that of Franklin as well, with the latter again serving as a counter-figure to the other two, as he had in the matter of responses to the Indian. Franklin, we are told, possessed a *"voluptuous* energy" which he had borrowed from his surroundings "without recognition . . ." (p. 153—italics mine). Impelling him was fear of the wilderness, of "the dance"—presumably the fertility dance of the Indians. He wished only to "touch" whatever he put his hand to (p. 155), "touch" here carrying the very opposite meaning of what it has in the chapter on Rasles, representing in Franklin's case only superficial contact. (Williams quite wonderfully applies this even to Franklin's interest in lighting, which he sees him as merely playing or "fooling" with.)

The precise significance of the sexual and matrimonial metaphors used by Williams to convey acceptance or rejection of the New World, personified as a woman, appears to shift. In some instances, e.g., that of Rasles, the metaphor remains metaphor, and is used to suggest the *intensity* with which America was lovingly regarded, or should have been regarded. But there is also a tendency in the book for the metaphoric to slide into the literal, and to involve actual sexuality or, rather, its denial. In the case of the Puritans, Williams explicitly presents us not only with a group blind to the beauty and uniqueness of the land they had come to, but also sexually repressed. The two qualities appear together again in that spiritual descendant of the Puritans, Franklin. For, after telling us of the tremendous inner restraint operating on Franklin's voluptuous energy, his mode of merely touching, Williams notes that he had "tentatively loosed himself once to love, to curiosity perhaps, which was the birth of his first son. But the terror of that dare must have frightened the soul out of him" (p. 156). Fear of the New World in general and fear of sexuality in particular are here clearly joined. A closely related, if not identical, pattern can be seen in Williams's description of Washington, when we consider it together with the chapter on Franklin which it immediately precedes. Washington is viewed as a man of great sexual attractiveness and a strong sexual drive, the latter being part of a tremendously passionate potential, "a mad hell inside that might rise, might one day do something perhaps brilliant, perhaps joyously abandoned—but not to be thought of" (pp. 141–142). Franklin and Washington would appear to be linked together in Williams's mind when he says "The character they had (our pioneer statesmen, etc.) was that of giving their fine energy, as they must have done, to the smaller, narrower protective thing and not to the great, New World" (p. 157). In all these instances, there is a connection made between a refused commitment to that world and the repression of sexual energy.

If the wedding and marriage metaphors of the book tend to approach the literal, a similar process occurs with the underlying personification of the American earth as woman. Presumably originating as a device for showing the depth of love or fear occasioned by the New World, the earth-woman comes to be ranged alongside the actual American woman, sisters in rejection. Denial of the New World stands joined by Williams to denial of woman's sexuality. The latter has resulted in our not having had true women in America "since pioneer Katies . . ." (p. 178). Made by our Puritanism to regard their desires as evil, American women have evolved into beings "fit only to be seen by the box, like Oregon apples, bright and round but tasteless—wineless, wholesale" (p. 183). The wife of Houston is a case study. Williams speculates that the cause of Houston's breakup with his white bride was "a disproportion between them; a man of primitive vigors loosed upon her in private, she was overborne by him in some manner, or she refused to be overborne" (p. 212). "There are no women—Houston's bride is frightened off . . ." (pp. 154–155). (Houston's happy marriage to another white woman is completely ignored.)

Williams's view of the status of the American woman explains the stress he places on Aaron Burr as a man who took women seriously. Burr was to the American woman what Boone was to the American earth—an appreciative lover. Burr's contemporaries regarded women as "necessary but not noble, not the highest, not deliciously a free thing, apart, *feminine,* a heaven;—afraid to delve in it save like so much dough. Burr found the spirit living there, free and equal, independent, springing with life" (p. 205).[33] That his appreciation of them included the sexual is pointed up by Williams's statement that the "obscene flesh in which we dig for all our good, man and woman alike, Burr knew and trusted. Here he lived, giving and receiving to the full of his instinctive nature" (p. 207). *In the American Grain* values loving recognition of the American woman as well as of the American earth.[34]

There are two women in the book whose presence suggests that for Williams the true female possesses robustness and bold assertiveness, and that possessing these, she is an expression of the American earth. About a third of the chapter on Eric the Red is given over to Eric's daughter, Freydis. Pregnant, and confronted by the hostile Skrellings, she "stripped down her shirt and slapped her breast with her bare sword" (p. 4). The Skrellings retreat in terror from this spectacle. Freydis's ability to assume a violent role is again shown in her calling for an ax to kill the women belonging to a household against which she has brought unjust accusations. This Nordic Amazon, at once admirable and terrible, may be said to link up with a woman presented for our approval later in the book. At the end of the chapter given over to Williams's meditation on the nature of the American female, we are told of a Sachem of mixed blood, Jacataqua, scarcely eighteen years old, being attracted to the young Aaron Burr, then fighting in the French and Indian War. She opens a conversation with him thusly: " 'These,' with a wave of her brown hand toward Howard [an American captain] and the group of officers, 'these want meat. You hunt with me? I win'' (p. 187). Williams tells us that on this occasion Burr was at a loss before a woman for the first and last time in his life.

That Williams shows himself drawn to such formidable figures as Freydis and Jacataqua is of a piece with his conception of the genius of the American continent. He says that the Aztecs' religious artifacts and customs, including the practice of human sacrifice, displayed "the realization of their primal and continuous identity with the ground itself . . . [of] the mysterious secret of existence whose cruel beauty they, the living, inherited from the dead" (p. 33). Cruel beauty is what the "She" in the De Soto chapter exhibits, being lavish both in her gifts and punishments: "every arrow has upon its barbs a kiss from my lips" (pp. 48–49). Traversing the wilderness alone, Boone, according to Williams's image of him, experiences both an ordeal and an ecstasy. Later, Indians will offer him companionship, but they will also kill his son. Boone accepts both. Such acceptance of the dual nature of the American continent, its beauty and its terror ("Terror enlarges the object, as does joy"—p. 174), is what the book as a whole is urging.

This acceptance may be said to take two diverging forms in the work. On the one hand, it is associated with Boone's solo quest for elbow room, a sojourning in the wilderness, and on the other, it is linked to a civilization, Montezuma's Tenochtitlan, with its delicate and beautiful style. Williams is certainly drawn to the Aztec culture, to its rootedness and flowering in an accepted native place. However, most of his heroes in the book are not seen as integrated into a rooted culture, but move beyond such a setting as explorers and individualists. If there is any final choice in this matter, it would seem to lie on the side of the individual. For even with Tenochtitlan, what finally fascinates Williams about the Aztecs is the realization of their achievements in one man—Montezuma.

The historian, Williams complains, is too ready to portray men "in generic patterns," determined by environment or circumstance. He asks: "Are lives to be twisted forcibly about events, the mere accidents of geography and climate?" He answers that it is "an obscenity which few escape—save at the hands of the stylist, literature, in which alone humanity is protected against tyrannous designs" (pp. 188–89). What Williams is saying, I believe, both here and through the method of his book taken as a whole, is that studies of the past should preserve the contours of the individual, be responsive to his particular style, and allow him some measure of autonomy, that history is best treated as biography.[35] When it resists being treated as such, when, e.g., Williams finds the Pilgrims functioning as a group with no individual leader discernible, he is contemptuous. American history for Williams is not a matter of mass movements, political and economic developments, sectional conflicts, evolving institutions—it is primarily a matter of the individual.[36] This is why his book repeatedly focuses on a particular man, and why it adopts a different form or style for each of its chapters (sometimes letting the subject speak for himself through his own writing).[37] We move from the intense, bitten-off sentences of Red Eric, to the stately narrative describing Montezuma and his civilization, to the swooning speech of De Soto's "She," to the epigrammatic characterization of Benjamin Franklin. *In the American Grain* proposes to restore our history to us through vivid renderings of the personalities, tensions, drives, and delights of individual persons. In his prefatory note Williams says: "Everywhere I have tried to separate out from the original records some flavor of an actual peculiarity the character denoting shape which the unique force has given." The syntax here is a little gnarled, but the interest in individual particularity is clear enough. To be sure, Williams does not treat the past purely as an array of discrete, unrelated entities; he does not conceive of himself as simply making a series of separate excursions. His mind is by no means completely free of assumptions that would encourage the use of the historian's generic patterns, and he does look for certain designs within history which are relevant to his own day. But the book is so composed as to call our attention to particular men in their relationship to particular times and places.

Williams' personification of the American earth as a woman, that turning of historical materials into myth, is admittedly a nebulous affair and may well make historians jeer. It suggests at times a sexual interpretation of our past without an explicit commitment to a consistent, overall theory of cause and effect. At the same time, this personification allows Williams to focus attention on something the historian might neglect, the genius of the American place as it has impinged on various individuals during the course of our history. The personification reinforces the use of the different styles in helping create a sense of the inner being of Williams' historical figures, transforming public effigies into private persons. Williams strives simultaneously to keep his eye on the public world and on the single, separate self, setting in motion an interaction between the two that engages the deepest, most intimate aspects of the self, or that exhibits its personality. Concern with the large structures of the past and with overall developments is subordinated to a concern for the quality of private experience.

NOTES

1. See *The Selected Letters of William Carlos Williams,* ed. John C. Thirlwall (New York: McDowell, Obolensky, 1957), pp. 185–88.

2. William Carlos Williams, *In the American Grain* (New York: New Directions, 1956), p. 109. Italics and capitals in the original. Subsequent references to the book will be followed by the relevant page numbers in the text of the chapter itself.

3. *The Autobiography of William Carlos Williams* (New York: Random House, 1951), p. 146.

4. See, e.g., Williams, *Autobiography,* pp. 174–75, and *Selected Letters,* pp. 224–27.

5. *Selected Essays of William Carlos Williams* (New York: Random House, 1954), p. 157. Actually, statements similar to these can be found in Eliot. But he made them with his adopted England in mind, while Williams was thinking of his native America.

6. Williams, *Selected Letters,* p. 185.

7. Originally he had hoped to do a second volume, beginning with Jefferson and coming up to "the present day to end with Pancho Villa" (*Autobiography,* p. 237). But the poor sales of *In the American Grain* caused him to cancel his plans.

8. See also Williams, *Autobiography,* p. 178.

9. Even when Williams is supposedly presenting the sources themselves, he sometimes does so in a way that historians would find very dubious. On occasion he will excise or combine materials from his documents without acknowledging that he is doing so, interpolate details that are not in the original, cite as a fact something that is a matter of conjecture, or get a date or place name incorrect. In his fine book, *William Carlos Williams: An American Artist* (New York: Oxford University Press, 1970), James E. Breslin criticizes me for speaking of Williams's imagination "playing over the documents." (Breslin was responding to the appearance of this remark in the original form of the present chapter, *"In the American Grain: William Carlos Williams on the American Past,"* American Quarterly 19 (Fall 1967): 499–515.) In saying this, my primary purpose was not, as Breslin believes, to indicate that Williams did not have a good grasp of the documents, but to suggest the manner in which he used them. Also, Breslin says that in my claim that the book did not have a single, monolithic thesis but exhibited several concerns, I failed to see "either the coherence or the profundity of Williams's book. In the struggle between will and the land the book does have a unifying center . . ." (Breslin, p. 237). I still fail to see how Breslin's formula covers Williams's chapters on John Paul Jones, the slaves, Edgar Allan Poe, or Lincoln, among others.

50 THE IMAGINED PAST

10. Williams spoke of having used *"The Long Island Book"* as his source (*Autobiography*, p. 178). There is no book by that title so far as I have been able to determine. Williams undoubtedly meant the *Flateyarbok*, or *Flat Island Book*. He appears to have read as well the *Saga of Eric the Red*. Both of these works can be found, in translation, in the first volume of *Original Narratives of Early American History* (New York: Charles Scribner's Sons, 1906), a series that seems to have supplied Williams with several of his sources.

11. The principal source for Williams's chapter on De Soto is *The Narrative of the Expedition of Hernando De Soto, by the Gentleman of Elvas*. He could have found this in *Spanish Explorers in the United States 1528–1543* (which is the third volume of *Original Narratives of Early American History*), or, as Breslin claims, in *Narratives of the Career of Hernando De Soto* (New York: A.S. Barnes & Co., 1904), ed. Edward G. Bourne. The translation of this narrative is, in the second volume as well as the first, not by Bourne, as Breslin mistakenly says, but by Buckingham Smith.

12. Williams's attack on Franklin's values is an explicit one, but it may be that he was undercutting him implicitly by following the Franklin chapter with John Paul Jones's account of the battle between the *Bon Homme Richard* and the *Serapis*. For even though Jones's account is, technically, that of a victory, it seems much more a tale of confusion, ineptitude, and treachery, with his own ship ending up in worse condition than the *Serapis*. Placing the Jones chapter where he does, Williams may be advancing an implicit commentary on Franklin's image of a world in which the determined, energetic self cannot but meet with a successful ending, a world that is not intrinsically flawed. Such an interpretation of the juxtaposition of the two chapters is particularly suggested by the fact that Jones's ship was named after Franklin's Poor Richard.

13. See Williams, *Autobiography*, p. 178.

14. Breslin points out that Williams gives only part of Mather's remarks on the appearance of witches, and that Mather stressed the need to proceed cautiously in detecting them. Williams "gives no sense of the tortured ambiguities of his real stand." Breslin, pp. 107–8.

15. From letter written by Rasles, in *Lettres édifiantes et curieuses,* 34 vols. (Paris: N. Le Clerc, 1738), 23: 212. Williams may have first come across Rasles's letters in the English translation found in the Reverend William Ingraham Kip's *The Early Jesuit Missions in North America* (New York: Wiley and Putnam, 1846), but Williams cites the original French. See *In the American Grain*, pp. 120, 121.

16. Rasles tells of using snowshoes for the first time, thinking he would never be able to walk with them. But he exhibited such expertise that the Indians could not believe it was his first time on snowshoes. On another occasion, he saved himself from drowning by following the example of his Indian companions, leaping from one block of ice to another to get across a river. Williams was unquestionably entranced by such items as these.

17. Robert Penn Warren, *How Texas Won Her Freedom: The Story of Sam Houston & The Battle of San Jacinto* (San Jacinto Monument, Tex.: Sam Jacinto Museum of History, 1959), pp. 2, 12.

18. *The Autobiography of Sam Houston*, ed. Donald Day and Harry Herbert Ullom (Norman, Okla.: University of Oklahoma Press, 1954), p. 5.

19. Thomas Morton, *New English Canaan* (Boston: Prince Society, 1883), p. 256.

20. John Filson, *Life and Adventures of Colonel Daniel Boon* (Brooklyn: C. Wilder, 1823), p. 37. I do not know the particular edition of Boone's life Williams might have used.

21. *Autobiography of Sam Houston*, p. 6.

22. *Voyages of Samuel de Champlain 1604–1618*, ed. W. L. Grant (New York: Charles Scribner's Sons, 1907), p. 73. This is the third volume of *Original Narratives of Early American History;* see fn. 10.

23. John Filson, *The Discovery, Settlement and Present State of Kentucke* (New York: Corinth Books, 1962), pp. 71–72. This is a modern edition. The appendix to this book, containing Boone's *Life*, first appeared in 1784.

24. *Conquest: Dispatches of Cortes from the New World*, ed. Irwin Blacker and Harry Rosen (New York: Grosset & Dunlap, 1962), pp. 71–72. This was obviously not Williams's source for Cortez; he used *The Despatches of Hernando Cortés*, trans. George Folsom (New York: Wiley and Putnam, 1843). But in Folsom he could have read of "hearts taken from the breasts of living persons . . ." (p. 117). See also the next two citations in the text, drawn from Folsom.

25. *Despatches of Cortés*, trans. Folsom, p. 281.

26. Ibid., pp. 326–27.

27. Moreover, in direct contrast to Williams's contention that in the Indian we find "open, free assertion," Parkman speaks of the Indian's "dread of public opinion. . . ." Francis Parkman, *The Jesuits in North America in the Seventeenth Century* (Boston: Little, Brown and Co., 1875), p. xlix; see also p. 256.

28. This is apparently based on an actual conversation Williams had with Larbaud. See Williams, *Selected Letters*, p. 60.

29. Parkman, *Jesuits in North America*, p. 246.

30. Williams, *The Great American Novel* (Paris: Contact Editions, 1923), pp. 54–55. Notice the use of "penetrated his soul" in the passage just quoted; "penetrates" is a recurring term in *In the American Grain*, used very much as it is here.

31. Williams's conception of Raleigh as desperately in love with Elizabeth may seem strained, particularly to those who regard Raleigh's letter to Sir Robert Cecil, saying his heart was broken because imprisonment in the Tower had separated him from the Queen, not as a sincere expression of love but as a ploy to restore him to Elizabeth's favor by appealing to her vanity. See *Sir Walter Ralegh and His Colony in America*, ed. Reverend Increase N. Tarbox (Boston: Prince Society, 1884), p. 47.

32. Ibid., p. 54.

33. Williams's image of Burr was probably shaped, at least in part, by Burr's letters to his beloved daughter, Theodosia. These show him as continually occupied with her education and development.

34. M.L. Rosenthal has noted Williams's "special interest in women" as one of the "overriding preoccupations relevant to all of [his] work." *The William Carlos Williams Reader*, ed. M.L. Rosenthal (New York: New Directions, 1966), pp. x–xi.

35. It may be his desire to stress the autonomy of a particular kind of man, the artist, that accounts for the book's paradoxical chapter on Poe. For after telling us that in Poe, the local, the genius of the American place, found its first great

expression, Williams pictures Poe as desiring to be connected with no particular place, and makes the "local" an expression of Poe's own soul. Williams's contradictory treatment may have been the result of a reluctance to see the good artist's work as simply an "accident of geography and climate," even while he desired the American artist to be expressive of his surroundings.

36. Williams repeatedly shows a hostility towards men in the mass. Recurring in the book is an opposition between the gifted individual—e.g., Red Eric, Columbus, Poe—and the group.

37. See Williams, *Autobiography*, p. 184.

2

The Doomed Design:
William Faulkner's *Absalom, Absalom!*

The single most imposing work of historical literature produced in twentieth-century America is William Faulkner's *Absalom, Absalom!* While it does not employ an especially large cast of characters and makes limited use of panoramic effects, it manages, through an artful selection of materials, and the variety and intensity of its presentation, to convey the sense that it is furnishing a massive and authoritative picture of an entire society. It does this even while pointing up the difficulties of attempting to reconstruct the feelings and motives of those who have passed into history. Telling, in its shifting way, of the prodigious efforts of Thomas Sutpen to shape his "design," i.e., to create a grand place for himself and his progeny in the Mississippi of the mid-nineteenth century, the book itself is prodigious. (Recognized as such, it has received much illuminating scrutiny by various critics, and not wanting to go over ground already well covered any more than I have to, I will not attempt anything like a full acount of the novel.)[1]

Allen Tate once spoke of "the past in the present" as being "the pervasive Southern subject of our time."[2] *Absalom, Absalom!* may be said, with some qualification, to constitute an example of this. Faulkner has not chosen to plunge us directly into the past, but to have his historical materials twice removed, so to speak. They are filtered through a

53

group of characters who are set in a "present" of 1909–10 (the book itself appeared in 1936). But those materials are so intensely felt that the past becomes their present, and that present, in a way, becomes ours.

The story wastes no time in establishing an impression of how strong a presence the past constitutes for its latter-day characters. Moving at once into its strenuous prose, the novel provides us with a series of paradoxical juxtapositions or oxymorons. We find ourselves, on a *hot* afternoon, in a *hot* airless room in the house of Miss Rosa *Cold*field. There is a deadness inside the room, but the chamber is simultaneously vibrant. It is latticed with "yellow *slashes* full of dust motes . . ."[3] At the same time, the intense life outside the room partakes of the deathly. There is "a wistaria vine *blooming* for the *second* time that summer on a wooden trellis before one window, into which sparrows came now and then in random gusts, making a *dry vivid dusty* sound . . ." (p. 7—my italics). The spirit of the dead Thomas Sutpen, Rosa's brother-in-law, is evoked by her "outraged recapitulation" but is itself "quiet inattentive and harmless . . ." (p. 8). Later in the book, Miss Rosa's auditor, Quentin Compson, who is attempting to create his own version of the past, will be located in a space opposed to that of Rosa, in the sense that it is a room in the North (at Harvard) which is intensely cold, where he can feel "the chill pure weight of the snow-breathed New England air on his face. . . ." But along with this he can taste the dust he encountered on a "furnace-breathed" Mississippi September night of the preceding year (p. 362). The "cold New England night" is on his face but his blood runs warm (p. 373). The effect of these oppositions and juxtapositions is to create the central paradox of the presence of the past.[4] The characters from "history" are indubitably dead, and at the same time are undeniably alive in the consciousness of the living, so alive that they dominate that consciousness. The double nature of the historical characters is beautifully captured in Faulkner's ambiguous phrase, "victorious dust" (p. 8).

The presence of the past is heightened by Faulkner's having committed only a relatively small portion of the book to an omniscient narrator, the bulk of it to characters who relate the historical events by talking to a listener—Rosa to Quentin, Mr. Compson (Quentin's father) to Quentin, Quentin and Shreve (his Harvard roommate) to each other. However far the style of any given narrator may stray from ordinary modes of speech—and frequently the style seems to stray as far as possible—we are always conscious that one character is *speaking* to another. For all of these narrators the past is no further than their voices. So most of the book may be said to come to us in the form of oral history; and in the act of telling, a given narrator is at once in the present and in the past. If the past seems to permeate the very air of the story at times, it is because that air is made up in part of the breaths of those who have told and those who are telling of the bygone events. Quentin already knows part of what Miss Rosa tells him because "It was a part of his twenty years' heritage of breathing the same air and hearing his father talk about the man Sutpen . . ." (p. 11).

As Faulkner has arranged his book, the past has displaced almost completely any present of their own that the narrators might have. They exist only to tell of what has already happened or what they think has happened. Even something that at first promises to occur in the "present," the visit by Rosa and Quentin to the decayed Sutpen mansion, is so handled by the story that it comes to be related by Quentin after it has already occurred, and is transformed into an extension of history, the last chapter in the story of the rise and fall of the house of Sutpen.[5]

What the narrators tell us of the past is partly a matter of remembering events or what they have been told about them. But it is largely a matter of interpreting the known or of having to invent whole stretches of material in order to account for the actions of the Sutpen and the Coldfield families. For the past does not come to the narrators as a series of facts in clear relationship. The focus is not on sweeping movements or mass phenomena which have left substantial public evidence, but on the motivations and feelings of a few individuals who have left only an orally transmitted record of abrupt, mysterious actions. Mr. Compson, Quentin, and Shreve (but not Rosa) all feel the need to close the gaps in the scanty record; they all manifest the human desire to make sense of the things they do know. The past, then, engages not only their memories but their imaginations, as they strive to create a continuum out of the discontinuous materials they have been given. Their efforts to do so constitute the book's subject matter as much as the historical materials they grapple with.

They have, or at least Quentin has, what might be regarded as the advantage of contact with a participant in or witness to the actions of the past, Rosa. But her direct relationship to those actions serves to produce a version of what happened that obscures as much as it illuminates, a version that needs to be supplemented or qualified by the three other narrators (not that Faulkner gives the status of absolute truth to their versions either).

The style of Rosa's narrative is one of the astonishments of the book. In her style and what lies behind it we find that which makes her account inadequate, unsatisfactory. She does not so much talk to Quentin as she emits a high harangue at him. Her long sentences, their elaborate syntax, the tendency of many of them to try to say everything about their respective subjects before they agree to come to a halt, their melodramatic use of parallelism, their grandiose phrasing—all these seem designed to produce a linguistic medium that will make up by its inclusiveness and intensity for the emptiness of Rosa's life, past and present. That is to say, her speechifying serves as an attempted compensation for the experiential deprivations she has suffered. She talks of her life having ended forty-three years before, " 'since anyone who even had as little to call living as I had had up to that time would not call what I have had since living' " (p. 18). She makes the most of what has happened to her, but that consists largely of what has not—she was robbed of an ordinary childhood (her mother died giving birth to her), she was never courted or loved by a man, she never married. She *was* engaged to Sutpen but that engagement had none of the usual pleasures or satisfactions, and ended traumatically. The compensatory nature of her narrative is perhaps best illustrated by her rendering of her encounter with Clytie (Sutpen's illegitimate daughter by a Negro woman). Rosa has rushed out to the Sutpen house after hearing that Sutpen's son, Henry, has killed his sister Judith's suitor, Charles Bon. Rosa confronts Clytie at the foot of the staircase, which Clytie tells her not to mount. Clytie puts a restraining hand on her and Rosa is outraged, but at a word from Judith, her niece, she does not persist. The incident, in its actual elapsed time, could not have been a matter of more than a few seconds, but in Rosa's recounting of it she gives it an extraordinary duration.

The lush hysteria of her general account produces a version of the past that incorporates fairy-tale elements: a Prince Charming (Charles Bon) and an ogre (Sutpen). She experiences a vicarious romance through identifying with Judith in her relationship to Bon. More important is her conception of Sutpen as a heartless demon. Her first account in the story ends on a note of implicit outrage at his behavior, as she tells of Henry and Judith, when children, viewing their father in bloody contests with his slaves. But her image of him is based primarily on his treatment of her—he had proposed that they marry only if she first bore him a male child. She shows some self-awareness of her demonizing, but she persists in it. If little has happened to her, she can maximize what she *has* experienced by making Sutpen's behavior towards her epically horrendous. In this way she becomes a person who can at least lay claim to extraordinary victimization. She gives us, in the course of her re-creations, a Sutpen who is larger than life but who is impossibly inhuman, an abstraction of evil (and she simply leaves dangling the matter of Henry's killing Bon).

A kind of cooling-off of Rosa's overheated accounts is effected by the use of an omniscient narrator at the beginning of the book's second section. Of Sutpen's fighting with his slaves, presented as outrageous by Rosa, that narrator detachedly observes, "on occasion he doubtless pitted his negroes against one another and perhaps even . . . participated now and then himself—that spectacle which, according to Miss Coldfield, his son was unable to bear the sight of while his daughter looked on unmoved" (p. 40).

A more extensive qualification of Rosa's version of the past is provided by Mr. Compson's narrative. He points out how her own history served to condition the way in which she viewed Sutpen. Her birth coming at the expense of her mother's life, a fact for which she never forgave her father, and her upbringing by a bitter old-maid aunt caused her, in Mr. Compson's view, to look on Sutpen as a kind of Bluebeard, and on herself as "a breathing indictment . . . of the entire male principle" (pp. 59–60). Through Mr. Compson we can stand off and observe *her* instead of having to look through her frame of reference. Also, he enlarges the scope of the narrative. We move from Rosa's self-absorption to an account that tells us more of Sutpen's life than she did, and that explores at length the relationship between Henry and Bon, a matter that did not concern Rosa at all or at least one about which she had nothing to say. Mr. Compson conveys a sense of trying to be objective, of attempting to penetrate the lives and motivations of others. Not having been himself involved in the events he relates, he has no need to indulge in the self-pity and self-justification that color Rosa's account. In portions of his narrative we get a satiric detachment and humor, a tonal mode Rosa is not capable of.

A large portion of Mr. Compson's account is given over to his depiction of the Charles-Henry relationship, as he delivers an extended conjecture as to why Henry shot Bon. He posits a traumatic discovery on Henry's part that the Bon he had loved possessed an octoroon mistress with whom he had entered into a kind of marriage and by whom he had had a son. According to Mr. Compson, Henry could not tolerate a man in such a relationship marrying his sister, and although he loved Bon he killed him as the only way of preventing the marriage from taking place. To his credit Mr. Compson is skeptical about his own theory, aware that it does not satisfactorily explain the known facts. Something is missing, he admits. But his skepticism shades off too easily into an epistemological defeatism, a sense that strive as we may, we simply cannot fathom the past; the doings of those now dead are "inexplicable. . ." (p. 101).

Even so, he offers his version with considerable elaboration, presenting a melodrama of manners in which a rustic, inexperienced, excitable and puritanical Henry is played off against a sophisticated, world-weary Bon, product of a sybaritic New Orleans. Mr. Compson's narrative style may on occasion approach that of Rosa (the book itself acknowledges that the various narrators can sound like each other). But nothing could be more different from her breathless telling of separate incidents (all of which she seems to find outrageous and which virtually disappear under commentary, digressions, and rhetoric) than Mr. Compson's sustained, controlled depiction of the developing Henry-Bon relationship he posits. If he conceives of Bon introducing Henry in a leisurely, masterful way into the New Orleans octoroon world, taking pleasure in his control over his provincial friend's exposure, this corresponds to the manner in which Mr. Compson himself tells of the alleged events. Where Rosa theatrically gushes forth, Mr. Compson confidently spins a good story, taking his time.

It is astounding that after giving so much play to Mr.

Compson's version of the past, and making him appear so sophisticated a narrator, the book should disown his conception, or at least suggest that it is substantially distorted and incomplete. In writing *Absalom, Absalom!* Faulkner appears to have had narrative (and rhetorical) energy to burn, and he lavished it on the Rosa and Mr. Compson sections, only to then question the reliability of either of them as a narrator. (At the same time a certain residue of each of their versions remains in the compound offered by the book as a whole—having created their accounts, Faulkner could not simply obliterate them, and undoubtedly he did not want to. He surely wished Sutpen to retain some of the legendary dimensions he acquires when seen through Rosa's eyes, and he wanted to bring to us the immense differences in backgrounds that the Old South, as portrayed by Mr. Compson, could produce.)

There are two very dubious elements in Mr. Compson's re-creation of the Henry-Bon relationship. First, he imputes to Bon a passivity, imperturbability, and detached amusement in his commerce with the Sutpens that are a far cry from the view of him that Quentin and Shreve come up with, one based on evidence not available to Mr. Compson, and, the book suggests, one closer to the truth. (The characteristics Mr. Compson gives Bon may be seen as projections of his own nature.) The second questionable component in Mr. Compson's version[6] concerns the manner in which Bon enters the story. As Mr. Compson portrays him, Bon simply materializes in the most unlikely of settings. In Mr. Compson's words, Bon was "a personage who in the remote Mississippi of that time must have appeared almost phoenix-like, fullsprung from no childhood, born of no woman. . ." (p. 74). This is not simply the way Bon registers on those around him in Mississippi—this is, in effect, the nature of his genesis for Mr. Compson as well, who does nothing to supply him with a past beyond telling us of the existence of his octoroon mistress and his child. What his life consisted of before he acquired them, where he sprang from—these are simply left great blanks by Mr. Compson. In this he is doing what Rosa had done in telling of Sutpen. Here is the picture she left in Quentin's mind: "Out of quiet thunderclap he would abrupt (man-horse-demon) upon a scene peaceful and decorous as a schoolprize water color, faint sulphur-reek still in hair clothes and beard . . ." (p. 8). The suggestion in this is that Sutpen has come straight from hell, which of course tells us nothing at all about his origins. Rosa has made him for Quentin one *"who came out of nowhere and without warning . . ."* (p. 9; italics in original).[7] In fairness to Rosa, it should be said that this was the impression Sutpen made on the town, Jefferson, not simply on her, and one in keeping with Sutpen's appearance as described by the omniscient narrator: men of the town looked up "and there the stranger was," on horseback (p. 31), "man and beast looking as though they had been created out of thin air . . ." (p. 32). There is no doubt that this mode of appearance has a strong aesthetic appeal for Faulkner, and is an example of his fondness for abrupt effects (it is the alternation of such effects with delayed disclosures that help give the book its special narrative texture). But the novel undertakes to work against its own grain in this respect, forsaking the mystery and glamour attendant upon such appearances *ex nihilo* as Sutpen and Bon make, to create at considerable length a past for each of them. That creation is something other than Rosa's trivial notion of establishing a person's past. For her a past that is known and acknowledged is a manifestation of respectability—a person with an unknown past is a shady character. She tells us, in an unintentionally comic manner, that her father "knew who his father was in Tennessee and who his grandfather had been in Virginia and our neighbors and the people we lived among knew that we knew and we knew they knew we knew. . ." (pp. 16–17). The unfolding of the past of Sutpen and the past of Bon gets well beyond Rosa's prissy concern with genealogy. The recovery of each man's history figures as an act of the imagination that is at the same time a moral act.

For that is what contemplation of the past, at its best, *is* for Faulkner in this book. The facts about the past, simply taken by themselves, give the people in the book's present a man—Sutpen—who seems beyond human feeling, and an action—Henry's slaying of Bon—that is one of senseless violence. It is the self-appointed task, first of Mr. Compson, then of Quentin and Shreve, to attempt to enter into the circumstances of the historical characters, to imagine the quality of their experiences, to provide a context that will make the past seem something other than a grotesque legend, will make it the story of flesh-and-blood human beings, struggling with circumstances and/or with themselves. These narrators try to imagine themselves into the lives of others, so that what has happened will be seen as coming out of recognizable human needs and drives, with these including commendable motives. Thus, theirs is a generous use of the imagination. The effort at understanding moves toward becoming an act of forgiveness or of sympathy. Insofar as Rosa is content to regard Sutpen as past-less or to simply *assume* that his past is one of vague horrors, and insofar as Mr. Compson gives us a Charles Bon who is possessed of virtually no history, they have not made such an effort. But Mr. Compson at least *has* attempted to provide a context for Henry's shooting of Bon that makes Henry seem less a killer than an agonized and pitiful man acting out of principle. And it is significant that Mr. Compson should ask:

> "Have you noticed how so often when we try to reconstruct the causes which lead up to the actions of men and women, how with a sort of astonishment we find ourselves now and then reduced to the belief, the only possible belief, that they stemmed from some of the old virtues? the thief who steals not for greed but for love, the murderer who kills not out of lust but pity?" (P. 121)

It is given to Quentin to supply a past for Sutpen that is crucial to an understanding of his actions. To be sure he does this on the basis of information that Sutpen supplied to Grandfather Compson, but as that past comes to us it is out of Quentin's mouth, and Quentin may be said to fill in the spaces between the facts, and to supply commentary on them. We do not really get close to Sutpen before Quentin's creation of him. It is given to Quentin and to Shreve to supply a past for Bon, and to provide a fuller context for Henry's murder of him than Mr. Compson was able to give (he was not in possession of all the evidence). In so doing, Quentin and Shreve may be said to function as hero-historians, committing their imaginative energies to a strenuous recovery of the past.

The pattern of the narratives, then, takes roughly a three-part form, a kind of tonal thesis-antithesis-synthesis (I exclude the passages of omniscient narrative). We begin with Rosa, who was a participant in the past but whose status as such has distorted her view of Sutpen. We then go to Mr. Compson who is perhaps too detached and too ready to turn his account into a picturesque story featuring a dandyish Bon who is himself too detached (though as already indicated Mr. Compson does not come over only as such).[8] We then move to Quentin, and then to Quentin and Shreve who, in an extraordinary collaboration, immerse their sensibilities in the discontinuous materials they have to work with, doing so with a maximum of sympathy. This is not to say that the book fully vouches for the truthfulness of their joint re-creation, but it does seem to endorse the spirit of their undertaking. Between them they give us a Bon who, far from being the cool, amused sophisticate of Mr. Compson's rendering, is an anguished young man, desperately seeking some sign from Sutpen that would acknowledge him as his son. They give us a Henry tortured by the thought that Bon, who intends to marry his sister, is part Negro. This Henry agonizedly determines to kill the friend he loves who is also his half brother. Before this, Quentin has given us a Sutpen whose monomaniacal "design," the creation of an estate and a dynasty, is not regarded merely as the plan of some ahuman, perverse being, but is seen as stemming from an experience of deep shock and humiliation in his boyhood.

There has been some disagreement over the relation of Sutpen and his design to antebellum Southern society. Ilse Dusoir Lind and Olga Vickery, among others, see Sutpen as an embodiment of that society or an extension of it.[9] Cleanth Brooks, on the other hand, argues that Sutpen's qualities and actions should be seen as typifying "frontier America in general," rather than "something specifically Southern. . . ."[10] It *is* the case that Sutpen is something of an exotic and an outsider so far as the Southern townspeople of Jefferson are concerned, and that his enterprise has a willed, sensational quality that makes it seem unique. But at the same time Faulkner is unquestionably using Sutpen's design to comment on Southern plantation society. While it is true, as Brooks maintains, that the mountain milieu Sutpen derives from should not be regarded as Edenic, it is also true that his origins have so shaped him as to make him register with especial acuteness the nasty configurations of the plantation world he encounters after his family's descent from the mountains (a descent that may well be regarded as symbolic). He is employed, in a standard novelistic strategy, as the naive outsider through whom an alien society can be experienced and illuminated in a way it could not be by one who belonged to that society in the first place. What he brings down with him from the mountains is a simplicity connected with a sense of justice, fair play, and decency. These are outraged by his treatment at the hands of the slave society. Attempting to conduct what he regards as a piece of straight-forward, legitimate business in delivering a message from his father to a plantation owner, he is humiliated, told by a Negro servant, in effect, that he is not fit to enter the manor house through the front door but must go around to the back. This incident, of course, occurs in the context of his awareness that there are sharp differences not only between whites and blacks, but between whites such as his own family and the plantation owners. (Faulkner makes sure we are aware of the bafflement, frustration, and anger of the poor whites, which are expressed in their harassment of blacks.) However, in his boy's innocence, Sutpen had thought that men better off, which he believed to be simply a matter of luck, would not take advantage of the unlucky, would, indeed, be "tender" towards them (p. 226). He thought, in his heartbreaking simplicity, that the white man he was bringing a message to "would be as pleased to show him the balance of his things as [a] mountain man [who owned a fine gun] would have been to show the powder horn and bullet mold that went with the rifle" (p. 229). It is only when these expectations are violated that he becomes the monomaniacal creator of his design. Thus, even granted his special nature, his career *is* an indictment of the slaveholding South, of its treatment of whites as well as of blacks. Moreover, he is seen as part of that South in the very moving plot-strand of the book that involves Wash Jones and that proves a sharp turnabout in the story's treatment of the Civil War.

That war is in the background of much of the action, and occasionally we are given direct, if brief views of it. Those glimpses we get are strongly tinged by a *Gone with the Wind* sensibility. As Mr. Compson evokes the early stages of Southern mobilization, he talks of

> "what is probably the most moving mass-sight of all human mass-experience . . . the sight of young men, the light quick bones, the bright gallant deluded blood and flesh dressed in a martial glitter of brass and plumes, marching away to a battle." (P. 122)

He creates a picture of a glamorous democracy of men going

off to war, and tells of a tour made of Mississippi with the
segments of a company's flag, the sweetheart of each man in
the company helping to stitch the segments together. He
portrays Sutpen's daughter Judith, along with other Southern women, nobly tending the wounded and the dead. But
Faulkner, in general, has difficulty in keeping to a strictly
heroic line, and his depiction of the war characteristically
moves toward the comic when he has a letter of Bon tell of
the desperate capture of Yankee wagons by Confederate
soldiers, only to have it discovered that the wagons contain
not ammunition but stove polish. However, a more important and decidedly uncomic qualification of the glamorous and celebratory treatment of the war comes through
Wash Jones, a poor white in Sutpen's employ. In his early
appearances in the novel, Wash figures in a way that
encourages the reader to dismiss him as white trash, a sly and
funny figure of minimal importance to the action. He ultimately comes to have an important plot function, serving as
the murderer of Sutpen. But it is his commentary on Sutpen,
his state of mind preceding the murder (as re-created by
Quentin through Mr. Compson) that is of interest here. He
had originally worshipped Sutpen, who became a Colonel in
the Confederate army, and on Sutpen's return from the war
he continued to see *"in that furious lecherous wreck the old
fine figure of the man who once galloped on the black
thoroughbred about that domain two boundaries of which
the eye could not see from any point"* (p. 184; italics in
original). He thought that if God Himself came down to earth
to ride a horse He would look like the Colonel. He believed
that whatever Sutpen touched would be made right. But he
has to confront the fact that Sutpen has fathered an illegitimate child on Wash's young granddaughter, and that he is
repudiating the granddaughter and her newborn baby because the child is a girl, and not the male heir Sutpen is so
desperately seeking. It is for this reason that Wash kills the
Colonel. He now sees him as one of a class of men who were

undeniably brave, unquestionably war heroes, but who have now all become his enemy. Quentin tells Shreve that Mr. Compson had conjectured " 'that maybe for the first time in his life he began to comprehend how it had been possible for Yankees or any other army to have whipped them . . .' " (p. 290). Wash is imagined as having thought " 'Better if narra one of them had ever rid back in '65 . . .' " (p. 290). That is to say Wash is seen as having gotten beyond his once worshipful response to Sutpen, coming to perceive him as one of a group of men morally arrogant and blind. Wash moves from his original status as a comic figure, whose colloquialisms are humorously played off against the book's narrative rhetoric, to a position of stature and tragic dignity, in which there is nothing amusing about his bitter ruminations. This is a startling and powerful development in the novel, and should be taken as containing a strong criticism of the ruling class in the Southern plantation system, a class which supplied brave leaders, but leaders whose gallantry was expended in a war designed to defend an exploitative society. The oppressed Wash has come to see his oppressor clearly. A fearful holocaust follows as he kills not only Sutpen but his own granddaughter and her baby, then makes a suicidal rush at the men who have come to apprehend him.

Wash's cutting down of Sutpen provides the deathblow to Sutpen's design. That design operates in the story to engender events and developments which echo occurrences in Sutpen's own career and comment upon it, or which function as antidesigns or rival designs (Wash's murder of Sutpen can be seen as part of this pattern). So, for example, if the design began with what Sutpen took to be an affront to his humanity, through the denial of entrance at the front door of a plantation mansion, that design itself generates affronts to others, dramatized in similar terms. One of these involves Bon. When he makes his initial visit to the Sutpen house, as a friend of Henry's, Sutpen, according to the Quentin–Mr. Compson reconstruction, realizes he is his son by a marriage he had repudiated. For the moment it appears that Bon will be given the kind of entry Sutpen had been denied. Sutpen is pictured in this way:

> "he stood there at his own door, just as he had imagined, planned, designed, and sure enough and after fifty years the forlorn nameless and homeless lost child came to knock at it and no monkey-dressed nigger anywhere under the sun to come to the door and order the child away. . . ." (P. 267)

But while Bon gains entry, in a technical sense, he is denied true admittance in the sense that Sutpen will not acknowledge him as his son. Thus Sutpen, once turned away himself, is now turning away Bon. To drive the point home, Faulkner has Bon, in Shreve's re-creation, say to Henry: " ' "Then I knew that he did know [I was his son]. . . . But he didn't tell me. He just told you, sent me a message like you send a command by a nigger servant to a beggar or a tramp to clear out" ' " (p. 341). (The motif of the denied entrance has actually already recurred with reference to Wash—when he carries food up to the Sutpen house during the war Clytie stops him from entering, saying " ' "You aint never crossed this door while Colonel was here and you aint going to cross it now" ' " [p. 281]).

There are other echoes of the father's life in the son's. Sutpen's expectations of the white planter to whom he was bringing a message seemed very small to him. He only wanted to be treated with what he considered minimal decency. So, too, Bon's expectations of his father are small, pitifully so. He would settle for the tiniest gesture of recognition on Sutpen's part, but nothing is forthcoming. If Sutpen's behavior amounts to an awful denial of paternal obligations, that denial is duplicated in Bon's behavior toward *his* son. For while the terms are different, Bon's actions, which he knows will provoke his murder, constitute a denial of the obligations he has toward his child by the octoroon woman, as well as towards the woman herself (just as Sutpen denied *his* first wife).

Of course Bon is a victim before he forsakes his obligations. His victimization began well before Sutpen refused him recognition. For Sutpen so outraged his first wife by abandoning her that she brought Bon up conceiving of him only as something whereby to wreak revenge on Sutpen (such at least is Shreve's conjecture). The destruction of Sutpen becomes *her* design, and her conception of her son as a mere instrument corresponds to the way Sutpen regards others—Ellen Coldfield (his second wife), Rosa, and Wash's granddaughter. Denied recognition by Sutpen, Bon embarks on his own design, i.e., his own persistent enterprise, which is that of eliciting recognition by his father, and, when that enterprise is not successful, revenging himself on Sutpen by refusing to withdraw from his impending marriage to Judith.

Finally, to return to Wash Jones, Sutpen's destroyer, we find operating in him a desire that matches closely a crucial wish of Sutpen's. In establishing his grand estate, Sutpen is attempting to do right by his descendants. He wishes to insure that they will not have to endure the rejection and humiliation visited on him because of his poor white status (cf. his imaging himself taking in "the homeless lost child," referred to earlier). So, too, with Wash. Horrible as it is, his killing of his granddaughter and her baby proceeds, the book implies, from his desire to prevent them from continuing to receive shameful treatment, from being further victimized by the actions of whites more powerful than they.

These patterns and similarities, taken together, produce the sense of a hideous chain of cause-and-effect, with one violation of human dignity and feeling engendering another, until the whole Sutpen edifice collapses. History repeats itself, with *its* designs triumphing over Sutpen's. This element of repetition is strongly brought out by Rosa's encounter with a resisting Clytie, when she goes to find out what (i.e., who) has been hiding in the rotting Sutpen mansion. This confrontation brings to mind the time she rushed out to the house on learning that Henry had killed Bon (it turns out to be Henry who is in hiding). The two visits, considered as a pair, call to our attention the terrible consequences of Sutpen's ambition. That ambition manifested itself in what might be thought of as a design in black and white, a design requiring racial "purity," but one that circumstances did not respect, with a troublesome middle element being created through racial mixing. The attempt to deny or obliterate that middle ground proved more than the design could carry out and still survive. The book, alternating in its structure between focusing on Sutpen and focusing on Bon and Henry, shows how the original design entailed, first, a father failing his son, and then the son sabotaging the father's hopes. The generations interact, destroying each other. This is what the family's history comes down to.

Such, at least, is the conception arrived at by Shreve and Quentin in their extraordinary collaborative attempt to explain the actions of people of the past who have been kept alive for them by oral tradition (that their version may be wrong and reflect their own particular sensibilities is suggested by the book itself, but no more persuasive version is forthcoming). While Shreve, at times, seems as engaged by Southern history as is Quentin, it is the latter alone who bears the burden of that history at the book's conclusion. He may have unlocked the mysteries of the Sutpen saga, but he can hardly be exhilarated by what he has found. For even to persons as generous and sympathetic as Quentin and Shreve (and to some extent Mr. Compson), that saga only seems to add up to a hideous waste of energy, aspiration, and idealism. Shreve taunts Quentin with the figure of the last of the Sutpen line, Bon's idiot grandson, and asks Quentin why he hates the South. His tortured roommate can only think, in a protest that has become famous, and that undercuts itself, *"I dont. I dont! I dont hate it! I dont hate it!"* (p. 378; italics in original).

These are the book's last words, but the feelings of hatred
and anger they so strongly imply should not be taken as
defining the whole of the novel's attitude. It is true that an
enormous perversity has been shown at work throughout,
but one intertwined with distinction or greatness, even if of a
crazy sort. As each carries out what he feels he must,
proceeding from what began as an admirable intention,
Sutpen and Wash assume a tragic grandeur. The resinous
hearts of the book's characters, in their peculiarly Faulkne-
rian way, help feed what flames upon the night. To say this is
by no means to obliterate the thrust of Quentin's words,
whose placement, after all, gives them great weight, but to
point up the terrible compoundings the novel gives us, of
love and hate, generosity and inhumanity, self-respect and
self-destruction. We are left not with a resolution of them,
only with Quentin's anguish.[11]

NOTES

1. For good overviews of the novel see Olga W. Vickery, *The Novels of William Faulkner* (Baton Rouge, La.: Louisiana State University Press, 1959), and Ilse Dusoir Lind, "The Design and Meaning of *Absalom, Absalom!*," in *William Faulkner: Three Decades of Criticism*, ed. Frederick J. Hoffman and Olga W. Vickery (New York: Harcourt, Brace & World, 1963), pp. 278–304.

2. Allen Tate, "The Novel in the American South," *New Statesman,* 13 June 1959, 831.

3. I have used the Modern Library text of the novel (New York, 1951). Succeeding quotations from the book will be followed in the text of the chapter itself by the relevant page numbers. The page of the quotation just given is 7; the italics are mine.

4. Walter J. Slatoff's *Quest for Failure: A Study of William Faulkner* (Ithaca, N.Y.: Cornell University Press, 1960) shows how the coupling of opposing conditions or qualities is characteristic of Faulkner's imagination, and operates in a variety of contexts. I am simply pointing out how the oxymoronic materials I have noted relate to *Absalom, Absalom!*'s general preoccupation with the past.

5. Faulkner can create such an effect even when not using historical materials. See Jean-Paul Sartre's "Time in Faulkner: *The Sound and the Fury*," in Hoffman and Vickery, *William Faulkner,* pp. 225–32.

6. His tendency to make generalizations about women might be regarded by some readers as yet another doubtful element in his account, but I believe that in these he is speaking for Faulkner.

7. Much of the book, particularly when Rosa is speaking, is set in italics.

8. In addition to what has already been said about his version, we might note his account of Bon's son. There is an implicit pity running through it.

9. See the items cited in note 1.

10. Cleanth Brooks, *William Faulkner: The Yoknapatawpha Country* (New Haven, Conn.: Yale University Press, 1963), p. 427.

11. For an alternative reading of *Absalom, Absalom!,* it is recommended that the reader consult John T. Irwin's *Doubling and Incest/Repetition and Revenge* (Baltimore, Md.: Johns Hopkins University Press, 1975). Irwin approaches the book (as well as other Faulkner works) largely in Freudian terms. Quentin and Shreve, along with Sutpen, Bon, and Henry, are implicated in his scheme, which sees the novel largely as a complex struggle between fathers and sons. Irwin makes brilliant use of the Biblical story of David and Absalom in his reading of the book.

3

An Odor of Sartoris:
William Faulkner's *The Unvanquished*

"An Odor of Verbena," frequently anthologized as a short story complete in itself, also serves as the final chapter of Faulkner's *The Unvanquished,* a novel which appeared in 1938. In that chapter, an extended reference is made to Colonel Sutpen, who figures of course as a central character in *Absalom, Absalom!,* published two years earlier. The allusion to Sutpen only serves to point up the enormous differences between the two novels, in terms of both form and achievement. But while it is a much more conventional piece of storytelling and a much smaller accomplishment than *Absalom, Absalom!,* and while the whole of it has been less highly regarded than its concluding chapter, *The Unvanquished* has an interest of its own, revealing part of Faulkner's overall conception of the Southern past.

The book consists of a series of episodes ranging in time from 1863 to 1874, and related to us by Bayard Sartoris, who figures as a major participant in the work as well as its narrator. Coming from *Absalom, Absalom!* to the adventures Bayard speaks of, one is first struck by the decided absence of the earlier book's elements: the opaque narrative technique, the rhetorical inflation, the tortured questing for the truth of the past. (Such things would probably not have found favor with the readers of *The Saturday Evening Post,* where much of the book first appeared, in the form of stories).[1] It is almost as though writing *The Unvanquished* constituted a vacation for Faulkner, a respite from the strenuousness of *Absalom, Absalom!* Where the story of Colonel Sutpen seemed determined to build up and complicate its subject, to give its materials massiveness, intensity, and large significance, *The Unvanquished,* while drawing its subject matter mostly from the potentially great theme of the Civil War, is to a very large extent content to be relatively low-keyed, relaxed, diminutive.

This is immediately apparent in the treatment of the war action and of the invading Yankees (the story takes place in Mississippi). The Civil War set countrymen killing fellow countrymen, produced an enormous number of casualties, and caused destruction that went, at least in the South, far beyond the confines of limited battlefields. But Faulkner is apparently reluctant to tap these potential sources of drama and intensity. Neither Yankee nor Southerner kill one another before our eyes, though such deaths are alluded to. Much of the war action *per se* is occurring or has occurred offstage, and does not generate a sense of widespread death. It seems to involve, on the part of Colonel Sartoris, much more in the way of stealing Yankee horses than shooting their riders. When the Yankees appear on the home front, the basic locus of the action, they come on mostly as exasperated dupes, frustrated and defeated (in terms of the loss of material goods) by Southern wiles. They do burn down the Sartoris home (as well as others) but that burning is handled in a curiously muted way. For while one chapter concludes with the Yankees being called " 'bastuds' " because they have destroyed the Sartoris house,[2] the destruction takes place almost before we know it, and is not dwelt upon. There is very little bitterness directed against the invaders by either Faulkner or his characters.

Indeed, the Yankee presented most fully is made very attractive. Colonel Dick, knowing that the two boys, Bayard and his Negro companion Ringo, are literally hiding behind

Rosa Millard's skirts after having shot at one of his Union soldiers, pretends to believe the lady's assertion that there are no children present. He orders his men not to harass her (the story comes uncomfortably close to being a Confederate version of "Barbara Frietchie"). Later, the Colonel signs an order stating that the silver and mules taken from Rosa should be returned. He is the courteous, considerate gentleman from start to finish, admiring and sympathetic in his response to the Southern civilians. Faulkner's depiction of Colonel Dick would seem to partake of what one historian has found in a number of Civil War novels, the myth "of a war ruled by antebellum courtesies rather than military necessity. . . ." Such a view "avoided violence to the feelings of either North or South. . . ."³ There is certainly such avoidance here, and it constitutes one of the book's *evasions* of touchy and difficult subject matter. We are given a conflict flattering to both sides, a Civil War which turns out to be a war game more than anything else (the book opens with Bayard playing at war with Ringo, and this turns out to be a comment, intended or not, on much of the book).⁴

There *are* feelings of hatred and revulsion that get into the novel, but these are directed not against the Yankees, but against Southerners preying upon other Southerners. Grumby's Independents are a group of men who begin to loot and terrorize their compatriots as soon as the Northern soldiers are gone. They do not stop at beating women and children, and they end up murdering Rosa Millard. Here are villains of the deepest dye whom everyone can hate with a clear conscience. An easy target for easy feelings is thus provided, making for the complete displacement of the North-South confrontation.

One detects an evasiveness not only in Faulkner's handling of the war, but in his depiction of the relationship between Bayard and Ringo as well—this is part of the larger question of the book's presentation of the Negro. The two characters are twelve-year-old boys when we first meet them. They have long eaten together and slept together, and both call Rosa Millard, mother of Colonel Sartoris and grandmother of Bayard, "Granny." Bayard says of Ringo: "maybe he wasn't a nigger anymore or maybe I wasn't a white boy anymore. . . ." (p. 8). They live a kind of wartime idyll, sharing adventures that are a boy's dream. (The relationship between them links up with the interracial male pairings Leslie Fiedler finds so prominent in American fiction.) In the incident where they shoot at the Yankee soldier they handle the rifle together. During another episode they are riding on one horse, and the symmetry of the action further establishes an "equality" between them: "presently I caught Ringo and held him as he slipped off and then a little later Ringo caught and held me from slipping before I even knew that I had been asleep" (p. 68). Bayard says that the difference in the color of their skins didn't count for them, only the difference in their experiences (at one point Bayard is temporarily "ahead" of Ringo because he has seen a locomotive whereas Ringo has not). If anything, Ringo is regarded by Colonel Sartoris as the smarter of the two boys, and it is he who plays an active role in Rosa's scheme for getting mules from the Yankees under false pretenses. Ringo is a vivid presence in the book, a character of much charm, thoroughly engaging (Faulkner once said he grew up with a boy like Ringo). But apart from that, he has been made by the author into a wholehearted devotee of the old order, perhaps more of a Sartoris than the Sartorises themselves. When the two boys are journeying from home, Ringo trades a prized possession for some of the "Sartoris dirt" that Bayard has taken with him (p. 62). He is a great admirer of Granny. When he forges copies of the order Colonel Dick had given Rosa, he wants "to sign [General] Grant's name every time, and when Granny said that would not do anymore, Lincoln's. At last Granny found out that Ringo objected to having the Yankees think that Father's folks would have any dealings with anybody under the General-in-Chief" (p. 145).

He is plainly unsympathetic to the carpetbaggers who are trying to put Negroes into office. Finally, in "An Odor of Verbena," when Colonel Sartoris is murdered, it is Ringo who comes to inform Bayard and fetch him home, saying " 'we,' " i.e., he and Bayard, could get the Colonel's killer (p. 251).

But in that chapter, the last in the book, Ringo is ultimately relegated to the background. He and Bayard are both twenty-four now, and Bayard has left home to study law. Just what Ringo is doing is not specified (he is presumably still attached to the Sartoris family in some capacity). Given the prominence of Ringo's role and his relationship to Bayard in the preceding portions of the book, the subordination of these in "An Odor of Verbena" is striking. Such an effect was undoubtedly not intended by Faulkner, and could simply be the result of his bringing together the previously unpublished "Odor" and pieces of the book that had appeared earlier as separate stories. But he has given us *The Unvanquished* as a whole, and looked at as such, the book's shunting aside of the Bayard-Ringo relationship constitutes an evasion of a painful subject, namely, the presumable effects that their growing up and out of boyhood, their going the separate ways of white and Negro, have had on their friendship and their views of each other (this would have been particularly complicated by the changed status of the Negroes as a result of the war). Faulkner is certainly entitled to his focus in "An Odor of Verbena," which is the matter of Bayard's entry into moral manhood, but since the story does come as the concluding piece of a larger work, one looks, in vain, for the exploration of a relationship that has figured prominently hitherto. One gets the sense that Faulkner is trying to cover important ground too quickly, too skimpily, that he acknowledges his debt to his character without discharging it, when he has Bayard say that Ringo had changed so much during the time he was engaged in Granny's mule scheme that "I had had to do most of the changing just to catch up with him" (p. 248). What does the change in Ringo consist of, and how do he and Bayard relate to each other now? Only the white character is given a significant development. For if we are to go by what "An Odor of Verbena" does tell us, we see a Bayard who is capable of achieving moral independence, while Ringo seems arrested in a state of Uncle Tom-hood, defined only by his wish to avenge the Colonel's death. The two young men are not adequately placed in relationship to each other in the book's concluding chapter.

The intelligence and resourcefulness that Faulkner ascribes to Ringo in the course of *The Unvanquished* stand out all the more sharply because of the novel's generally condescending treatment of the slaves (the split here in the treatment of the Negro may remind the reader of the clashing elements that went into Mark Twain's portrait of Nigger Jim). For example, the elderly Joby functions exclusively as a comic black, humorously reluctant to do heavy work, and saying "Which?" when one would expect him to say "What?" He is pictured as being in a continual contest with Granny which she always wins. At one point he is portrayed with "his mouth hanging open and his eyes like two eggs" (p. 66), the very model of stage-Negro amazement. His son Loosh is described as having a head resembling "a cannonball . . . bedded hurriedly and carelessly in concrete. . ." (p. 4). (We cannot help laughing at this comparison, albeit guiltily.) Even Ringo does not escape such portraiture, and on one occasion when it is applied to him it robs him of potentially heroic status. He and Bayard have tracked down the infamous Grumby. Bayard is attacked by the outlaw who in turn is attacked by Ringo: ". . . I saw Ringo, in the air, looking exactly like a frog, even to the eyes, with his mouth open too. . ." (pp. 209–10). Later, he makes an appearance saying " 'I ain't a nigger any more. I done been abolished' " (p. 228).

Such touches are of a piece with Faulkner's distinctly unreconstructed view of the slaves leaving their masters when they hear of their emancipation. The subject enters in a comical way with Loosh's wife, Louvinia, striking him in the head when he says the Negroes will be freed, and telling him " 'You black fool!' . . . 'Do you think there's enough Yankees in the whole world to whip the white folks?' " Bayard's reaction to Loosh's statement is to tell Granny excitedly that the Yankees are coming " 'to set us free!' " (p. 26). So first, we have Louvinia's amusing distinction between white folks and Yankees, followed by Bayard's inability to distinguish between the status of the white Southerners and the slaves (this last is undoubtedly meant to be amusing also, but is hard to take). After thus availing himself of Bayard's one-time naïveté to try for a comic effect, Faulkner then makes use of the older Bayard's maturity to have him deliver a serious comment on the slaves' attraction to freedom (Bayard is recounting the story's events years after their occurrence, so the narrative is able to move from the child to the man). He speaks of "the impulse to move which had already seethed to a head among [the Negroes], darker than themselves, reasonless, following and seeking a delusion, a dream . . ." (p. 92). Faulkner's imagination is engaged by this view (one typical of many Civil War novels),[5] and he provides us with remarkable pictures of the blacks moving in groups along the roads and entering a river in quest of their freedom. We are given a vivid sense of an inexorable, though futile and irrational mass movement, but one wishes Faulkner had allowed his dramatizations to speak for themselves, had been less tendentious and condescending in his treatment of the slaves' drive toward freedom. Drusilla, Bayard's cousin, speaks contemptuously of the slaves tramping the roads all night, " 'waiting for a chance to drown in homemade Jordan . . .' " (p. 115). Granny lectures a number of slaves on their having left home, telling them to return where they came from. The two ladies appear to be speaking for the author.

Yet there is one notable exception to Faulkner's supercilious conception of the Negroes' hunger for liberty. When Granny asks Loosh if he is leaving the Sartoris home he says that he is: " 'I done been freed; God's own angel proclamated me free and gonter general me to Jordan. I don't belong to John Sartoris now; I belongs to me and God.' " Challenged by Granny on having revealed the whereabouts of the Sartoris silver, Loosh replies: " 'Where John Sartoris? Whyn't he come and ax me that? Let God ax John Sartoris who the man name that give me to him. Let the man that buried me in the black dark ax that of the man what dug me free' " (p. 85). This is a remarkable moment. A character has broken free of his author's general views and inherited prejudices to present with force and dignity a conception of himself which goes directly counter to the thrust of the story. A piece of Faulkner's imagination seems to have cut loose here and to be operating on its own. The reader finds it hard to believe that the Loosh speaking these lines entered the story possessed of a head like a cannonball embedded in concrete.

Perhaps Faulkner's generally condescending treatment of the slaves leaving their homes to seek freedom comes out of a view of slavery which, at least in *The Unvanquished,* does not make that condition seem an oppressive one at all. Certainly there is no abuse of Negroes at the hands of the Sartorises anywhere in the book. Also, the wartime conditions depicted seem to have made blacks and whites virtual equals, either in the form of the adventures shared by Bayard and Ringo, or of the common quarters inhabited by members of the two races after the burning of white homes. By such equalization of their condition, Faulkner would seem, as he does in the ultimate subordination of the Bayard-Ringo relationship, to be evading the great, painful fact of the

South's old order, the fact of slavery. In the one household beside that of Sartoris where we get a picture of the relations between whites and blacks, there is nothing to suggest the terrible forms slavery could take. The brothers Buck and Buddy McCaslin participate in an elaborate game with their slaves which allows the latter freedom of movement in the evenings. Also, Colonel Sartoris says that the McCaslins are possessed of ideas about social relationships well ahead of their time. In an anticipation of Ike McCaslin in *The Bear,* we are told of the brothers' conception that the people belong to the land and not vice versa. We are told, too, as a presumable extension of this notion, that the brothers have a scheme whereby the slaves will not be given their freedom, but will buy it in work on the plantation. Buck and Buddy have persuaded some poor white farmers to pool their meager land holdings "along with the niggers and the McCaslin plantation, promising them in return nobody knew exactly what, except that their women and children did have shoes, which not all of them had had before, and a lot of them even went to school." Here, too, there is an "equalizing" of whites and blacks, though under conditions of the greatest vagueness, and presided over by members of an upper class exhibiting a spirit of noblesse oblige. The McCaslins' plan seems to represent the book's prescription for the way the slaves should have been freed.

A spirit of noblesse oblige is at work, also, in Granny's disposing of the fruits of her successful swindling. (Repeatedly getting mules free from the Yankees under false pretenses, she sells them back to the Northern soldiers.) She distributes money and mules to her neighbors, but demands that they tell her how they will spend the money, what they will do with the mules, etc. Occasionally, she takes a mule from one person and gives it to another. She is the determined, courageous aristocrat, providing for the less resourceful around her, a Lady Bountiful. When she prays to God, she acknowledges the chicanery of her dealings with the Yankees, but defends it at the same time. Her address to God is a paradoxical thing, a defiant prayer. She is unquestionably admired by Faulkner and part of his portrait of the Old South at its best. (That portrait is highly sketchy, since what the book mainly gives us is the Old South being broken down by the war.)

Granny, or Rosa Millard, was cited by George Marion O'Donnell when he formulated his famous thesis about the Faulkner canon, saying that its unifying principle was "the Southern social-economic-ethical tradition," and that it exhibited "the conflict between traditionalism and the anti-traditional modern world in which it is immersed." The Sartorises are people who "act traditionally. . . ." Arrayed against them are "the invading Northern armies" and the landless whites, like Ab Snopes, who aim "to make the traditional actions of the Sartorises impossible."[6] O'Donnell treated *The Unvanquished* first in the development of his thesis, going on to apply his conception of the traditional versus the modern to a number of Faulkner's works, including almost all the major novels. O'Donnell's view proved an influential one, though it has been modified by others since, or called into question as applying to the whole of Faulkner. Putting aside the question of its validity for other of Faulkner's works, we can say that its accuracy with respect to *The Unvanquished* is so dubious that one wonders why it wasn't questioned from the very start. For while Sartorises and Snopes, who are key figures in O'Donnell's formulation, are both present in *The Unvanquished,* O'Donnell's description of the conflict between them, and the respective motivations they embody, does not cover the facts but, rather, misrepresents them.

We might first observe that the invading Northern armies do not represent a principle antagonistic to an "ethical tradition" embodied in the Sartorises. As has been already demonstrated, the chief portrait of a Yankee soldier is highly flattering. Moreover, it is precisely because the Yankees assume that the principle of returning confiscated goods to civilians is at work in the forged military orders Granny presents to them, that she is able to carry out her swindles. They are hardly the enemies of a "traditional" morality here. And just how traditionally ethical is Granny in her dealings with the Yankees? If anything, Sartoris and Snopes *share* a common ability to hoodwink, to outsmart, the invaders. Granny and Abner Snopes make a pair of natural partners until such time as Granny proves the victim of Ab's unscrupulousness with respect to her (only here does O'Donnell's thesis apply). There is in Faulkner considerable admiration for the shrewd dealer, and a delight in his or her manipulations (this is present even in *The Hamlet* where there is much sympathy for the victims of such manipulations).[7] Faulkner's treatment of shrewd operators was probably influenced by tales of outwitting that make up part of the body of "American humor." And while events in *The Unvanquished* ultimately take a terrible turn, the story of Granny's repeated victimization of the Yankees is colored by comedy, as when a Yankee lieutenant asks Granny not to turn a receipt he is giving her into a document that will eventually ruin him. By that point in the story he knows her way with Union Army paper forms.

The talent for outwitting is featured in *the* Sartoris, the Colonel himself. While he is undoubtedly brave, we are made just as conscious of his resourcefulness in *fooling* the enemy. In one episode he gains time for escape by acting like a dimwit. In another, he captures a group of Union soldiers by having Bayard and Ringo make a great deal of noise, giving the false impression to the soldiers that they are surrounded by Confederates. The incident ends with the Yankees sneaking off into the bushes in their underwear. As with the events centering on Granny, the episode is basically comic. Here, too, the focus is hardly on the operation of a traditional morality but on an amoral shrewdness. With the triumphs of both Granny and the Colonel, the reader is not witness to the display of an ethical tradition so much as a capacity to adopt to new circumstances, to improvise, to act in a way that has more to do with spiritedness and imagination than with morality. The results are largely amusing, and rather than adopt O'Donnell's view, it is more to the point to observe that Faulkner's treatment of the Southern past here partakes of the quality of American humor, its amalgam of heroism and comedy.

We should also note that there is a kind of comedy at work in one of the book's chapters other than the sort we have been viewing, and that this too goes counter to O'Donnell's thesis. It is not manifested in terms of Confederate triumphs over the Northerners, but takes the form of satire at the expense of the South. Such humor is not characteristic of the book as a whole, but it does figure as one component in Faulkner's presentation of Southern history. The section called "Skirmish at Sartoris" is largely concerned with the efforts of Bayard's Aunt Louisa to get her daughter Drusilla married to Colonel Sartoris. Drusilla, a cousin of the Colonel's dead wife, had ridden off to war with the Colonel's troop, acting as just one more soldier. Aunt Louisa was scandalized by Drusilla's action, and now insists that she and Colonel Sartoris must get married at once. The women of the town of Jefferson enter into a kind of alliance with Louisa to see that propriety is served. All of these ladies are treated as comic figures, their concern with what they regard as sacred social forms played off against the thoroughly unconventional behavior of Drusilla. Aunt Louisa may be said to embody a "traditional" sensibility, but, whatever O'Donnell might say about the matter, it is not seen by the story as anything to be honored. Aunt Louisa says her husband died in the war *"to protect a heritage of courageous men and spotless women . . ."* (p. 219, italics in original). Drusilla has flouted, in her mother's view, "all Southern principles of purity and womanhood that our husbands had died for . . ." (p. 222). (Aunt Louisa may be regarded as a spiritual

ancestress of Mrs. Compson in *The Sound and the Fury,* who
is preoccupied with the supposed worth of her family and its
good name, which she sees as threatened by the activities of
her daughter Candace.) Faulkner plainly cannot take Aunt
Louisa or her rhetoric seriously, mocking even her display of
mourning (she wears a black crepe bow on her umbrella and
carries around with her "a wad of some kind of black
knitting" (p. 232)—one thinks of Twain's satire of expressions of ostentatious sorrow in *Huckleberry Finn*). In her
comic obsession with getting Drusilla married, she seems to
represent for Faulkner a ridiculous elevation of propriety to
the supreme value in life, and in her statements about what
the Southern dead had sacrificed themselves for, she is seen
as advancing an absurd conception of the war.[8] These are
components of a Southern sensibility that Faulkner can only
laugh at.

Yet even as he shows a readiness to be amused here at the
genteel Southern woman's view of the world, Faulkner can
be accused of using the humor of "Skirmish at Sartoris" to
cloud the issues raised by another element of the South he is
presenting to us, the use of violence to maintain the political
status quo. Apart from the matter of Drusilla's marriage, the
chapter's principal concern is with Colonel Sartoris's response to the machinations of the carpetbaggers. Efforts are
being made by Northern whites to get the Negroes of the
town to become Republicans and vote a black man into
office as town marshal. The Colonel, along with the other
white men of the town, is determined that this shall not
happen. He ends up shooting the two Northerners who are
behind the scheme, saying he allowed them to fire first. He
and Drusilla appropriate the ballot box, and in the subsequent "election," all the white men vote against the
would-be Negro marshal. "Skirmish at Sartoris" ends with
the men cheering Drusilla and the Colonel. The book itself
appears to be endorsing the Colonel's action (he claims to be
working " 'for peace through law and order' " [p. 239]),

evading the question of the means he has employed in pursuing his goal. Faulkner reduces the pressure of such a question by intertwining the story of the ballot box with the comedy of Aunt Louisa confronting a Drusilla who has *forgotten* to get married in the excitement of the action taken against the carpetbaggers. The chapter appears to be presenting an unreconstructed Southern view of the voting episode, with the cheers of the men sounding "high and thin and ragged and fierce, like when the Yankees used to hear it out of the smoke and the galloping . . ." (pp. 241–42).

However, with the book's final chapter, "An Odor of Verbena," the critique of the Colonel that is conspicuous by its absence from "Skirmish at Sartoris" makes a notable appearance (that critique is not acknowledged at all in the O'Donnell thesis about Sartorises vs. Snopeses).[9] Bayard, now a law student, is called upon by a traditional code to avenge his father's killing (the Colonel has been shot by his one-time business partner, Redmond). He is expected to do so by his fellow townsmen, by Ringo, and most important, by Drusilla, who presents him with a pair of duelling pistols; she is described by him as "the Greek amphora priestess of a succinct and formal violence" (p. 252). However, when he goes to confront Redmond, Bayard does so with no intention of participating in a duel or killing him. This decision marks a significant break with the Sartoris mode.[10] It is obviously approved of by the story and this alone indicates that the way of Colonel Sartoris represents something less than the highest form of conduct for Faulkner. But "An Odor of Verbena" makes unfavorable judgments of the Colonel more directly.

Those judgments must operate against the formidable image of the Colonel that has emerged from the previous chapters. Even as it was being created, that image was partly recognized by Bayard as the subjective product of his younger self, but this distancing acknowledgment still left

the Colonel endowed with glamour. The objective facts of
the story display his courage and quick-wittedness. He rides
a horse named nothing less than Jupiter; it is described at one
point as standing in the dawn "as a mesmerized flame. . ."
(p. 69). Effects like this rub off on the man.

But the Colonel's participation in violence is confronted
by "An Odor of Verbena" in a way that is new to the book.
The chapter tells of how Drusilla, some time before his
death, had defended him as having a dream in which " 'all
the people, black and white' " would raise themselves by
their bootstraps (p. 256). Bayard, however, had wondered
how he hoped to accomplish anything good if he killed
people. Bayard reminded Drusilla that the carpetbaggers
Sartoris had shot before holding the election were " 'men.
Human beings' " (p. 257). Bayard refers to his father's
"violent and ruthless dictatorialness and will to dominate"
(p. 258), compares his eyes to those of "carnivorous animals" (p. 266), and sees the hands of the dead Colonel
colored by "the invisible stain of what had been (once,
surely) needless blood. . ." (p. 272). The moral question of
the Colonel's right to kill, an issue that had been allowed to
escape from "Skirmish at Sartoris," is being faced here.
Bayard decides that *he* does not wish to continue the pattern
of killing in confronting Redmond.

Yet in the last analysis, Faulkner shows a distinct ambivalence towards Colonel Sartoris (a figure based on Faulkner's own great-grandfather). The attraction that the Colonel
has for him is by no means purged in "An Odor of Verbena."
Faulkner cannot bring himself to reject this character clearly
and finally. Note, for example, the curious handling of
Sartoris's encounters with Redmond. There is one scene
which, confusingly, refers to a forthcoming meeting between
Redmond and Sartoris but not the one in which the Colonel is
killed. During this scene, the Colonel says he is tired of
killing and will go to see Redmond unarmed. In the en-

counter where he *is* killed, he is described as carrying his derringer in its usual concealed place but not using it. Thus, while the Colonel, after his death, is thought of as a man stained with blood, he has displayed, while still alive, a rejection of his usual ways. We have, then, simultaneously, an impulse in the story to judge the Colonel harshly, and a desire to present him favorably through his own expression of contrition. Also, while Bayard seems at one point to repudiate the Colonel's "dream" because of his father's readiness to employ violence in seeing it realized, he says, as the book draws to a close, that the dream was "something which he had bequeathed us which we could never forget. . ." (p. 291).

Finally, there is the symbolic gesture made by Drusilla. It is she who has most passionately expressed the desirability of Bayard's avenging the Colonel's death. When she realizes he is not going to shoot Redmond she becomes hysterical. Yet, ultimately, she pays tribute to Bayard's going unarmed to meet Redmond by placing a sprig of verbena on his pillow. While riding with the Colonel during the war, she used to gather the flower and wear it; it was "the only scent you could smell above the smell of horses and courage and so it was the only one that was worth the wearing" (pp. 253–54). The book concludes with Bayard's discovery of the sprig. In one way Drusilla's gesture can be interpreted as a realization by her that Bayard's course of action is an admirable one, superior to the violence she had originally espoused. But the means by which the gesture is made is linked inextricably to the courage of the Colonel. The odor of verbena takes its meaning from its association with his wartime activities, in which Drusilla shared. The odor evokes the Colonel, and Drusilla's gesture is that of one Sartoris paying tribute to another. So that her act of laying the sprig on Bayard's pillow expresses perfectly Faulkner's mixed feelings toward Sartoris. On the one hand there is the recognition of the courage Bayard has shown in taking a course of action so different from that characteristic of his father. But at the same time the Colonel's courage is evoked, and Bayard, in rejecting his father's way, is seen as being worthy of his father. Some critics would argue that there is a progression in the book from the young Bayard's romanticizing of his father to the adult Bayard's recognition of his father's defects. What is being argued here is that alongside its severe judgment of the Colonel, the book manages to retain much of the original glamour it had bestowed on him.

The ending of the book, then, contains a survival of the admiration for the Colonel as a representative of the Old South. In this respect, as well as others, *The Unvanquished* is very different from *Absalom, Absalom!,* where Quentin Compson's insistent cry that he does *not* hate the South strongly suggests just the opposite. The Old South in *Absalom, Absalom!* seems a much more terrible place than in *The Unvanquished,* having inhumanity as a part of its structure, as demonstrated in Colonel Sutpen's "design" for founding a dynasty. The recovery of the story of Sutpen oppresses Quentin intensely. In *The Unvanquished,* the past, even while rejected in one way, is also cherished, and there is a sense of reconciliation and closure at the book's conclusion as opposed to the open-ended pain that Quentin exhibits. The strenuousness and complexity of *Absalom, Absalom!* do not result in release, whereas the relative relaxation and simplicity of *The Unvanquished* produce a Southern past that can be at once rejected and loved, certainly lived with. Everybody would agree that *Absalom, Absalom!* is the greater work and that it acknowledges the cruelty, injustice, and conflicts of the past more fully than *The Unvanquished.* But the latter work is Faulkner's creature as well, and points up what might be called the Confederate component of his sensibility.

When, in a conversation about his great-grandfather and the Civil War, Faulkner was asked the sources of his history, he said:

"I never read any history . . . I talked to people. . . . When I was a boy there were a lot of people around who had lived through it, and I would pick it up—I was just saturated with it, but never read about it."[11]

While we need not accept this statement as the whole truth—there were works on the Civil War in Faulkner's personal library though not a very great number of them[12]—it is undoubtedly the case that Faulkner got much of his sense of the past from oral tradition. Such a source would have tended largely toward a glorification and defense of the past, and certainly influenced *The Unvanquished*. Insofar as it retains the mark of such influence the book is a measure of how far Faulkner had to go from his cultural starting point to be able to write a work like *Absalom, Absalom!* *The Unvanquished* itself is not completely subservient to a narrow, glorified version of the past, being a mixture of the celebratory, the comic, the satiric, and the critical, but it ends up accepting Southern history in a way that *Absalom, Absalom!* cannot.

NOTES

1. All but one of the chapters making up the book were first published in magazines.

2. William Faulkner, *The Unvanquished* (New York: Random House, 1938), p. 86. Further quotations from the novel will be followed in the text of the chapter by the relevant page numbers.

3. See Robert A. Lively, *Fiction Fights the Civil War* (Chapel Hill, N.C.: University of North Carolina Press, 1957), p. 44.

4. Irving Howe has remarked of *The Unvanquished* that "One must remind oneself that this is Faulkner's book about the Civil War." He asks: "was this the war that roused William Tecumseh Sherman to his burst of eloquence?" *William Faulkner: A Critical Study* (New York: Random House, 1952), p. 45.

5. See Lively, *Fiction Fights the Civil War*, p. 53.

6. George Marion O'Donnell, "Faulkner's Mythology," in *William Faulkner: Three Decades of Criticism*, ed. Frederick J. Hoffman and Olga W. Vickery (New York: Harcourt, Brace & World, 1963), pp. 82–83. O'Donnell's essay was originally published in 1939.

7. I cannot agree with those commentators on the book who solemnly talk of Granny's "corruption" in going into partnership with Ab Snopes. See Hyatt H. Waggoner, *William Faulkner: From Jefferson to the World* (Lexington, Ky.: University of Kentucky Press, 1959), pp. 174–75; also Andrew Lytle, "The Son of Man: He Will Prevail," *Sewanee Review,* 63 (Winter 1955): 131–32. See also O'Donnell, "Faulkner's Mythology," p. 83.

8. It should be observed that Aunt Louisa's view of the motives behind the war was not untypical of the actual South. See W. J. Cash, *The Mind of the South* (Garden City, N.Y.: Doubleday & Company, 1956), pp. 85–86.

9. O'Donnell says only that Ab Snopes made Rosa "betray herself into an act of self-interest such as his. . ." "Faulkner's Mythology," p. 83.

10. As with his treatment of *Absalom, Absalom!*, John T. Irwin, in *Doubling and Incest/Repetition and Revenge,* (Baltimore, Md.: Johns Hopkins University Press, 1975), sees the action here as a Freudian drama: "by defeating the man who killed his father, Bayard has proved himself a better man than his father; he has supplanted that overpowering, debilitating image of the father in the life of the son by psychically doing away with the threatening father-surrogate. In defeating his father's killer, Bayard is symbolically killing his father, and when Bayard confronts Redmond, the man who actually did what Bayard had unconsciously desired to do as an implicit part of his incestuous desire for his stepmother [Drusilla], i.e., kill his father, Bayard confronts a double of himself. It is a theme that Faulkner never tires of reiterating: by courageously facing the fear of death, the fear of castration, the fear of one's own worst insticts, one slays the fear; by taking the risk of being feminized, by accepting the feminine elements in the self, one establishes one's masculinity" (p. 58).

11. Quoted in Robert Cantwell, "The Faulkners: Recollections of a Gifted Family," in *William Faulkner: Three Decades of Criticism,* p. 57.

12. See *William Faulkner's Library: A Catalogue,* compiled by Joseph Blotner (Charlottesville, 1964).

4

Antebellum Rootedness:
Allen Tate's Images of the Old South

Looking back to the emergence in the 1920s of the Fugitives, a group of Southern writers centered at Vanderbilt University, Allen Tate said that "with us entering the world once more [after World War I] meant not the obliteration of the past, but a heightened consciousness of it."[1] The past he referred to was, of course, that of the South, a subject that figured in all the literary forms he practiced over a long career—reviews, essays, biographies, fiction, and poetry.

One of his earliest considerations of the Southern past is strikingly uncharacteristic of him in its detachment from and mockery of the old order, and might startle those readers whose perusal of Tate's critical prose has not gone beyond his collected essays. The piece called "Last Days of the Charming Lady,"[2] though agreeing with the view that portions of the antebellum South exhibited the "graces of living" more than other sections of the country, delivers an urbane but barbed commentary on the deficiencies of the Old South. Possessed of no meaningful religion, thin and derivative in its literary and intellectual productions, it was, Tate says, informed by only a single idea—the worth of its political-economic system. It had no capacity for self-criticism, no ability to throw off old assumptions and adopt new ones. In this essay, published in 1925, Tate is plainly dissociating himself from a then current nostalgia which he

92

found as devoid of the critical spirit as was the Old South for which it pined. Help for the modern South would have to be supplied by the Southern writer's pursuit of a cosmopolitan culture. Feeling himself "a foreigner at home," that writer would, before discovering a tradition "somewhere in the United States," have to "first see himself, if at all, through other eyes."[3]

In the very same year that Tate published "Last Days of the Charming Lady," the South was being widely and unfavorably viewed through the eyes of others because of the Scopes Trial. This apparently did not sit well with Tate. According to Louise Cowan, the Northern ridicule of the South was one cause (another was Tate's negative reaction to New York City) for his distinct shift in attitude toward his native region, a change he underwent along with John Crowe Ransom and Donald Davidson. "At the end of 1925 . . . these three still considered themselves, as writers, disengaged from their society. But by the spring of 1927 they . . . were to affirm a positive belief in the principles of the Old South."[4]

In 1925 Tate had described the antebellum South as producing mediocre imitations of Europe, and the modern Southerner as unlikely to have "a native culture compounded of the strength and subtlety of his New England contemporary's."[5] But by 1930 he was saying that the Old South was ignorant of Europe and could afford to be so "because she *was* Europe; that is to say . . . was trying to take root in a native soil," whereas it was New England which had been culturally parasitic on Europe.[6] Moreover, his original comparison of Southerner and New Englander, made only in passing and to the detriment of the former, had evolved in Tate's writings into an historical drama of conflicting regional sensibilities, with Tate emerging as the acerbic advocate of the South. He played off John Adams, as a prototypal New Englander, against Thomas Jefferson. The latter had relied on "custom, breeding, ingrained moral decision," while Adams had been forced "to think out from abstract principle his role at a critical moment of action."[7] Tate obviously thought the Jeffersonian approach superior. The escape from ideas that he had charged Dixie with in 1925 had been adroitly transmuted five years later into a virtue:

> The Southern mind was simple, not top-heavy with learning it had no need of, unintellectual and composed; it was personal and dramatic, rather than abstract and metaphysical; and it was sensuous because it lived close to a natural scene of great variety and interest.[8]

The year before this statement appeared, he had said, answering the "prejudice" he attributed to New England which saw Southerners as unlettered, that the South was simply "wary of new and crank ideas. . . ."[9] He asserted this in his book on Jefferson Davis. In that work, interestingly enough, Davis's flaw seems to be that he was too much the Northerner. His mistake, according to Tate, "the mistake of all theorists, rests upon the assumption . . . that the abstractions must be looked to first of all."[10] While Tate did not retract the derogatory remarks he had made about Southern literature in his "Charming Lady" essay,[11] the writing of the Davis book as well as of his biography of Stonewall Jackson had apparently helped provide him with the sense that the Old South, considered as a totality, a way of life, rather than in terms of its literature, was a kind of Eden.[12]

This Eden had been violated by an abstraction-ridden, morally arrogant North (the "North" and "New England" were virtually identical terms for Tate at this time). The North interpreted the Constitution "by abstract right. The South interpreted it historically, literally."[13] The Northern economy had lived off the South's. Getting so much, the North "began, under a panoply of moral purpose, to wonder why she didn't get more: why not get it all?"[14] That moral purpose was expressed in terms of "abstract right," which only leads to self-interest, as opposed to the "historical sense," which creates the genuine feeling of obligation ascribed by Tate to the Old South.

That region's superior morality was inseparable, in Tate's view, from its economic and social structures. Its order was that of "a stable, landed society" (as the defending theoretician of that society, Calhoun was named by Tate, with undoubtedly self-conscious extravagance, as "the Christ . . . of political order in the United States" while Andrew Jackson served as the "Anti-christ").[15] The plantation was conceived of in the South as "fixed productive property rather than as negotiable wealth. . ."[16] For the antebellum Southerner, wealth was "a collection of physical objects" rather than the abstract medium of money.[17] "Men were bound by their responsibility to a definite physical legacy— land and slaves," and in the Lower South such a binding produced a "genuine ruling class" in which power and responsibility were identified with each other.[18] (In a review of John Crowe Ransom's poetry written in 1927 Tate said that "the code of noblesse oblige" was one of Ransom's qualities that connected him with the culture of the eighteenth-century South;[19] for Tate that *noblesse* had apparently carried over to the next century.) If Tate appears to be celebrating a society of sharp class distinctions, he is. He spoke of "pure democracy" as a "political monstrosity. . . ."[20] (In his celebration of a hierarchical social order swallowed up by the events of history, Tate can be compared to Cooper.)

Antebellum man had supposedly approached a unity of being that stands as an ideal for Tate. There was, he claimed, no split between the economic basis of that man's life and his moral being. The land was "the primary medium through which man expressed his moral nature. . . ."[21] (In the region of his own upbringing, Tate said, a Kentucky more "back-

ward and Southern . . . than Tennessee or North Carolina,"
one's identity was bound up with the land, with the place one
came from, and had very little to do with money.)[22]

Not only was there unity of self in the Old South Tate
presented, there was a unity among the classes as well, such
ties distinguishing "a civilization from a mere social
machine."[23] Tate cited Ulrich B. Phillips's *Life and Labor in
the Old South* as showing "the astonishing, interwoven
homogeneity of southern society, in which all interests were
bound up into a whole—an answer to the economists who
have wondered why the poor whites followed Lee as faith-
fully as the rich. . . ."[24] The Old South, as Tate imagined it,
served as a rebuke not only to the North which went to war
against it, but to the United States of the twentieth century,
which had gone the way of the marauding Yankees (the
"New South" being only an extension of the North).[25]

For, as opposed to the South's one-time physical and
moral rootedness in the land, Tate found modern America
characterized by the domination of industrialism and its
concomitant cities. The economic order was marked by
irresponsible finance capitalism and absentee landlordism.
One's moral being and life style were divorced from the
economic base that supported them or were in conflict with
it. Rather than generating a unified society of hierarchically
arranged classes, industrialism had produced an atomized
society. The industrial laborer enjoyed only a dubious kind
of freedom. He did not feel himself located in an institution
or class, and he attempted to fill the resulting "void" with the
consumption of cheap goods. The industrial machine was
geared to manufacturing these goods, while the higher values
of society were "degraded."[26]

Tate's critique of modern America had a great deal of
validity. But what of the slavery that the Southern economic
order he admired had rested on? In 1959, in an article on the
Southern novel, Tate referred to the "curse of slavery," and
mocked books which depicted Negroes as "spoiled by

having been deprived of the benefits of slavery."[27] (There could not have been very many serious books of that kind appearing at the time Tate wrote this.) Three years later, he complained that the portrait of the Old South found in the works of Donald Davidson, a fellow Agrarian, "always seemed to me to leave about half of the Old South out of the account: the half, or third, or whatever the figures were, that included the Negro."[28] The impatience with "the figures" here is notable, and may be seen as going counter to the statement in which it is found. At any rate, these remarks about slavery come late in Tate's career. One might complain about *his* portrait of the Old South that if it does not fail to take account of the Negro, it portrays him and the institution of slavery in highly dubious ways, sometimes giving us Allen Tate as Stephen Foster.

Stonewall Jackson and *Jefferson Davis* both put forth the claims (though neither is especially concerned with the subject) that slave-owning in the Old South was characteristically benevolent. It was to the planter's interests to keep the slaves healthy and contented. But the ties of "association and affection" between master and slave "exceeded all considerations of interest."[29] In a review of a book on the Old South Tate said: "Not all planters were alike. One sat in his stately gallery in shirt sleeves . . . playing with Negro children; another kept punctilious order, and died with the words: I could never forget that I was born a gentleman."[30] A charming unbending or a dignified propriety—these categories will apparently do for distinguishing among the planters. Looking hard for some second thoughts about slavery in Tate's nonfictional prose, one finds the concession that there were "too many cases of separation" of husbands and wives, but this is immediately followed by the claim that planters did their best to keep families together.[31] There *were* two injustices in the system, Tate admits. The first was "the humiliation of the name—slavery; the other was that it gave the talented individual little chance to rise."[32] As stated, the first "injustice" seems trivial (here is Nominalism with a vengeance). The second is seen as operating only in relation to a potential elite. That slavery might in some way have harmed or stunted a man who was not "talented" does not seem to have occurred to Tate here or most other places.

Tate shows a similar blindness in other remarks on Negro slaves. He seems to view them from an unreconstructed white man's perspective almost exclusively, i.e., he considers them in terms of their ability or inability to satisfy white needs. Thus, in 1935, in an essay "The Profession of Letters in the South," he sees the Negro as having constituted "a barrier between the ruling class and the soil. . . . The white man got nothing from the Negro, no profound image of himself in terms of the soil." So that the black man failed to furnish a desirable aesthetic component for the white imagination. Also, he had a "thinning influence upon the class above him. . . ."[33] What a curiously inverted and unfeeling way of looking at the matter. But it is of a piece with what might be called the overseer's-eye-view of the slaves that Tate had shown in *Jefferson Davis:* "The Congoes and the Angolas from the far south were tractable, but they were stupid and shiftless. The Eboes were even stupider. . . ."[34] The one conception of the black that Tate seems able to respond to favorably, that, indeed, almost seems to hypnotize him, is the Negro as good servant. In *Stonewall Jackson,* for example, he refers to a Negro servant as devoted—"he particularly loved young Marse Tom."[35] The house-slaves were chosen, he tells us in *Jefferson Davis,* for their good servant qualities. Only "the most intelligent and most courteous" were selected.[36] But the good servant could function in other capacities as well. There was, for example, Davis's black overseer, James Pemberton. "James was a remarkable man, but there were thousands like him. Almost every family could boast of a servant as honest, as faithful, and as intelligent as James."[37] During the Civil War, many families "were completely dependent upon the exertions of some slave who had chosen to share their fortunes."[38] We shall presently see this preoccupation with the good servant—and his opposite—reflected in Tate's novel *The Fathers*.

If at any time between his "Charming Lady" essay of 1925 and that novel's appearance in 1938 Tate manifested a consciousness of the genuine evils of slavery and the desirability of abolition, it was only a glimmer. Passing remarks in *Stonewall Jackson* and *Jefferson Davis* attempted to get the South off the hook by presenting the problem of freeing the slaves as defying resolution. For example, Tate said that Jackson did not know how the slaves could be freed; he only knew it could not be done quickly.[39] In *Jefferson Davis* Tate asserted that the problem of who would "control and care for" the slaves if they were freed was insoluble.[40] This conjoining of freedom and control may strike one as paradoxical, as does Tate's attack on people in New England who desired "to destroy democracy and civil liberties in America by freeing the slaves."[41] His contempt for the Abolitionists was unmistakable, and he dismissed John Brown as a "homicidal maniac."[42] Far from being a chink in the armor of his defense of the Old South, slavery served Tate as a weapon in attacking Northern industrial society, both of the nineteenth century and of today. If the black man had been freed, Tate claimed, he would have been exploited. In the North this was beginning to happen to the "free" white man.[43] The modern industrial laborer, as a rule, had no greater chance than the slave to better himself, and on the whole "the modern system is probably inferior to that of slavery; the classes are not so closely knit; and the employer feels responsible to no law but his own desire."[44]

All in all, then, starting with a cool, mocking detachment from the Old South, Tate quickly reversed himself and sprang to its defense, through his reviews, his essays, and two biographical works. He seemed to be defining his own, second, approach in declaring that when the historian looks

"at his own background . . . the best should be made of it."
Also, he said, "the past should be magnified in order to keep
the present in its place."[45] The past for him was that of the
Old South, the present the hated industrial order of the North
and the New South.

It is the Virginia of the Old South that serves as the setting
of Tate's sole novel, *The Fathers*. The full intentions of this
work can be arrived at only if we keep in mind the attitudes
we have been examining in Tate's nonfictional prose.

The book may be said to focus on two houses or families in
the Old Dominion, the Buchans and the Poseys, who are
played off against each other. This seems like an eminently
novelistic arrangement, but literary considerations aside,
Tate's choice of it undoubtedly stemmed from his sense of
the Southern past. He located "the center of the South" in
the family, and this was "no less [true] for Robert E. Lee
than for the people on Tate's Creek Pike; for Virginia was a
great aggregate of families that through almost infinite
ramifications of relationship was almost one family."[46]

The Buchans and the Poseys link up. George Posey
marries Susan Buchan. Her brother Semmes plans to marry
Jane Posey, George's sister (though events prove otherwise). Lacy Buchan, the book's narrator, is also in love with
Jane. But the Buchans are distinctly different from the
Poseys, and it is this difference that generates the crucial
events.

The Civil War serves in the book mainly as a catalyst. We
are given no overall view of the struggle. The events leading
up to it, and its manifestations, are localized, kept largely
within the confines of the two families or at most the
immediate neighborhood, with only marginal treatment of
the larger context in which the war is occurring.[47] (In this
respect the book is something like *The Unvanquished*.) The
Yankees make an appearance, but only in brief, isolated
instances, with the exception of the burning of a mansion
(which seems to be an obligatory event in most Civil War

fiction), and even *that* takes place offstage. The real drama lies within the individual Buchans and Poseys and their families, though Tate wants us to see his characters' private lives as shading off into the public realm, and the qualities and interaction of the two families as engaging issues that are historical in scope. The genuineness of that engagement is open to question.

Major Buchan is the patriarchal head of his family, living at Pleasant Hill, a kind of plantation (curiously not designated as such by the narrator but only as a "place"—could this be a sign of Tate's reluctance to look closely at the economic basis of the family's existence?)[48] Pleasant Hill has come to the Major through his mother. Here, as in his essays, Tate posits an intimate relationship between the Major's family and their "place," a relationship that is seen as prevalent among the people of their class: "we always spoke of the Carters of Ravensworth, the Carys of Vaucluse, the Buchans of Pleasant Hill."[49]

The Major rules over his place and his family and his Negroes with firmness but also kindness. He is always dignified, always polite. His presence has a kind of unforced potency; when he walks into a roomful of people "his quiet entrance . . . silenced them like a pistol shot" (p. 97). He experiences no tension between his own nature and the code by which he lives. That code is a blood-possession, something he does not have to think about or learn; he simply embodies it. Lacy ascribes to him the quality of "high innocence" (cf. the way of life designated in Yeats's "A Prayer for My Daughter"). That innocence, however, hardly equips him to understand the realities of the political world, of a country headed for a momentous schism. There is no difference, he believes, that cannot be settled by men of intelligence and good will meeting together.[50] His Cousin John thinks that men like the Major are at once the glory of Virginia and the element that will ruin the Old Dominion through their failure to understand that reason and moderation will not suffice. But if the Major's innocence blinds him to reality, so much the worse for reality. Late in the book Lacy, the youngest son of the Major, gives voice to this *ubi sunt:* "Men of honor and dignity—where are they now? I knew gentlemen in my boyhood but I know none now. . ." (p. 210). The context makes it plain that he is thinking primarily of the Major, and his statement reflects at least one of the book's attitudes toward Buchan as a representative of the Old South.

The novel attributes to the Major and his life style the quality of impersonality. His particular being has been absorbed by a way of life, a set of social rituals and a code of honor, larger than himself (see p. 210 of the novel). George Posey, on the other hand, is nothing but the personal, particular, and individual. He operates out of his desires and impulses, unchecked by the rules of the game that the Major lives within automatically.[51]

The alienness of Posey's presence in Buchan's world is partly manifested at the level of manners. George fails to make the proper inquiry when coming to call at Pleasant Hill, and gives young Lacy a gun without first securing the Major's approval. At the tournament he competes in and wins,[52] instead of fitting the wreath that symbolizes victory on his lady's head, he drops it into her lap and laughs. Challenged to a duel, and seeming to accept, he simply knocks his challenger down instead of exchanging shots with him. On the day of Lacy's mother's funeral, George abruptly departs before the burial (he is greatly agitated by her death and unable to subordinate his feelings to the social needs and forms of the occasion). Lacy is enough of a Buchan to register George's going off as "extraordinary and violent. . ." (p. 14). Though the Major tries, at one point, to rebuke Posey—"what papa had said to him would have blasted off the earth most of the people I knew"—he is totally unaffected. The Major's domain does not extend to him. He does not even appear to be acquainted with its rules.

He is set off from the Buchans in other respects. If the Major is innocent of the ways of business, George is not. He can, among other things, translate slaves into monetary terms; the Major is incapable of doing so. In addition, as older members of the Buchan clan point out more than once, George, unlike themselves, has been raised in "town." His father had owned considerable property, but when George was still a boy, had "left the land. . ." (p. 5). We are undoubtedly meant to link this background with George's lack of rootedness in a place like Pleasant Hill (as well as with his contempt for those who concern themselves with " 'the honor of Virginia' " (p. 107)). Indeed, he exists at the other extreme, that of pure mobility, striking Lacy as "a man always riding off somewhere" (p. 150). (Before the funeral of the Major's wife, Posey had literally ridden off.) His lack of identification with a place is explicitly connected to the "personal" quality of his feelings. Place or land is seen as providing a desirable curb or boundary to the operations of the ego. George, however, "knew no bounds" (p. 179). In Lacy's mind, he is associated with a precipice or, in a variation on the image, with a "chasm" or "abyss" that Lacy sees as lying beneath the conventions of civilization (pp. 43–44, 185–86). Operating only from within himself, Posey is invested with a quality of intense solitude by Lacy, who regards him as being a stranger everywhere. (It might not be farfetched to think of Posey as akin to Faulkner's Joe Christmas, who is also cut off from a land-rooted life, and an alien wherever he goes.) Posey's acute aloneness and individuality function both as an awful burden for him and as a destructive force for others. In a vision, Lacy's grandfather tells the boy that George is "alone like a tornado" (p. 268).

At the same time, the book makes a case for Posey. Indeed, the split in attitudes he induces in Lacy and in the novel may be said to constitute one of the work's principal tensions. Lacy has never been able to tell himself that George "was not right about everything . . ." (p. 132).

Something of the glamour of the Byronic hero attaches itself to Posey in the course of Lacy's narrative (this is the other side of the disapproval of his aloneness). He is accorded as well the glamour of physical heroism. Also, if he violates the code of society when he knocks down John Langton, the man who challenged him to a duel, the reader can only rejoice that Langton, a thorough bully, is receiving his comeuppance. The book appears to acknowledge the irony that Langton had functioned as a dominant figure at the tournament of chivalry. This is one instance of the novel's recognition that the life-style of Virginia's landed society has its contradictions, and Posey, the individualist, is given a pleasing triumph over a member of that society.

Moreover, while the Buchan world from which he stands apart is celebrated for its civility, generosity of spirit, and capacity for enduring life's crises through its ceremonies, there is an occasional quality of mischievous humor in the rendering of its inhabitants which serves to qualify the celebration, and which, in effect, tips the book towards Posey's position outside of that world. We are told, for example of old Uncle Armstid who only says "Hanh?" in response to any question addressed to him. A Mrs. Gunnell usually manages to hold her trumpet to the wrong ear in trying to catch the conversation around her at the Buchan house. She is described at one point as having a fly running up and down her nose; nearby, a Mr. Broadacre is asleep, exuding alcoholic fumes. Earlier in the book, he had inadvertently swallowed some tobacco juice while addressing a crowd, but in the course of his orotund speech the "sound of his own voice had restored his equanimity" (p. 66). Not only do we get these bits of human comedy but also a couple of humorous remarks at the expense of the Buchan assumptions. Lacy tells us that in growing up he had been given the distinct impression that "God was a Virginian who had created the world in his own image" (p. 129). Lacy's mother had a set way of washing china. If this ritual had been discredited or even questioned, she would have felt that the purity of womanhood was in danger, that religion and morality were jeopardized, and that infidels had wickedly asserted that the State of Virginia (by which she meant her friends and kin) was not the direct legatee of the civilization of Greece and Rome. (P. 184)

This is used by Lacy as an example of his contention that "people living in formal societies, lacking the historical imagination, can imagine for themselves only a timeless existence . . ." (p. 183). Such remarks as these point to the psychological gap that exists between Lacy and his world. That gap is filled by his admiration of George Posey, the man, he tells us at the book's conclusion, that he loves more than any other.[53] If the Major's ordered, civilized world stands as an ongoing rebuke to the anarchy and violence of Posey's life, Posey's passionate, impatient and fearless behavior stands as a critique of the bland assumptions and static perfection of the Major's mode of life.

The complex attitude that emerges here suggests that Tate's view of the Old South was less one-sided than his "Agrarian" posture indicated. (The significance of the book's title is, probably, that both Posey and Major Buchan are spiritual fathers of Lacy, and of Tate himself, though it might also be argued that the title is ironic, for no viable father-principle emerges from the novel.) We should remind ourselves again of the irreverence Tate displayed toward the South in his "Charming Lady" essay, and the quick reversal of tone in his subsequent writings. We might speculate that the attitude he expressed in his essay was never fully relinquished but had to be suppressed in the espousing of his Agrarian views, and was only allowed to emerge again as a component of the more complicated stance that we find in his novel.[54] Moreover, we should note that Tate's critique of the modern social and economic order, which included the New South, met with an adverse response in that region. He was in the position of being at once hostile to the North and not really able to call the existing South his own. Such isolation might well have led him to sympathize with the ever-alienated Posey,[55] even though that character apparently represented to him the coming of a hated modernity to the South.

Commentators on *The Fathers* agree in seeing Posey as so representative.[56] The novel, in their view, appears to be implying that the old order crumbled not so much because a superior Yankee force was brought to bear upon it, but because of a disintegrating element present *within* it, a new sensibility, exemplified in Posey, which was impatient with the stasis, rootedness, unworldliness, and subordination of self to custom that it found in the existing society. The rejection of these things entailed the embrace, in effect, of a Northern or modern way of life.

Such a conception undoubtedly lies behind the book, but one wonders whether the critics would have been able to see it without a knowledge of the cultural position Tate had assumed as an Agrarian years before the book's appearance.[57] It is true that Posey is symbolically linked to the North through his carrying of carpet bags, and that he is a man of the town rather than the countryside (though that aspect of him receives little dramatization). But how much else is there in the novel *per se* to give him the kind of representative and historical significance that everybody agrees he has?[58] If anything, the presentation of Posey's background, regarded by the book as important in explaining his behavior, strikes one not as grounded in a historical situation, but as a curious mutation of a literary mode, the Gothic. The Posey family is depicted through a mixture of this mode and humorous variations on it. The resulting sometimes-comic Gothic operates as a peculiar presence in the novel, and distinctly undercuts, or at least dilutes, the historicity Tate undoubtedly wished Posey to possess.

Reexamining the way in which the Posey family is first brought to our attention, we might well wonder if Tate's conception of this family did not change in the course of his writing *The Fathers,* and if he failed to go back and make the revisions necessary to a consistency in its portraiture. We are told that the Poseys were "a respectable family . . . quiet, presentable . . . like the Buchans, undistinguished . . . unexceptional" (pp. 4–5). Lacy says he cannot understand why they developed as they did. Later, however, certain Gothic elements emerge. Reference is made to Jarman Posey, George's uncle, who lives in a remote room of the Posey house, communicating with the family through servants. It turns out he is engaged in writing a history of man's struggle to build a civilization after the ice age. He is so cut off from everything that he might as well be living in that period. Rozier Posey, George's father and one-time head of the family, had died while his son was still a boy, but there were "tales of his secrecy of action and brutality of character" that help explain, for Lacy, the "extreme refinement of sensibility" that victimized his wife "and George too in his curious way." (Lacy appears to be claiming that the development of that refinement was a reaction to Rozier's brutality.) Lacy goes on to say, in clear contradiction of his earlier characterization of the family as "unexceptional," that they "did not live the normal life of their times—that, I suppose, is what it all comes down to" (pp. 177–78). When Lacy goes to the Posey house, he finds it a "world of closed upstairs rooms, a world where people communicated only through their infirmities . . ." (p. 182). While walking in the upstairs hall, Lacy sees peeping out at him through a partly-opened door "a dim face that seemed to have no support below it, being wedged tightly between door and jamb" (p. 170). All this is decidedly creepy. But while Tate may be creating a Poe-esque effect here (is Posey a pun on *Poe?*), an un-Gothic humor is incorporated in the treatment of the family. Milly George, George's aunt, having come to Lacy's mother's funeral, jerks her head aimlessly, "like a chicken pausing alertly between scratches" (p. 96). Nobody has ever seen her "eat anything but overripe bananas" (p. 184). The family members seem to share in a withdrawal from reality, comically depicted. If the oncoming war is mentioned, George's mother has a "spell," and Aunt Milly just says "Thank you, honey," taking her bananas and closing her door. When a runaway slave appears, to pay his respects to George's mother after a considerable absence from the household, she forgets he has ever been away before he even leaves her presence. She "could not admit that common people were real" (and if poverty, childbirth, or money were referred to in front of Milly, *that* lady would "vaguely sniff . . ." [p. 184]). When George's mother dies, presumably of a fright, Lacy attempts in vain to communicate this fact to Jarman, who thinks he is talking of a death years before. In such moments, the family does not exude a Gothic weirdness or ominousness, but only a ridiculous self-absorption.

But whether *echt* Gothic or largely comic, the Posey family would appear to have shaped its scion George in a crucial way. The dotty atomism of the family is regarded as having thrown him back on the purely "personal," cutting him off from "piety . . . order . . . elaborate rigamarole . . ." (p. 180).[59] The ladies of the family "had let their social tradition lapse in personal self-indulgence . . ." (p. 184). Tate's wishing us to regard George as the product of these ladies reduces him to a case history—which is not the same as being historically representative. There is a large gap between Tate's apparent intention to present George as typifying modern man or "Northern" values, and the novel's grounding his character in the nature of his particular family. The Poseys simply do not join up with history, not, at least, in a way consistent with Tate's intention. If anything, the Posey ladies seem representative of a pampered, idealized Southern womanhood that may indeed have constituted a significant historical entity, but which was hardly a class to be blamed on the North.[60]

There is yet another difficulty in Tate's handling of the Poseys. They are supposed to present a contrast to the Buchan family, with its sociality, conventions, rituals, and its ordering head. But at one notable point in the book the attempt to distinguish between the two families is subverted by the appearance of an inadequacy common to both of them. On the very same page where we are told of the Posey ladies' self-indulgence and evasion of reality, of Milly's diet of overripe bananas, we are also told of the silver-polishing ritual of the Major's wife and its concomitant assumptions, of her believing that "her small world held life in its entirety. . ." (p. 184). Are not these ladies, whether Posey or Buchan, all encased in incredibly small, smug existences?

A similar breakdown in the distinction between the two families occurs in the awful episode involving George, Semmes (an older brother of Lacy), and Yellow Jim, the runaway Posey slave. The two white men have removed Jim from the Posey house after he has unintentionally frightened George's mother to death, and has traumatized George's sister Jane (in a nice touch, Aunt Milly has slept through it all). Semmes is under the impression that Jim is being removed so that he can be shot. As Jane's fiancé, he apparently believes that he has priority in the matter (is this because the possible violation or attempted violation of Jane takes precedence over the mere death of George's mother?) He proceeds to kill Jim. He in turn is shot to death by George, who, it turns out, never intended to kill the slave. Semmes has acted out a code, a prescribed ritual: "An engaged man had to see that a negro who had insulted his affianced bride got properly killed" (p. 270). George, as usual, has acted out of his impulsive and violent individualism. But does the distinction finally matter? Is the Buchan-Posey dichotomy of any significance here? Each mode of life has produced a corpse.

The episode with Jim brings into focus the novel's treatment of slavery (a treatment that is likely to make many contemporary readers uncomfortable, though previous commentators on the book have shown no signs of such a reaction). Here, again, Tate is interested in distinguishing between Major Buchan and George Posey. The Major's handling of slaves is presented as a case of pure noblesse oblige. He never addresses his slaves by diminutives or nicknames; he leads his wife's servant by the hand into Mrs. Buchan's funeral procession, placing her ahead of the immediate family; he honors the desire of a slave to stay at Pleasant Hill rather than move into town with the family, because he always subordinates discipline to feeling; he directs his personal servant, Coriolanus, as a matter of daily ritual, to rest after his few minutes of dusting. He neither buys nor sells slaves (those he possesses have presumably been inherited), and he has freed some of his blacks. Or at least he thinks he has—without his knowledge, Posey, conducting his business for him, has sold them. Posey has also sold one of his own slaves, Yellow Jim (the magnificent horse Posey rides has come to him through that sale). George regards the Major's refusal to buy or sell Negroes as "a kind of fastidious self-indulgence at the expense of his posterity. . ." (p. 134). His descendants would eventually have to sell the slaves or free them at a financial loss to themselves. While the book, in general, would appear to be setting the Major's humanitarianism against Posey's abstract approach—Posey regards the blacks as "liquid capital"—it refuses to make a choice in the matter of the Major's refusal to indulge in slave-trading. Lacy asks "was not George Posey right about this? And was not papa also, in his own fine way, right?" (p. 134). Moreover, the heirs' entitlement to have their father's estate come down to them intact, the *holding* of slaves (as opposed to dealing in them), is simply never questioned. One might pass this off by saying that Lacy embodies the contemporary Southern slaveholder's attitude, and that this is Tate's narrator speaking, not the author himself. But there is virtually nothing in the book that encourages us to make this distinction with respect to the question of slavery.

The bulk of the passing references to blacks in *The Fathers* is condescending when not contemptuous, and tends toward the use of stereotypes. We get the following: "trifling negro girls" who have broken the Poseys' good glassware (the Negro as shiftless); a black boy laughing and slapping one of several "young wenches," who giggles (the Negro as light-hearted); a mulatto girl who is willing to let Lacy "have it" (the Negro as sexually loose); a "stout buck" who pounces on a piece of ham thrown to him and lies on the ground "until he had gorged it all" (the Negro as animalistic—see pp. 205, 9, 73, 52, respectively, for these references). Such blacks as the last one cited are regarded by Coriolanus, the Major's servant, as an " 'ornery passel of niggers,' " in an interesting example of black snobbery (p. 53). Lacy believes he finds "a trace of insolence" in a black he meets who claims to be free (p. 188), and when he encounters another such, who expresses his indifference to the Confederate soldiers' having " 'Skeddaddled,' " Lacy says, "Free nigger. . ." (p. 261).

With respect to the blacks who have not been freed, *The Fathers* appears to relegate them to one of two categories: the good servant and the bad servant (see my remarks concerning the good servant, p. 98 above). It does not conceive of any other mode for them. The shining example of the good servant is Coriolanus. A pseudoequality is conferred upon him when Lacy says of his daily napping in the same room in which the Major reads: "In this way the two old friends enjoyed each other's company" (p. 127). A notable instance of the bad servant is Blind Joe, who belongs (significantly?) to George Posey. He whines, wheedles, leers, grins evilly, or shows his teeth like a cur. He is delighted at the plight of Jim, who is facing death, and when he gets a chance to desert his master he does so. Lacy wonders at one point why things could not have worked out so that Joe had been in Jim's place. This bad servant seems to be the character the book despises most.

The black who offers the most interesting possibilities of characterization, and whose presence carries the promise of a scrutiny of the slavery system rather than an unquestioning assent to it, is Yellow Jim (who is actually George's half brother). But this promise is not fulfilled. Lacy does make the observation that Jim was humiliated by Posey's having traded him for a horse and some cash; worse, Jim had felt betrayed, for his status as a slave had only intensified his loyalty to the Poseys. Lacy sees Jim as "tortured" (p. 206). But this sympathetic notation of Jim's feelings comes soon after a pair of rather dubious statements. In the first, Lacy has called Jim "the best negro I ever saw" (except for Coriolanus), basing this on Jim's having cleaned Lacy's boots, brushed his clothes, and toted warm water upstairs for his bath. In the second statement, Lacy has said that he doubted if Jim "would have been as good as he was if his white blood. . .had not been good" (p. 205). What, exactly, had been so good about Rozier Posey's blood is a mystery, in light of the little we are told of him.

Still, some basis for a dramatization of the evils of slavery has been established through the treatment of Jim. His being marked for death because he has allegedly made some sort of improper advance to Miss Jane is immensely ironic. For he used to dote on her, taking pride in the medals she won at school. From the time Jane, irrationally, began to fear Jim's presence, he felt he could do no good. When Jim reveals this to Lacy his tone becomes "manly and his posture erect" (p. 230). Lacy apparently prefers this to the note of self-pity he had heard earlier in Jim's speech, but neither Lacy nor the book seems to detect the irony of associating manliness with the adult Jim's unthinking worship of a vapid adolescent, for that is what Jane is. (Nor does the book question Jim's attributing whatever happened in his encounter with Jane to the "nigger" in him.) The good servant conception has manifested itself again in the "manly" statement, and serves to dissipate what seemed to be emerging, at least shakily, from the book—an acknowledgment of the implications of Jim's situation and of the injustice awaiting him.

The feeble signs the novel gives of detecting the evils of slavery in relation to blacks are replaced by its seeing those evils as, ultimately, victimizing the whites. Lacy has a vision of George astride Yellow Jim "whose face was as white as his master's." But the point of the vision seems to be that "they ran over a child in white," presumably Jane (p. 227). (Tate seems not to have escaped the sentimentalizing of the young Southern belle.) Atha, a slave belonging to the Poseys, is made to say " 'I ain't white folks, praise be de Lawd' . . ." (p. 243). This, from the *mother* of Jim, with her son facing death. Finally, after Lacy has made one of the most important moral observations of the book, namely, that ". . . Yellow Jim had been used by us all," he goes on to ask: "What had we done to Yellow Jim more than we were . . . doing to ourselves?" (pp. 244, 245). The whites become the moral beneficiaries of this statement, insofar as such a view puts aside as the crucial question the matter of the slaves' victimization. Also, the responsibility for that victimization has been shifted from the Old South (Major Buchan) to that of Northern or modern man—George Posey. All this should strike us as sleight-of-hand rather than as a genuine illumination of history.

Turning to Tate's poems, we find that one of them, "Records," contains details matching the description of the grandfather Lacy sees in a vision that comes to him late in *The Fathers*. As in the novel, the stately ancestral figure, here a great-grandfather, encounters a fat man with stringy hair and cold gray eyes. While in *The Fathers* the encounter appears to serve as an ominous foreshadowing of the coming of the Yankees, in the poem it generates a *frisson* whose significance is not quite clear. Tate may be suggesting the dissolution of a desirable social order, represented by the great-grandfather, and the rise of a grubby new one, represented by the fat man. Be that as it may, "Records" is relatively rare among Tate's poems in placing us squarely *in* the past. Generally, those of his poems concerned with history are set in the present, with the speaker looking backward.

This is true even of "To the Lacedemonians," where the speaker, while having been an active participant in the past (he is an aged veteran of the Confederate army) has lived on into a period well removed in its qualities from the old days that engage his musings. The poem begins with a distinct sense of his alienation from his current circumstances:

> The people—people of my kind, my own
> People but strange. . . .

There are unmistakable echoes of T. S. Eliot's "Gerontion" in "To the Lacedemonians." We find these in the line "Old man: no memory; aimless distractions," as well as in the windy ambience of Tate's poem. But one crucial difference between the two works is that Eliot's speaker cannot recall a meaningful past where Tate's can. He has, so to speak, heaved a cutlass. Using that past as a standard, the old soldier delivers an indictment of the present South that has a familiar ring if we come to the poem from a reading of Tate's essays or *The Fathers*. The past, the veteran tells us, displayed qualities of rootedness, dignity, chivalry, and a strong sense of connection with one's kin. Contemplating his present surroundings, he finds a repulsive mobility and rootlessness, luxury without elegance, eyesight without vision, and a mere propinquity of mediocre beings, huddled together out of a common fear, rather than men in meaningful relationship with each other (here, too, are echoes of Eliot's poetry). The old soldier and his fellow veterans are able to elicit the tribute of "wonder" from the young men

who stare at their parade. But that is all. For in the present
South

> All are born Yankees of the race of men
> And this, too, now the country of the damned. . . .

In place of the brooding of "Gerontion," that focused on
human weakness and inadequacy as traits recurring through
history, and that indicted the speaker as much as anybody
else, we have here a mere crankiness which employs a
virtually unqualified glorification of the Southern past as a
rebuke to a worthless present. The speaker himself is not
implicated. Tate's poem is simplistic in a way that Eliot's is
not.[61]

As already indicated, Tate's poetry about historical events
or situations typically involves only a *sense* of the past,
rather than a direct immersion in or recall of it. But that
sense, figuring as a kind of atmosphere, can strongly suffuse
the sensibilities of Tate's modern-day speakers. A good
example of this is "The Oath," which gives us a man, who
seems to be Tate himself, and a companion, musing by a fire
at twilight. Two ancestors of the speaker are evoked in the
opening lines, forcefully presented and connected by patterns of alliteration and assonance:

> . . . Uncle Ben's brass bullet-mould
> And powder-horn and Major Bogan's face

They figure as examples of the "animated dead" who, the
speaker's companion implies, are more alive than the living:

> . . . Who are the dead?
> Who are the living and the dead?

The poem can be seen as an example of Tate's nostalgia for
the past, and his concomitant repudiation of the present.
Viewed in this way, it can be regarded as of a piece with "To

the Lacedemonians" and with the general strain of Tate's
mind that has been traced thus far in this chapter. But there is
another kind of connection between "To the Lacedemonians" and "The Oath," in the way in which the past, so to
speak, invades and energizes the present in the two poems.
This is manifested in "To the Lacedemonians" by the
intensity of the speaker's celebrations of the Confederate
effort and his disgust with the contemporary scene. In "The
Oath," the question of "Who are the dead?" is followed by
the speaker's meditation on the "ageing fury of a mountain
stream," and a sense of

> . . . the dark pounding its head
> On a rock, crying: *Who are the dead?*

Just after this the speaker's companion turns "with an
oath—By God it's true!" Both men may be said to have
received a transfusion of energy from the past, even if that
energy may be one of despair. The quiet evening scene has
been transformed into a passionate one, and, paradoxically,
the asking of the rhetorical question that would appear to
condemn the "living" utterly, has succeeded in making
those so condemned more genuinely alive.

The poem that Tate chose as the opening work of two
editions of his collected poems seems, on the face of it, far
removed from a concern with the American past. It is
entitled "The Mediterranean" and focuses on the figure of
Aeneas, the legendary founder of Rome. But the title of the
very next poem "Aeneas at Washington," would suggest
that this European culture-hero is, in Tate's imagination,
connected with America, and it turns out that he is linked for
Tate with the Southern past. "Aeneas at Washington"
transports its subject from a Troy falling before the Greek
onslaught to the banks of the Potomac. The poem ends with
Aeneas thinking of "Troy, what we had built her for." The
curious conjunction effected by the poem can be explained

by a remark Tate made in a tribute to Faulkner. He spoke of "The Greco-Trojan myth (Northerners as the upstart Greeks, Southerners as the older, more civilized Trojans). . . ."[62] We might also keep in mind the identification Southern planters made between themselves and the ancient Romans. Seen in this light, "Aeneas at Washington" may be regarded as another lament for the destruction of the Old South. Its ostensible allusion to Troy's downfall—"That was a time when civilization / Run by the few fell to the many"—is ultimately a reference to the passing away of an "aristocratic" Southern culture. The "Blue Grass" cited by Aeneas is undoubtedly meant to bring to mind Tate's native Kentucky as well as Troy's "glowing fields."

"The Mediterranean," referring like "Aeneas at Washington" to a vegetation that seems to be growing in America, presents the past in a somewhat different way. Here there is no suggestion of a lost South which, like Troy, represented a pinnacle of civilization. Rather, America in its entirety, at least by implication, is considered as representing a falling-off from the classical civilization of the Mediterranean. That civilization offered the opportunities for heroism. America, on the other hand offers only an inane material over-abundance:

> Fat beans, grapes sweeter than muscadine
> Rot on the vine: in that land were we born.

A similar disposition to see an absence of the heroic in American history, or at least to question a glorification of that history, can be found in "To a Romantic." Addressed to Robert Penn Warren, the poem finds him too ready to assign grandeur to men of the past:

> As if the sleepy dead
> Had never fallen to drowse
> From the sublimest talk
> Of many a vehement house.

Warren, the poem claims, thinks "the dead arise / Westward and fabulous. . . ." In place of this view, the poem offers its own reductive definition:

> The dead are those whose lies
> Were doors to a narrow house.

Here the dead are made to bear the burden of having helped create what has become our oppressive present. The statement is sweeping, but the poem refuses to flesh out its pronouncement, content simply to make it.

There is one Tate poem which departs significantly from those treatments of the past we have been looking at (as well as from most of the works considered in this book). "Message from Abroad" concerns itself not with heroic or distinguished figures from the past, emblazoned on the records, nor with the fall from heroic modes. It contemplates, rather, those who have left little or no trace of themselves, sunk in a common anonymity. They stand behind or below the usual historical categories and placements: "Provence, / The Renascence, the age of Pericles. . . ." They are "lost, / Not by poetry and statues timed. . . ." Tate provides an American example of such lost persons, taking as his starting point a passage from a work published in 1799, *Traveller to America.*[63] Their only memorial consists of a ruined habitation. They are not available to Tate's inner eye. Theirs

> was a secret fate,
> . . . .
> What did you say mornings?
> Evenings, what?[64]

It is possible to see a kind of guilt operating in the poem (this is a tentative reading). The speaker is delivering his meditation from Paris. He seems to be indicating that his going to Europe has succeeded in obliterating the red-faced man who serves as the prototype of the anonymous dead of the poem. Cleanth Brooks suggests that this is simply the result of Europe having more history than America.[65] But the speaker can be seen as suggesting that if he had not indulged his taste for the Old World, he might indeed have been able to imagine into existence the red-faced man. That man has been "drowned" in the ocean the speaker crossed to get to Paris. Like Williams composing *In the American Grain* even as he sojourned in Europe, Tate may have been intent on keeping up a connection with America while physically removed from it, through reminding himself of the obscure, uncelebrated masses of the American past. They at once haunt his imagination and elude it.

In contrast to the situation in "Message from Abroad," the speaker in "Ode to the Confederate Dead," Tate's best known poem, is located in his native setting, standing outside the gate of a cemetery containing the graves of soldiers. He knows of the historical events in which they participated. But while not separated from the dead because of a removal in space or a lack of knowledge, he feels alienated from them because theirs was a sensibility he cannot share.[66] The Confederate dead possessed "vision," knew "arrogant circumstance." The Ode's echoes of Eliot's "The Love Song of J. Alfred Prufrock" (e.g., the repetitions of "know," a slight variant on the recurrent "known" of "Prufrock") suggests that the speaker suffers from an inhibiting sensibility which, he recognizes, cuts him off from the heroism of "the immoderate past. . . ."[67]

But perhaps the strongest source of the oppression the speaker feels is his consciousness of the condition of death. The "rumour of mortality" of which he speaks is not merely a rumour; it is a fact. Conceived of as heroes, the Confederate soldiers exist for him in a state of *definition*, but it is a state on the point of dissolution, just as the autumn leaves, an important presence in the poem, are driven to their ironic "election in the vast breath. . . ." The definition and the dissolution provide the poem with its central tension.[68]

The Confederate dead bring to the speaker's mind Stonewall Jackson and the names of individual battles, the stirring list of "Shiloh, Antietam, Malvern Hill, Bull Run." But these separate battles get gathered up into an indiscriminate "thick-and-fast. . . ." Later in the poem, the speaker says, referring to the dead soldiers:

> The singular screech-owl's tight
> Invisible lyric seeds the mind
> With the furious murmur of their chivalry.

Note the use of *singular* and *tight* here as contributing to a sense of definition or form. But it is a precarious sense; "murmur" undercuts the force of "furious." If we have form here it appears on the edge of breaking up (the very next line returns us to the leaves, which figure as a kind of refrain object in the poem, emblems of mortality).

The condition of precarious form has been established at the very beginning of the poem:

> Row after row with strict impunity
> The headstones yield their names to the element.
> The wind whirrs without recollection. . . .

The formal organisation of the graves ("Row after row") is both given "strict impunity" and seen as yielding to the dissolving elements. (Even the "Row after row" itself, with its effect of piling up, can be regarded as threatening the definition of a given row.) The opening words of the passage just quoted are repeated in a variant manner in the lines that tell us of

> . . . the inexhaustible bodies that are not
> Dead, but feed the grass row after rich row.
> Think of the autumns that have come and gone!—
> Ambitious November with the humors of the year,
> With a particular zeal for every slab,

> Staining the uncomfortable angels that rot
> On the slabs, a wing chipped here, an arm there. . . .

Here, the state of definition of the dead is maintained as the poem insists that they are not dead. But the passage furnishes us with a delayed rhyme for the "not" of "not/Dead" in "rot," subverting its original assertion. Also, "Row after row" is echoed later in the poem by "Rank upon rank, hurried beyond decision," which is soon followed by the leaves flying in the wind. Once again, then, the formalized status of the soldiers is giving way to death's formlessness. (We might compare this with "To the Romantic Traditionists" where the "strict forms/ Of will" of the traditionists yield before the poem's consciousness of death.)

At its close, the "Ode" is dominated by its awareness of the "ravenous grave" guarded by a snake "who counts us all!" Contemplation of the past here does not furnish the viewer with a sense of a precious society gone down before a Yankee assault. Nor, to differ with Tate and those critics who have swallowed his comments on the poem whole, does the focus on the past serve to provide a sense of a tradition-less contemporary society. To meditate on the past here is, primarily, to arrive at the horrifying consciousness that men who made history are lying in the earth.

NOTES

1. Allen Tate, "*The Fugitive* 1922–1925: A Personal Recollection Twenty Years After," *Princeton University Library Chronicle*, 3 (April 1942): 83.

2. Allen Tate, "Last Days of the Charming Ladys" *Nation*, 28 October 1925, pp. 485–86.

3. *Ibid.*, p. 486.

4. Louise Cowan, *The Fugitive Group: A Literary History* (Baton Rouge, La.: Louisiana State University Press, 1959), p. 240.

5. Tate, "Charming Lady," *Nation*, p. 486.

6. Allen Tate, *Essays of Four Decades* (Chicago: Swallow Press, 1968), p. 572.

See also Allen Tate, *Jefferson Davis: His Rise and Fall* (New York: Minton, Balch & Co., 1929), p. 87.

7. Tate, *Essays*, p. 571.

8. *Ibid.*, p. 573.

9. Tate, *Jefferson Davis*, p. 38.

10. *Ibid.*, p. 132.

11. Indeed, he restated his negative judgment ten years later; see Tate, *Essays*, p. 527.

12. At the same time, one of Tate's formulations of Southern superiority, namely, that the South thought in images rather than abstractions, may well have been influenced by one of the developments in modern poetry, the rise of Imagism.

13. Allen Tate, *Stonewall Jackson: The Good Soldier* (New York: Minton, Balch & Co., 1928), p. 60.

14. Tate, *Jefferson Davis*, p. 47.

15. Tate, *Stonewall Jackson*, p. 38. See also his *Jefferson Davis*, p. 48.

16. Tate, *Stonewall Jackson*, p. 17.

17. *Ibid.*, p. 12.

18. Tate, *Jefferson Davis*, p. 55.

19. Allen Tate, "The Eighteenth-Century South," *Nation*, 30 March 1927, p. 346.

20. Tate, *Jefferson Davis*, p. 208.

21. Tate, *Essays*, p. 556.

22. *Ibid.*, p. 581.

23. Tate, *Jefferson Davis*, p. 56.

24. Allen Tate, "Life in the Old South," *New Republic*, 10 July 1929 p. 212.

25. Tate wrote to Donald Davidson that " 'the chief defect the Old South had was that in it which produced . . . the New South.' " Quoted in Cowan, *The Fugitive Group*, p. 244.

26. *Jefferson Davis*, p. 43.

27. Allen Tate, "The Novel in the American South," *New Statesman*, 13 June 1959, p. 831.

28. Allen Tate, "The Gaze Past, the Glance Present," *Sewanee Review* 70 (Autumn 1962): 673.

29. Tate, *Jefferson Davis*, p. 43.

30. Tate, "Life in the Old South," p. 211.

31. Tate, *Jefferson Davis*, pp. 42–43.

32. *Ibid.*, p. 43.

33. Tate, *Essays*, p. 525.

34. Tate, *Jefferson Davis*, p. 39.

35. Tate, *Stonewall Jackson*, p. 8.

36. Tate, *Jefferson Davis*, p. 41.

37. *Ibid.*, p. 42.

38. *Ibid.*, p. 214.

39. Tate, *Stonewall Jackson*, p. 40.

40. Tate, *Jefferson Davis*, p. 47.

41. Tate, *Stonewall Jackson*, p. 25.

42. *Ibid.*, p. 57.

43. *Ibid.*, p. 39.

44. Tate, *Jefferson Davis*, p. 43.

45. Tate, "Life in the Old South," p. 212.

46. Tate, *Essays*, p. 588.

47. One of the book's sections ends on a portentous, public note—"The Confederate flag over Arlington was gone"—but there is something hollow about this. The context has not really prepared us to respond caringly to this fact. Howard Nemerov has justly remarked that for Tate "the situations of history are family or at least local situations, not paradigms composed of least common denominators called wars, truces, migrations and laws." "The Current of the Frozen Stream," *Sewanee Review* 67 (Autumn 1959): 587.

48. Pleasant Hill is based on an actual site connected with Tate's family. See Radcliffe Squires, *Allen Tate: A Literary Biography* (New York: Pegasus, 1971), p. 14.

49. Allen Tate, *The Fathers* (Chicago: Swallow Press, 1960), p. 135. Subsequent quotations from the novel, published originally in 1938, will be followed in the text of the chapter itself by the relevant page numbers.

50. As he did with John Crowe Ransom, Tate links Major Buchan to the eighteenth century.

51. Arthur Mizener focuses on this aspect of the novel in his "Introduction" to *The Fathers*, pp. xv–xviii.

52. Such tournaments, inspired by medieval joustings, are still held in Virginia. See Blakey Green, "Jousting Tournaments in Virginia: The Age of Chivalry Lives On," *New York Times*, 22 August 1971, p. 58.

53. Lacy reminds one of Nick Carraway in *The Great Gatsby*. While Nick disapproves of Gatsby, he clearly loves him.

54. At this point we might take note of Tate's remark that while his reaction to a new magazine was to reject it as " 'hokum,' " this response was " 'checked . . . by an opposite tendency to sympathize with almost anything revolutionary, sensible or not, and at the same time to derogate conservatism of all kinds.' " Quoted in Cowan, *The Fugitive Group*, p. 69.

55. See John L. Stewart, *The Burden of Time: The Fugitives and Agrarians* (Princeton, N.J.: Princeton University Press, 1965), p. 405.

56. See, e.g., Mizener, "Introduction" to *The Fathers*, pp. xiv–xv, and Radcliffe Squires, "Allen Tate's 'The Fathers,' " *Virginia Quarterly Review* 46 (Autumn 1970): 649.

57. An irony emerges here—a work by a man identified as a "New Critic" requires a context beyond the book itself to be fully understood. But of course, Tate as a critic is inadequately defined by that label.

58. It has been pointed out that Posey regards slaves as commodities to be sold if economic considerations so dictate, while the Major cannot treat them this way. But are we to take these attitudes as "Northern" and "Southern" respectively? The whole question of the book's treatment of slavery will be taken up shortly.

59. There is some suggestion that George suffers from a too-present mother and, by implication, an absent father, an authority figure like the Major. But as with the

sexual strain of Lacy's consciousness, this particular psychological approach is not fleshed out in the book.

60. See W. J. Cash, *The Mind of the South* (Garden City, N.Y.: Doubleday & Company, Inc., 1956), pp. 97–98.

61. But we should note that in another poem, "The Ancestors," Tate appears to indicate that human failure of nerve is a characteristic of the past and the present.

62. Allen Tate, "William Faulkner 1897–1962," *Sewanee Review* 71 (Winter 1963): 163.

63. Such, at least, is what the epigraph to "Message from Abroad" indicates. I have not been able to locate this work.

64. Pablo Neruda's *The Heights of Machu Picchu* is also concerned with anonymous masses of the past, but conceives of them as those exploited to produce architectural grandeur. There is no such slant in Tate's poem. He seems, simply, struck with the poignancy of lives that have been blotted out and sealed off forever from our apprehension.

65. See Cleanth Brooks, *Modern Poetry and the Tradition* (New York: Oxford University Press, 1965), p. 99.

66. Tate has written an extended commentary on the poem in his essay "Narcissus as Narcissus" (*Essays,* pp. 593–607) which sees the speaker as exemplifying a cultural situation rather than embodying an individual sensibility. I think it best to concentrate on the poem as it appears on the page and not simply accept that essay in toto. Considered in itself, "Ode to the Confederate Dead" does not really carry the heavy freight of subject matter—solipsism, narcissism, the "entire society" of the Confederacy versus the fragmented society of the twentieth century—that Tate's essay assigns to it. Tate himself seems uneasy in claiming that the "poem is 'about' solipsism . . ." (*Essays,* p. 595).

67. Here, unlike "To the Lacedemonians," the speaker *is* in the position of Eliot's Gerontion, who is conscious of heroism in the past and of the absence of it in his own life. The wind in Eliot's poem, taken over in "To the Lacedemonians," makes its appearance in this work as well, which appears just after "To the Lacedemonians" in Tate's *Poems* (Denver: Alan Swallow, 1961).

68. Tate's comments on the poem coincide at least in part with this reading.

5

"It Happened in Extraordinary Times": Eudora Welty's Historical Fiction

Recurring as a kind of signature in a number of Eudora Welty's works are references to the Natchez Trace—a one-time buffalo path, later an Indian trail, and after that an artery for white settlers. Part of its interest for her lies in its historic character: "Why, just to write about what might happen along some little road like the Natchez Trace—which reaches so far into the past and has been the trail for so many kinds of people—is enough to keep you busy for life."[1] The Trace figures in *The Robber Bridegroom,* a novella, as well as in the stories "A Still Moment" and "First Love," all three narratives set in a period when America was still possessed of a frontier, a wilderness. These works, along with "Asphodel" (which mentions the Trace) and "The Burning," a story of the Civil War, constitute a category of "historical" fiction in the Welty canon whose qualities have not been adequately defined.

The American past as it comes to us through these stories is clearly set off from the ordinary and from our own time; it is made to preserve a distance and apartness rather than to display some familiar, "universal" qualities that would connect it easily to us. This is a result of the stylization of its treatment, either by the self-conscious choice of literary modes drawn from earlier periods, or by a narrative voice or technique aimed at creating a dreamlike or visionary ambi-

125

ence (to be sure the latter approach can be found in some of Welty's stories of our own time, but the past *always* seems to call forth from her an overtly stylized or special treatment).

The resulting rendering of the past reveals some striking stresses and discord, split attitudes, a sense that Miss Welty stands among much of her materials unable to come to some dominant, coherent conception of them. Such, at least, seems to be the case with *The Robber Bridegroom,* "Asphodel," and "The Burning." "First Love" does impose a dominant tone on its subject but at the cost of an obscurantist depiction of the past. It is only in "A Still Moment" that Miss Welty combines throughout tonal wholeness and clarity of presentation, creating a powerful image of our history.

The Robber Bridegroom relates the adventures of Jamie Lockhart, a romantic outlaw-hero, his sweetheart Rosamond, her father Clement, and others who roam the forest through which runs the Natchez Trace. In the final chapter, Rosamond, seeking Jamie, comes upon a postal rider who proceeds to relate a tall story about " 'the grandfather of all alligators. . . .' "[2] The tale has no relevance to Rosamond's situation. But its inclusion points up *The Robber Bridegroom's* fascination with the exuberant storytelling abundance of American frontier folklore. A spirit of play is at work in the alligator tale as in much of the book, and will not be curtailed by any exigencies of the plot. Appropriately enough, the teller of the tall story turns out to be Mike Fink, one of the most famous characters of the frontier legends. He had figured prominently in the first chapter but had disappeared. His reentry near the end of *The Robber Bridegroom,* his eventual throwing off the role of the mail rider, and his restoration to his "original glory," may be taken as recapitulating the thrust of much of the book, that is, its attempted resurrection of the milieu and sensibility present in the Mike Fink legends, among others. The novella cannot be thought of apart from its sources in folklore. Reviewing the book, Alfred Kazin stressed the joy Miss

Welty took "in the world she has restored," and spoke of her keeping in view "the comedy and poetry embedded in it."[3]

However, focusing on these aspects of the work, Kazin (as have other critics) slighted a significant element both of *The Robber Bridegroom* and of the folk materials that lie behind it, namely, the elements of cruelty and violence that Constance Rourke has spoken of, many American tales exhibiting "the broad, blind cruelty of the backwoods."[4] For example, the pride in marksmanship that figures prominently in Western folklore could take some dubious forms. In one story, Davy Crockett proves the trueness of his aim by shooting off a tomcat's ears; to outdo him, Mike Fink shoots off the tails of a group of pigs. On another occasion, Mike was reported as having shot off the heel of a Negro's foot because it protruded too far to suit him.[5] In one of the tales recounting it, this outrageous act is absorbed and neutralized by the generally comic context in which it occurs. Something similar occurs in *The Robber Bridegroom* when we are told of a landlord, encountered by Clement, Rosamond's father, who has lost his right ear through its having been pinned to a market cross as punishment for his horse-stealing. The next landlord Clement finds has had his left ear shot off during some trouble he had gotten into. The third landlord met has two "large ears" (p. 4), and this is a sign to Clement of his scrupulousness. The sequence as a whole is funny, with the first two landlords furnishing a comic reference point of symmetrical earlessness, though each man's loss is, if taken by itself, hardly amusing. Here, as in the frontier tale, an event or detail of physical injury, disturbing in itself, has had its character dissolved by comedy. Another example of this process, or something akin to it, occurs in the episode where Salome, Rosamond's wicked stepmother (a character drawn from fairytales), is captured by Indians and made to dance until she drops dead. During her dance, she casts off her petticoats until she is "as naked as a plucked goose," and then stands "blue as a thistle" (p. 163) just before dying. Her body is tied to a "bony pony . . ." (p. 164). These comic or near-comic notations form a curious amalgam with the events described, and remind us of Constance Rourke's observation that many American folk tales "verged toward that median between terror and laughter which is the grotesque. . . ."[6] At moments, Miss Welty's story moves towards that median, though at other times it finds itself simply at the pole of terror. Clement tells of his son having been dipped into boiling oil by his Indian captors, with the boy's mother looking on. In another episode, it is seriously proposed by one character that a young woman be sliced down the middle, and in yet another an Indian girl is drugged, raped, dies on the spot and has her little finger cut off. So while *The Robber Bridegroom* is full of highjinks, and delights in its often outrageous re-creation of the tall tale as well as the fairytale, it shares with those two forms the inclusion of horrors, as well as the neutral, matter-of-fact recounting of those horrors.

Kazin asserted that the fairy-tale element of the story gives us what "the solemnity of history can not give us."[7] But the story itself is capable of turning solemn on us, at least flirting from time to time with a number of serious themes. There is, in particular, a rendering of Clement's thoughts which constitutes something of a formal surprise. The major mode of the book has been so much in the domain of the playful and/or the pell-mell, and given over to the particular, that we are surprised when the narrative stops long enough to have a character deliver himself of a somber, sustained, generalizing meditation. Clement says to himself, in part:

"Massacre is hard to tell from the performance of other rites, in the great silence where the wanderer is coming. Murder is as soundless as a spout of blood, as regular and rhythmic as sleep. Many find a skull and a little branching of bones between two floors of leaves. In the sky is the perpetual wheel of buzzards. A circle of bandits counts out the gold, with bending shoulders more slaves mount the block and go down, a planter makes a gesture of abundance with his riding whip, a flatboatman falls back from the tavern door to the river below with scarcely time for a splash, a rope descends from a tree and curls into a noose. And all around again are the Indians.

"Yet no one can laugh or cry so savagely in this wilderness as to be heard by the nearest traveler or remembered the next year. A fiddle played in a finished hut in a clearing is as vagrant as the swamp breeze. What will the seasons be, when we are lost and dead? The dreadful heat and cold—no more than the shooting star." (P. 144)

Such a passage does not seem covered by Kazin's description of *The Robber Bridegroom* as capturing "the lost fabulous innocence of our departed frontier, the easy carelessness, the fond bragging and colossal buckskin strut."[8]

But it would be hard to come up with any formulation of the book's character that does apply to all its parts. Undoubtedly conceived as a piece of high-spirited mimicry, not a direct rendering of the past so much as of the past's own fantastic forms, the book sometimes throws off its chosen mode of *jeu d'esprit* and becomes somber, allowing itself to be at least momentarily dominated by the oppressive material that had been comically contained in the originals. Insouciance falters as the frontier becomes a place of casual slaughter.

The book exhibits its divergent elements right through the conclusion. We have a fairy-tale ending with Rosamond and the robber bridegroom happily married to each other, possessed of beautiful twins, and living in a beautiful house. But this conclusion is not without its flickers of bitter comment, as in the passing mention of the "hundred slaves" they own, or in the observation that the husband's "transfer from bandit to merchant had been almost too easy to count it a change at all" (p. 184). And yet, the assertion that the husband was a hero and had always been one appears to be offered without irony, the book seeming reluctant to simply debunk the heroic. Perhaps Miss Welty is implicitly confessing her novella's divided nature when she has Clement refuse the couple's offer to have him live with them; he chooses to sail home instead. Clement has been the vehicle of the story's mournful, thoughtful strain. He does not, can not, fit in with the fairy-tale lovers. Welty seems intent on retaining an image of the past as fabulous and joyous without being able to relinquish a sense of its horrors. The story ends on a note of unresolved ambivalence.

If a mixture of modes, the tall story and the fairy tale, is present in *The Robber Bridegroom,* the same may be said of "Asphodel," the modes here being those of Greek tragedy and romantic historical fiction. Here too we find a mixture of tones, and the ultimate effect of the historical re-creation (the story appears to center on an event in antebellum Southern plantation society) is ambiguous.[9]

The three ladies who recount the story of the courtship, marriage, and separation of Miss Sabina and Don McInnis, their voices sometimes speaking singly, sometimes in unison, function in the manner of a Greek chorus. Like that chorus, they seem to have little or no life of their own, existing primarily as narrators of and commentators upon the notable doings of the two personages who monopolize their thoughts. The setting contributes to the "classical" Grecian flavor of the story. Asphodel, a mansion, is a "golden ruin" still possessed of its Doric columns (p. 95). The house had at one time contained statues of Venus, Hermes, and Demeter. As in a Greek tragedy, a curse of heaven is called down by Miss Sabina on the head of McInnis, among others, and in an incident possibly meant to summon up classical myths of women deranged under the influence of wine, Miss Sabina acts in a frenzied manner, throwing an ink pad against a wall, which leaves "a purple mark like a grape stain. . ." (p. 108).

The manner of the chorus's narration tends, at one level,

to impart a larger-than-life quality to McInnis and Miss
Sabina. On the night of his wedding, the chorus says,
McInnis " 'stood astride . . . astride the rooms, the guests,
the flowers, the tapers, the bride and her father. . .' " (pp.
99–100—first ellipsis in original). After he has been unfaithful
to her, Miss Sabina drives him away with a whip, and
becomes, according to the chorus, " 'remote from us and
grand' " (p. 103). The two are not flesh and blood creatures
but function as legendary figures (to be sure, the legend
partakes of melodrama).

At the same time, one can find touches in the story which
serve to undercut the classical, legendary quality we have
been pointing to. Shortly after the three narrators, Phoebe,
Irene, and Cora, are described as "looking modestly upward
to the frieze of maidens" on Asphodel's facade, they are
designated as "all old maids, in hanging summer cot-
tons. . ." (p. 96). We get an enumeration of the disasters that
befell the children of Sabina and McInnis, which may be
seen, at least in retrospect, as taking on a comic excess.
Following the recounting of these misfortunes, Phoebe says
" 'Who can tell what will happen in this world!' " The
statement seems typical of choral utterances in Greek
tragedy, but where those are delivered in a mournful manner, the statement here is made by a character who immediately afterwards "looked *placidly* up into the feature-
less sky overhead" (p. 101; my italics). McInnis appears
suddenly, naked, at the picnic of the three old maids, and
they flee across a field. "With the suddenness of birds they
had all dropped to earth at the same moment and as if by
magic risen on the other side of the fence, beside a 'No-
Trespassing' sign" (p. 110). The inclusion of the sign does
not consort well with the legendary mode the story has
seemingly been trying to establish, and the movement of the
three ladies may be thought of as a parody of choral unison
("they had all dropped to earth at the same moment"). The
action that follows also serves to dispel the mood of high

seriousness the ladies' recounting had been striving for. McInnis is described as being " 'naked as an old goat' " (p. 110), and the three women are comically pursued by a herd of goats: "There were billy-goats and nanny-goats, old goats and young, a whole thriving herd. Their little beards all blew playfully to the side in the wind of their advancement" (p. 111).

Apart from these matters, belonging to the narrative frame, the core of the story, the legend of Miss Sabina, is touched by comedy. She is described as dominating the town, its " 'whole population—white and black, men and women, children, idiots, and animals—even strangers. . . . At the May Festival when she passed by, all the maypoles became hopelessly tangled, one by one' " (p. 105). Ruth Vande Kieft says solemnly that this shows Miss Sabina "has a way of spoiling anything pagan, such as an old fertility rite."[10] But surely Welty is working in a comic vein here, producing the caricature of a matriarch (although the chorus is presenting her in all seriousness).

Concentrating on its comic elements, we might conclude that the story is mocking the Southern tendency to subject the past to inflation and melodramatization. "Asphodel" can be taken as suggesting that such grandiose imaging is compensation for the undernourished lives of those who turn history into legend (cf. my remarks, pp. 56-58 on Rosa Coldfield's version of Thomas Sutpen in *Absalom, Absalom!*). But the trouble with such a view of the story's intention is that it collides with elements in the narrative that are not the products of the chorus's sensibility but apparently meant to operate as objective presences. At its start, the story establishes, indeed insists upon, a certain magical, tranced atmosphere: "It was a cloudless day. . . . It was noon, and without a shadow the line of columns rose in perfect erectness from the green vines. . . . It was a golden ruin. . . . The sky was pure, transparent. . ." (p. 95). "There was not a shadow. It was high noon" (p. 96). "Above them the six columns seemed to be filled with the inhalations of summer and to be suspended in the resting of noon" (p. 97). These are the observations, not of the old maids, but of the narrator. And at the very end, after the comically jarring episode of the naked McInnis and the herd of goats, we get this: "[Phoebe's] voice was soft, and she seemed to be still in a tender dream and an unconscious celebration—as though the picnic were not already set rudely in the past, but were the enduring and intoxicating present, still the phenomenon, the golden day" (p. 113). The comic, the "rude," the disruptive, are subordinated here to a softening, glamorizing process; the very elements that appeared to constitute a humorous, critical corrective of the old maids' concocted version of the past are smoothed away, and we are left with the magical atmosphere originally established in the story. (We should also note that the very figure whose sudden, earthy appearance would seem to undercut the chorus's representation of the past as high legend, himself suggests something beyond ordinary history, the mythical figure of Pan.) If Miss Welty was attempting to mock the tendency to convert history into myth, she appears to have succumbed to that tendency herself. It is possible, of course, to read the "golden day" passage that concludes the story not as the narrator's description but as something ascribed to Phoebe. However, the story does not allow a clear-cut distinction between narrator and character to be made here.

Where the mansion in "Asphodel" is burned down by the headstrong Miss Sabina as part of a private drama, the house in "The Burning" is put to the torch as part of the larger destruction of the South wrought by the Civil War. "The Burning" is set in Mississippi at the time Sherman's army is cutting a fiery swath through that state. Ruth Vande Kieft has deftly described "the strange, perverse-seeming narrative technique" of this story.[11] But it is more than the narrative technique that makes the tale rather difficult to grasp as a whole. "The Burning" is a mosaic not only of story pieces but of tonal fragments, and these never come together to produce a coherent design and attitude.[12]

One thing *is* clear, although that clarity is achieved at the expense of "The Burning" approaching too closely to *Gone with the Wind:* the Yankee soldiers are portrayed as nothing but despicable, contemptible louts who loot, rape, and destroy. The laugh of one of the soldiers who come to the house of the sisters Theo and Myra consists of his already hanging jaw dropping "still lower." Another soldier pursues Myra with "his red eyes sticking out. . ." (p. 29). At one point both men laugh, "jolting each other so hard that for a second it looked like a fight" (p. 32). The soldiers who carry booty from the house are implicitly connected with dogs fighting over bones. A drummer boy commits an act of gratuitous destruction, wringing the necks of two pet peacocks.

But once we move away from the unambiguous, unsparing portrait of hateful Yankee invaders, we are on uncertain ground. How, for example, are we to regard the two sisters, particularly Theo? At times in the story they seem like Gothic first cousins to the sisters Octavia and Clytie in an earlier Welty work, "Clytie." Theo, like Octavia, is the imperious, dominating member of a weird household; Myra, like Clytie, is weak and infantile. Miss Theo strikes poses and is made to say things like: " 'No man in the house. . . . Brother—no word. Father—dead' " (p. 31). Her imperiousness is given an amusing formulation when we are told that "the flat of Miss Theo's hand came down on mankind with a boisterous sound" (p. 30). These Gothic and comic elements (cf. the mixture in Tate's *The Fathers*) serve to keep us at an emotional distance from Theo, making her look bizarre, ridiculous, pretentious. Yet there are moments in the story when it would seem we are being abruptly asked to regard her with admiration or pity. She, along with Myra, is given dignity and pathos as the sisters watch the looting and destruction of their house. But her plan to commit suicide together with Myra is marked by a display of the self-congratulatory and ostentatious. Then, quickly following Theo's comic failure to hang herself (". . .Miss Theo came sailing down from the tree. She was always too powerful for a lady") is a description that makes her situation seem horrible, not funny: the slave Delilah "believed Miss Theo twisted in the grass like a dead snake until the sun went down" (p. 42). The ridiculous and the awful have been juxtaposed (not fused) and it is hard to know what to feel about all that has happened.

After the deaths of the two sisters, "The Burning" concentrates on Delilah. This new centering generates effects different from those coming out of the story's earlier treatment of the slave, and the difference adds to our confusion as to just what impression of the Civil War South Miss Welty is trying to convey. In the portions of the story where the sisters were still alive, Delilah seemed merely an obedient slave, somewhat simpleminded, regarded by others, both the sisters and the Yankees, as someone who existed only to be used. When the house was going up in flames (the slaves having participated in its looting along with the soldiers), Miss Theo had looked down at Delilah, who was peeping around her mistress's skirt, and said " 'Remember this. You black monkeys' . . . " (p. 35). This last phrase, which might be taken as an expression of white racism assigned to a particular *character,* comes to mind later when Delilah is described by the *narrator* as participating with unquestioning alacrity in the hanging: "Delilah, given the signal, *darted* up the tree and *hooking her toes* made the ropes fast . . . " (p. 40; my italics). The terms used here would appear to establish her, from the *story*'s viewpoint, as a black monkey indeed. (Later, she thinks of the child taken from her as "her black monkey" (p. 45). The tone in her use of the phrase is presumably different from that of Theo but the repetition of wording is notable, particularly since that repetition did not occur in the earlier version of the story.)[13] The image of

Delilah is hardly enhanced when we are told that after Miss Myra has been mounted on her back preparatory to hanging, the slave "was seized by the ribs and dragged giggling backwards . . . " (p. 41). While there is no question but that Delilah is presented as a victim up to the event of the sisters' suicide, it is also true that she is made to seem rather ridiculous and virtually without dignity.

But once the sisters are out of the way, Delilah is invested with a sensibility that we have not been prepared for and that gives her a sudden substance. She has three striking visions (more of these in a moment), and exits from the story with a "Jubilee cup" set on her head, undertaking some sort of journey. Alfred Appel, Jr., basing his remarks on the earlier version of the story, has claimed to see in her an endurance that is "not only stoic, but mystical, even saintly. . . . " He finds in "The Burning" the suggestion that "through their suffering, the Negroes are to be 'the chosen people' of the 'new' South."[14] This is a strained reading of either version of the story, having at best a minimal basis of support. It takes no account of the slave woman's depiction in the greater part of the work (nor of the explicit linking of slaves and soldiers in the looting of the house). Appel seems overly anxious to make a Dilsey-figure out of Delilah (or Florabel, as she is named in the earlier version). Her setting out on a journey at the end of the story is too vaguely presented to carry much weight. At the same time, there is presumably some significance in her act. But what is it? Welty's handling of Delilah has not been sufficiently firm or coherent for us to be able to say.

This uncertainty extends to the story's overall conception of the Old South. The fragmented, confusing presentation of the sisters, presumably representative of part of the old order, has already been discussed.[15] There are, in addition, Delilah's visions. She gazes into the portion of a Venetian mirror that has survived the burning of the house:

gold gathered itself from the winding water, and honey
under water started to flow, and then the gold fields were
there, hardening gold. Through the water, gold and honey
twisted up into houses, trembling. She saw people walking
the bridges in early light with hives of houses on their
heads, men in dresses, some with red birds; and monkeys
in velvet; and ladies with masks laid over their faces
looking from pointed windows. Delilah supposed that was
Jackson before Sherman came. Then it was gone. (P. 44)

The scene seems festive and precious, its disappearance a
loss. As Delilah continues to look into the mirror, she sees

minnows of light . . . quivering, leaping to life, fighting,
aping old things Delilah had seen done in this world
already, sometimes what men had done to Miss Theo and
Miss Myra and the peacocks and to slaves, and sometimes
what a slave had done and what anybody now could do to
anybody. (P. 44)

This second vision is somewhat ambiguous. Its noting of
"what men had done . . . to slaves" would seem to indict the
South, but that observation is part of a larger one whose
other phrases apply to what the *Yankees* had done (*and* the
Yankees had raped Delilah). At best, this second vision
qualifies ever so slightly the affection for the old order
coming out of the first vision; its main effect is to reinforce
the first vision by picturing the present of the story, the Civil
War and its destruction of the old order, as a horrendous
time. But earlier, before the entry of the Yankees, the mirror
had reflected a scene in the house that seemed vacuous and
somewhat ridiculous:

There in the mirror the parlor remained, filled up with
dusted pictures, and shuttered since six o'clock against
the heat and that smell of smoke they were all so tired of,
still glimmering with precious, breakable things white
ladies were never tired of and never broke, unless they

were mad at each other. Behind [Delilah] the bare yawn
of the hall was at her back. . . . (P. 30)

Where do all these mirror images, taken together, leave us?
Finally, Delilah has a vision of an army of winged creatures:

bees saddled like horses out of the air, butterflies har-
nessed to one another, bats with masks on, birds together,
all with their weapons bared. She listened for the blows,
and dreaded that whole army of wings—of flies, birds, ser-
pents, their glowing enemy faces and bright kings'
dresses, that banner of colors forked out, all this world
that was flying, striking, stricken, falling, gilded or black-
ened, mortally splitting and falling apart, proud turbans
unwinding, turning like the spotted dying leaves of fall,
spiraling down to bottomless ash; she dreaded the fury of
all the butterflies and dragonflies in the world riding,
blades unconcealed and at point—descending, and rising
again from the waters below, down under, one whale made
of his own grave, opening his mouth to swallow Jonah one
more time.

This description is remarkable, stunning in itself. It may be
meant to recall some of the details of Delilah's first
vision—the honey and hives, the birds, the masked ladies. It
generates a marvelous sense of apocalypse, but does not aid
us in finding the story's judgment of the time and the place.
Too many diverse elements in the story—comedy and
nobility, grotesquerie and pathos, absurdity and dignity—
have jostled for our attention, and a real synthesis has failed
to emerge.

No such problem of fragmentation occurs in "First
Love"; the story is virtually all of a piece in its depiction of
Aaron Burr. But like the other works we have examined, this
one presents the past in a way that endows it with a
difference, a strangeness. As was the case with "Asphodel,"
the early portions of "First Love" insistently strive for a
dreamy, drugged atmosphere, a portentous ambience
("Whatever happened, it happened in extraordinary times,

in a season of dreams. . . " [p. 3]). From its beginning, the story is plainly trying to create a sense of the charged and special in its portrayal of Burr, apprehended through the eyes of Joel, a boy observer. The eyes, not the ears—Joel is deaf. As though in compensation, his eyes are filled to capacity by Burr, who is not so much a person in the story as he is a presence, radiant himself and the cause of radiance in others. Here is Joel first discovering Burr in his inn-room late at night: he "opened his eyes to see the whole room shining brightly, like a brimming lake in the sun" (p. 10). The lighting effects that are made to play about Burr are so extraordinary that the man would almost seem to be endowed with the Shekinah. Godlike, too, are the qualities of the primal and ineffable assigned to a gesture by Burr:

> To Joel it was like the first movement he had ever seen, as if the world had been up to that night inanimate. It was like the signal to open some heavy gate or paddock, and it did open to his complete astonishment upon a panorama in his own head, about which he knew first of all that he would never be able to speak—it was nothing but brightness, as full as the brightness on which he had opened his eyes. (P. 11)

One check upon the godlike status given to Burr is the story's conception of him as a tragic figure, the dreamer of a great but doomed dream. (This is based on the historical Burr's planning of a vast, vague adventure in the American West which never came off.) If light is used to make him seem beyond the human, it is also employed to suggest his tragic dimension. Thus, we are told that as Burr talks with Blennerhassett (a party to his plans) in Joel's room, "Lights shone in his eyes like travelers' fires seen far out on the river" (p. 16). When Joel goes down there, the river "would leap suddenly out of the shining ice around, into its full-grown torrent of life, and its strength and its churning passage held Joel watching over it like the spell unfolding by night in his room" (p. 18). He thinks: "Was any scheme a

man had, however secret and intact, always broken upon by
the very current of its working? One day, in anguish, he saw
a raft torn apart in midstream and the men scattered from it''
(p. 18). Later, Blennerhassett stands in the firelight of Joel's
room with his wife, "like creatures balancing together on a
raft. . . '' (p. 24). Juxtaposed, these passages link the river
with both the glory of Burr's Western scheme, suggested by
the light, and with its destruction. A slight touch of undercutting is provided when Burr's flotilla, intended to help
carry out his plans, is described as a puny affair. But this
effect is dissipated as the story unfolds, and it had been
preceded by one more in keeping with the overall celebratory tone of "First Love": Joel sees on the river "a chain of
great perfect trees floating down, lying on their sides in
postures like slain giants and heroes of battle, black cedars
and stone-white sycamores, magnolias with their leavy
leaves shining as if they were in bloom, a long procession''
(p. 21). These symbolic objects are more appropriate to the
story's conception of Burr than is his actual flotilla. One is
presumably supposed to be left with the sense of a magnificent failure.

What exactly were the details of Burr's grand scheme?
What was he trying to accomplish? Was it treasonous? These
questions, still matters for speculation by historians, the
story does not attempt to answer. While we are potentially
privileged by our being placed in a room where Burr holds
nightly conferences with Blennerhassett, we are deprived of
any concrete reconstruction of the past through the device of
Joel's deafness, the story being told from his point of view.
And a device it certainly appears to be, chosen deliberately
to stand between us and any specific formulation of Burr's
plans. Burr exists for us as a creature of glamorous gestures.
Nothing so specific, so fixed, as an actual utterance by him is
allowed to encroach on the *mystery* assigned to his being.
After Joel's first witnessing of Burr, the boy "was seized and
possessed by mystery" (p. 13). Watching Burr and Blen-

nerhassett on another occasion, "he could see that the secret was endlessly complex. . . ." (p. 14). Welty does not attempt to have a sense of mystery and complexity emerge from direct presentation, but simply insists on its presence in Burr's unheard eloquence. Burr "might have talked in another language, in which there was nothing but evocation" (p. 16). This is, perhaps unwittingly, a description of the story's own mode. To a large extent, it attempts "nothing but evocation." We are told that in Burr's face "there was every subtlety and eloquence, and no features. . . ." (p. 16). The story itself suffers from too much in the way of "elo-quence," too little in the way of features. (When we are presented with a circumstantial paragraph telling us of the time and place of Burr's trial for treason, it comes as a shock.)

Perhaps "First Love" is implicitly justifying its refusal to give concreteness and particularity to Burr's scheme, and thereby to Burr, when it says:

> If love does a secret thing always, it is to reach backward, to a time that could not be known—for it makes a history of the sorrow and the dream it has contemplated in some instant of recognition. What Joel saw before him he had a terrible wish to speak out loud, but he would have had to find names for the places of the heart and the times for its shadowy and tragic events, and they seemed of great magnitude, heroic and terrible and splendid, like the legends of the mind. But for lack of a way to tell how much was known, the boundaries would lie between him and the others, all the others, until he died. (P. 28)

The issue is somewhat confused by Joel apparently being a mute, but that is not the essence of the matter. "First Love" may well conceive of itself as reaching back with love to a man of an unknowable time, discovering that it is impossible "to find names for the places of the heart and the times for its shadowy and tragic events. . . ." The story is at once committed to its own portentous eloquence, its mode of evocation, and to the notion that Burr's mystery lies beyond the powers of language to express. Failing to make him sufficiently real, "First Love" asks too much of us, implicitly insisting that we, like Joel, love and admire Burr. In contrast, what we are called on to admire in "A Still Moment," we can, and ungrudgingly.

Where someone like Walter Savage Landor brings together in his writings figures of high European culture and has them engage in "Imaginary Conversations," Welty, in "A Still Moment," assembles three men associated with the American wilderness and has them engage in silence. Their failure to converse dramatizes the separation between them, their nonintersecting conceptions of the land in which they find themselves, their American atomism.

It is not that they fail to speak at all. When James Murrell, a legendary nineteenth-century outlaw, meets Lorenzo Dow on the Natchez Trace, he rides along with him, talking continuously. Dow was an evangelist and another legendary figure of the last century. (A biographer has claimed that at his death in the 1830s "he was probably the most widely travelled man in America, and certainly the most widely known." Associated with him are "dim fables of weird and mysterious powers.")[16] Dow does not respond to Murrell, whose talk, rather comically, centers on a *silent* man— himself, spoken of as another—who has committed evil deeds. Murrell plans to murder Dow. The two dismount in silence at a great oak tree and are joined there by yet another legendary personage, John James Audubon, the remarkable naturalist and artist. Dow makes a statement about God having created the world, but apart from that, the three have fortuitously come together in "a still moment." (Presumably, they never met each other in real life.)

A snowy heron descends to feed in a marsh and rivets the gaze of all three men. The different ways in which they view the bird are extensions of their respective modes of vision, as these have been depicted by the story up to this point. For Dow, as for the American Puritans, the wilderness and its creatures are of no value or interest in themselves, but acquire significance as *symbols* of God's order and will (the wilderness as a whole is to Dow but a symbol of the human heart). Earlier in the story he had greeted the appearance of fireflies as "signs sent from God that he had not seen the accumulated radiance of saved souls because he was not able, and that his eyes were more able to see the fireflies of the Lord than His blessed souls" (p. 74). The heron itself is interpreted by Dow as a sign of God's love and of His "Nearness" (this is somewhat ironic when we remember the story's having said of Dow's relation to his wife that "He found it effortless to love at a distance"—p. 74). Apart from its symbolic content, the forest for Dow is but mere space to be traversed as he goes from one camp meeting to another.

The actual Murrell had been branded as a horse thief, and this seems to have filled him, in the words of a biographer, with "a passion for revenge."[17] He conceived of a white-led Negro rebellion in the South, which would satisfy that passion and also make him fabulously rich. Welty's portrayal of him draws strikingly on this historical background. When he looks at the heron, Welty has him shade his eyes, the gesture thrusting into his vision the brand "H.T." on his thumb. He "looked at the bird with the whole plan of the Mystic Rebellion darting from him as if in rays of the bright reflected light, and he stood looking proudly, leader as he was bound to become of the slaves, the brigands and outcasts of the entire Natchez country . . ." (pp. 86–87). In her use of the branded thumb, Welty presents Murrell as seeing essentially nothing but himself. Moreover, despite his self-image as a creature of light, the story has continually linked him with darkness. (Audubon thinks of Murrell's eyes as "the dark kind that . . . saw neither closeness nor distance, light nor shade, wonder nor familiarity. They were

narrowed to contract the heart, narrowed to make an avert-
ing plan"—p. 85). For Murrell, the wilderness is nothing but
an "impediment" (p. 80).

Only to Audubon (whose entrance into the story is pun-
ningly connected with light), a man of enlarged eyes, is it
given to really see the white heron as well as other birds. He
also hears them, as opposed to Dow, whose ears are open
primarily to *inner* voices. Audobon's visual apprehension is
connected with the intimacy of touch: his eyes "embraced
the object in the distance and he could see it as carefully as if
he held it in his hand" (p. 87). Distance becomes nearness
here, as opposed to the absence of either in Murrell, and to
the dubious "Nearness" felt by Dow.

Each of the characters in the story is essentially a loner,
and each is possessed of an overwhelming vocation: "What
each of them had wanted was simply *all*. To save all souls, to
destroy all men, to see and to record all life that filled this
world . . ." (p. 88). It is as if the immensity of America had
provoked in each a response commensurate in scope. But
despite their experiencing a momentary union of peace as
they look at the heron, Audubon is ultimately separated from
and placed above the other two. Murrell is a monstrous
egotist and so is Dow, though in a more subtle way. Audubon
alone has a properly alert and appreciative awareness of a
world outside himself or men in general (he has a vision of the
Natchez Trace and its creatures as having existed "before
man ever knew where he wanted to go . . ."—p. 82). He has
a "care for looking outward . . ." (p. 92). In addition, it is
only Audubon who is capable of experiencing a chastening of
his overwhelming ambition (Murrell is unchanged by the still
moment, and Dow, while responsive to the bird's beauty,
theologizes his experience and remain unshaken in his
views). Audubon recognizes that he will never be able to
reproduce in his drawing the beauty of the living bird. But he
is not crushed by this thought. He departs from the story
ideally open to his surroundings, "noting all sights, all

sounds, and was gentler than they as he went" (p. 92). (He reminds us of the heroes of *In the American Grain*.) His presence in the story has condemned the religious denial or perversion of the American place, as exemplified by Dow, and the ruthless use of that place for self-aggrandizement, as exemplified by Murrell. "A Still Moment" celebrates Audubon's reverence for the wilderness which the others have so despised or denied, the story using its blatantly contrived and stylized meeting of the three men to produce a vivid paradigm of basic American responses to the American earth.

NOTES

1. "An Interview with Eudora Welty," in *Writers and Writing* (New York, 1946), p. 290.

2. Eudora Welty, *The Robber Bridegroom* (Garden City, N.Y.: Doubleday, Doran & Co., 1942), p. 170. Subsequent quotations from this book will be followed in the text of the chapter by the relevant page numbers.

3. Alfred Kazin, "An Enchanted World in America," *New York Herald Tribune Books*, 25 October 1942, p. 19.

4. Constance Rourke, *American Humor* (Garden City, N.Y.: Doubleday Anchor Books, 1953), p. 52.

5. See Walter Blair and Franklin J. Meine, *Half Horse, Half Alligator* (Chicago: University of Chicago Press, 1956), p. 89.

6. Rourke, *American Humor*, p. 49.

7. Kazin, "An Enchanted World in America," 19.

8. Ibid.

9. "Asphodel," as well as "First Love" and "A Still Moment," can be found in *Selected Stories of Eudora Welty* (New York: The Modern Library, 1954). Quotations from these stories will be followed in the text of the chapter by the relevant page numbers. The reader should note that *Selected Stories* contains two collections of stories, and that the pagination begins anew with the second collection. It is that collection which contains "Asphodel," "First Love," and "A Still Moment."

10. Ruth Vande Kieft, *Eudora Welty* (New Haven, Conn.: College and University Press, 1962), p. 58.

11. Ibid., pp. 154–55.

12. "The Burning" can be found in Eudora Welty, *The Bride of the Innisfallen* (New York: Harcourt, Brace & Co., 1955), pp. 28–46. Subsequent quotations from this story will be followed in the text of the chapter by the relevant page numbers.

13. The earlier version appeared in *Harper's Bazaar* 85 (March 1951).

14. Alfred Appel, Jr., *A Season of Dreams: The Fiction of Eudora Welty* (Baton Rouge, La.: Louisiana State University Press, 1965), pp. 139, 140.

15. It should be further noted that, adding to the confusion, there is a baby in the family whose race and parentage are a matter of dispute, and we never do discover the facts. He is either white or black, the child of Myra or her disgraced brother (or both?).

16. Charles Coleman Sellers, *Lorenzo Dow: The Bearer of the Word* (New York: Minton, Balch & Co., 1928), p. 3.

17. Ross Phares, *Reverend Devil: A Biography of John A. Murrell* (New Orleans, La.: Pelican Publishing Co., 1941), p. 17.

6

A Murderer in the Family:
Robert Penn Warren's *Brother to Dragons*

In *Brother to Dragons* Robert Penn Warren attempts to interpret, not a piece of historical evidence, but the absence of such, a glaring gap in the records left by Thomas Jefferson. Although Lilburn Lewis was Jefferson's nephew, those records fail to make any reference at all to Lilburn's horrendous axe-killing of a slave named George in the year 1811. Here, said Warren, in talking about the genesis of the work, "was Jefferson's family. The philosopher of our liberties and the architect of our country and the prophet of human perfectibility had this in the family blood."[1]

Brother to Dragons does not interpret Jefferson's silence as an expression of indifference to the murder. On the contrary, it sees him as having been traumatized by the event, so profoundly shaken that he felt compelled to disassociate himself completely from it, even while it caused him to undergo a total reversal of his assumptions about the nature of man and his societal possibilities. By giving prominence to Lilburn's gory act of murder and its effect upon Jefferson, Warren is clearly placing his approach to history at a far remove from a D.A.R. glorification of the past: "to the pious mind/ Our history's nothing if it's not refined."[2] Also, his book does not exhibit what he calls "the benign indifferency/ Of the historical imagination . . ." (p. 10).

147

The form of the work is a daring one, an attempted fusion of dialogue, drama, and descriptive, narrative, and meditative poetry, a combination not unlike that found in the source of Warren's title, the *Book of Job*.[3] Moreover, there is a genuine variety in the verse of the characters, ranging from the literate plenitude of Jefferson's speeches, which often take the form of high rhetoric, to the colloquial simplicities of Lilburn's brother-in-law. There are a few cases in which we feel a sense of disjunction, a wrenching jump from one verbal mode to another, but in general Warren has done a remarkable job of maintaining both variety and continuity among the work's voices. At one extreme those voices become mechanically highfalutin, at another saccharine-simple, but all in all there is a considerable quantity of varied and effective poetry, including powerful formulations of idealism and disillusionment, magnificent evocations of nature, vigorous and efficient narrative, and moving utterances coming out of the reconstructed dramatic circumstances.

Warren's own description of the form of *Brother to Dragons* can be found in a prefatory note to the work:

> It is in dialogue spoken by characters, but it is not a play. The main body of the action is in the remote past—in the earthly past of the characters long dead—and now they meet at an unspecified place and at an unspecified time to try to make sense of that action. (P. [XIII]).

This statement does not cover one of the characters in the poem, R.P.W., the poet himself, representing at times twentieth-century man. He both comments on the actions recounted and converses with the other characters, principally Jefferson. For the most part, Warren's insertion of himself into the poem works well, providing a flexible device for interrogation, discussion, commentary, and evocation. As one who has not only investigated the documents of the case, but who has sought out the site of the Lewis homestead, scene of the murder, he conveys a sense of being a man for whom the past is a living and significant presence. But he is not completely integrated into the work. He has endowed himself with an independent existence, largely through his thoughts and recollections of his personal experiences and relationships, particularly with respect to his father. This material has an interest of its own, but some of it raises questions that are outside the main story or else attempts a forced connection with it.

The relationship between R.P.W. and Jefferson is a shifting one. In their earliest exchanges, the poet seems sardonic and impatient with Jefferson, feeling free to cut him off in mid-sentence. At other times, the book allows Jefferson to make points at the expense of R.P.W. Elsewhere, the two are seen as capable of agreement or at least of disagreeing in a civil way and as intellectual equals. But often R.P.W., along with the work as a whole, seems out to *get* Jefferson, to indict and humble him up to, and possibly including, the very last. It is almost as though Warren has adopted Jefferson's own fierce dictum (one that the work is presumably questioning), uttered early in the book: "There's no forgiveness for our being human" (p. 24).

Just what in Jefferson has deserved the harshness with which he is treated? It would appear to be not so much his supposedly misguided assumptions about man's potential nobility and the possibility of a just society in which men regard themselves as brothers; it is the vanity, the self-flattery behind those assumptions. At least such vanity is imputed to Jefferson by his nephew Meriwether Lewis (of the Lewis and Clark expedition), who accuses his uncle of having but wished "To prove yourself nobler in man's nobleness./ Yes, in man's nobleness, you'd be the noble Jefferson" (p. 106). This charge is supported by Jefferson's sister Lucy (Lilburn's mother), who can be taken in the later portions of the poem as speaking for Warren. In her version of the accusation, she tells Jefferson that the report of the murder, showing "What evil was possible even in the familial blood,'' made him fear that he himself was capable of such an act, and caused him to renounce Lilburn completely. She avails herself of a metaphor that links Jefferson to Lilburn, indeed that substitutes Jefferson for Lilburn as killer:

> In vanity and virtue and your fear,
> You struck. You struck Lilburn down—and yet strike
> Poor Lilburn down, and over and over again, the axe
> Falls. . . .
> . . . .
> And as George was to Lilburn, so Lilburn is to you,
> And as innocence was all Lilburn wanted, it is all
> You yourself want, or have wanted. . . .
>
> (P. 190)

Thus, the historical fact of Jefferson's silence on Lilburn is converted by the poem into an assertion that he felt anguish over the murder and rejected his nephew; these responses in turn are interpreted as the expression of vanity. Such is the sequence, or a portion of it, by which Jefferson's hands are metaphorically dipped in blood. Even granting Warren's interpretation of Jefferson as guilty of great vanity, one wonders whether that characteristic has ever been formulated in such fierce, extravagant terms as those applied to Jefferson by his sister.

But Jefferson is connected to Lilburn and made to seem as guilty as he by more than Lucy's metaphor. That connection is one of the central conceptions of *Brother to Dragons,* which sees the two men not only as blood relatives but as kindred spirits, closely related in their basic needs.[4] They must be able to believe in an ideal, an abstraction. Once that ideal crumbles before the facts, it is replaced, in the case of Jefferson, by its inverse, and in the case of Lilburn by the combination of such an inverse with a passionate desire to keep some original ideal intact. Thus, under pressure of his knowledge of Lilburn's act, Jefferson moves from a belief in the glorious possibilities of mankind to a belief in the unredeemable evil of human nature. Lilburn, he says, "is an absolute of our essential/Condition . . ." (p. 93). Lilburn, who wants to believe in the angelic purity of his wife, is appalled when he finds she has enjoyed some unnamed sexual act he has performed upon her: " 'now I see when angels/Come down to earth, they step in dung, like us./And like it' " (p. 80). For him the world is " 'a sty' " (p. 70). (These statements link up with Jefferson's consciousness of the earth's "ordure" [p. 7].) Lilburn's desire for an ideal absolute expresses itself in his desire to keep the memory of his mother intense and inviolate. The breakage of her possessions and their disappearance from the family home is regarded by him as a desecration, a blotting out by the slaves of the fact of her death, a death whose agony for him he wishes to hold at its original pitch. When his slave George breaks a favorite pitcher of his mother, he kills him.

But where *Brother to Dragons* moves toward a harsh indictment of Jefferson, it shows, even while pointing up Lilburn's perversity and cruelty, a distinct inclination to soften its judgment of that murderer. Warren may be revealing a preference for a lost violent soul like Lilburn to a mere theoretician like Jefferson. Also, the very act of fleshing Lilburn out, plucking him from his obscure place in the past and trying to account for his actions, serves to transform him from a monster in an historical footnote into a human being.

Warren has interestingly intertwined an implicit Freudian approach with a consideration of the Southern racial situation of the time to show the psychological and cultural forces besetting Lilburn. He is pictured as having two mothers, his actual mother, Lucy, and his black wet nurse, Aunt Cat. (Warren tells us that the latter is a character wholly of his own invention.) Over the years, the Negro woman had fought a silent struggle with Lucy for Lilburn's love. But where Lilburn's attachment to his white mother is excessive, overwrought, Oedipal perhaps, he cannot accept his one-time relation with Aunt Cat. Confronted with his mother's death and at the same time with Aunt Cat's recollections of having once given him suck, he repudiates her milk, saying " 'now I'd puke it out, the last black drop,/ I'd puke it out—oh, God! my mother's dead' " (p. 91). He then spits, attempting to purge himself of that in him which comes from Aunt Cat. Warren has created here a vivid image of a man straining for a racial purity (and behind that, perhaps, for a sexual one). Later, as R.P.W. reconstructs the story, it is another act of spitting by Lilburn, this time indicating his contempt for his slaves, that moves Aunt Cat to recall his rejection of her and to set off the revelations that will lead to Lilburn's exposure as the murderer of George. As hard and cruel a man as it depicts Lilburn to be, the poem shows him, at least in part, the product or victim of a culture of terrible contradictions, one which set up the most intimate relationships between blacks and whites, and at the same time drew the sharpest distinctions between them. To point up Lilburn's position as victim, Aunt Cat is not allowed by Warren to function simply as a poor, repudiated black mammy, but is conceived of as a potent figure who "asked for" Lilburn's act of spitting by her "proclamation and triumph/ Over the fallen adversary [the newly dead Lucy]. Then no wonder/ That Lilburn struck in rage, and outrage, back" (pp. 91, 92).[5]

Apart from seeing Lilburn as intensely acted upon, thereby softening our judgment of him at least somewhat, the poem is surely sympathetic to Lilburn's act of murder as an example of attempting escape from the complexities of the soul:

Any act at all, the bad, the good, affords,
Or seems to afford, the dear redemption of simplicity:
The dear redemption in the mere fact of achieved definition,
Be what that may.

(P. 56)

That the achievement of definition even in terrible deeds has its attraction for the poem, while not receiving its ultimate approval, is indicated by R.P.W.'s invoking of the dark in a section that leads up to the murder scene:

> Let now the night descend
> With all its graduated terrors,
> And in its yearning toward absoluteness now amend
> The impudent daylight's velleities, and errors
> . . . .
> For all life lifts and longs towards its own name,
> And toward fulfillment in the singleness of definition,
> So in the dark now let
> The dark flame lift, unfolding like a flower,
> And let the darkest flower bloom like flame
> Whose beauty hangs unmoving in our eye,
> For all achieved perfection can only proclaim
> The thrust toward timelessness, in Time.
>
> (P. 121)

There are other elements of the poem that indicate its sympathy for Lilburn. In trying to keep the memory of his mother's death alive, Lilburn is viewed as desperately hanging onto a hurt threatened with dissolution by the processes of nature. The spring, bringing back the grass over Lucy's grave, seems to make of her death nothing—April for Lilburn is indeed the cruelest month. His violence is regarded as a desperate attempt to maintain contact with the reality of pain, and, R.P.W. adds, "all we ask in the end is that: / Reality" (p. 113). Moreover, R.P.W. describes Lilburn as "at the last, / . . . only trying to know what the good thing was . . ." (p. 69). R.P.W. further contends that it is the destroyer who is in most need of love, and that "destruction's but creation gone astray . . ." (p. 99). Finally, when Jefferson exclaims that he would have killed Lilburn had he been on the scene, Meriwether Lewis suddenly appears to charge Jefferson with having, in effect, murdered *him*. He attributes his own death by suicide (a version Warren chose as opposed to the theory that Meriwether was killed) to his having acted upon Jefferson's notions about the goodness of men; this led him to an overwhelming disillusionment. The ideologue now stands in for the actual axe-murderer, as the whole matter of Lilburn is abruptly displaced by the question of Jefferson's responsibility for Meriwether's death, this becoming a central issue. Lilburn's most violent critic, Jefferson, is now the accused, as Warren strikingly inverts the relative historical positions of the two men, elevating the despised Lilburn and bringing low the mighty Jefferson. In the *Book of Job,* the stricken protagonist is robbed of his once enviable position through Satan, acting with God's permission. In *Brother to Dragons,* Warren plays God and Satan to Jefferson's Job.

But where Job protests his downfall, Jefferson ultimately consents to his. The shrill, angry, sometimes nearly hysterical, tone he exhibits in much of the poem is replaced by one of quiet sadness. Jarred out of his revulsion at the display of evil in *others,* the human race in general, his nephew in particular, he acquires a new humility. He recognizes that his dream was "but a reflex of my vanity . . ." (p. 193). The appearance of the accusing Meriwether has provided the emotional impetus for Jefferson's transformation, but it is his sister Lucy, acting as a kind of *raisonneur,* who brings Jefferson to his new perception. Thoroughly humble herself, she admits that her love for her son was imperfect and that she thereby contributed to his actions. She insists that Lilburn is but a reflection of Jefferson's own capacity for evil and that Jefferson must recognize this: "whatever health we have is not by denial,/ But in confronting the terror of our condition" (p. 192).

Vanity considered as a terrible flaw, the need for humility, the sense of the capacity for evil in all men—these concerns that run through Warren's poem testify to what might be called a Christian cast of mind. Some critics have seized on these elements and expressed them in terms that go beyond those actually employed in the book itself, speaking of "original Sin" and "God's grace."[6] (*Brother to Dragons*, together with such responses, may be seen as partaking of that religious sensibility that emerged in American literary culture after World War II, reaching its fullest development in the 1950s—Warren's book was published in 1953.) From a Christian orientation, Jefferson, in his eighteenth-century Utopianism, may be regarded as having failed to recognize certain Christian truths until he is made aware of them by Lucy. But critics who think in these terms are more Christian than the book itself, believing the work to adhere more fully and neatly to a religious sense of the world than it actually does. Warren is not applying a purely Christian perspective to a particular chapter of American history. There are other aspects of his sensibility operating here that work outside such a perspective.

Consider the poem's references to "glory." (A couple of these are mixed in with what might be termed religious allusions, but the conception of glory is hardly contained by those allusions.) Jefferson found glory in his vision of men's possibilities at the convention in Philadelphia which led to the writing of the Declaration of Independence. This particular manifestation of the quality could well be subsumed under a Christian reading of *Brother to Dragons* which would see that glory as an illusion. But what of the extended reference to glory that comes out of R.P.W.'s recollection of an incident in his boyhood when somebody shot a wild goose flying all by itself "and seized it, hugged it, ran/ Three miles to town and yelled for joy . . ." (p. 19)? (Jefferson had spoken of experiencing joy in Philadelphia.) Drawing on this episode, R.P.W. says "the only/ Thing in life is glory." He goes on to state that

> the one thing that man fears
> Is the terror of salvation and the face
> Of glory. But that face is all.
>
> (P. 20)

He has juxtaposed glory with a Christian conception, but if anything, the value that has been grounded in a secular context, glory, a delight in "the world's magnificence" (p. 20), is dominant.

Late in the work, with the story of Lilburn already concluded and the transformation of Jefferson brought to its completion, the poem, taking some four pages to do so, goes on to tell of what happened to Isham, Lilburn's brother. The materials in no way relate to Jefferson's acquisition of humility and recognition of his capacity for evil. It is as though one side of Warren, not expressed in his treatment of Jefferson, insists on asserting itself in the form of a narrative coda, the tale of Isham's adventures, spoken by the man himself. He tells of his escape from jail, and his riding to New Orleans, where he joined Jackson's forces and shot the prettily dressed British soldiers.[7] He yelled

> at the cotton bales.
> I jumped up high and waved my cap and yelled.
> I yelled for glory, how we killed and slayed. . . .
>
> (P. 200)

Later in the poem, in a kind of recapitulatory passage somewhat reminiscent of Whitman's catalogs of experience, R.P.W. says "We stood at the cotton bales, and yelled for glory." He goes on:

> We have yearned in the heart for some identification
> With the glory of the human effort, and have yearned
> For an adequate definition of that glory.
>
> (PP. 213–14)

The passage continues, speaking of the "necessity of virtue," and coming up with what one critic has called "the series of Christian paradoxes that form the thematic resolution of the work" (these will be quoted later).[8] But the somber statements that he refers to do not seem to link up with the question of glory, certainly not the glory Isham spoke of. That term seems to designate some joyous bursting forth of a man's energies, which are self-delighting, their own justification. They are unrelated to the questions of guilt and innocence, vanity and virtue, that the paradoxes deal with. If, at one level, the poem wants to apply to both past and present a wisdom expressed in Christian paradoxes, at another it links history and the poet's own experience in terms of a continuity of delight, moments of joy complete in themselves and not brought under a religious rubric. Warren seems to have wanted some integration of these two levels, bringing together the theme of glory and what might be called the theme of virtue in the following lines:

> If there is glory, the burden, then, is ours.
> If there is virtue, the burden, then, is ours.
>
> (P. 211)

But juxtaposition and parallel phrasing do not constitute a genuine integration. The glory the poem speaks of in connection with the goose shot down or with Isham's fighting at the cotton bales does not, in those contexts, carry the mournfulness of a "burden." That burden is, at best, an afterthought. So Warren's materials here fail to fuse.[9]

Another, related split can be found in the responses evoked by American history at different points in the poem. During one exchange, R. P. W. and Jefferson collaborate, in effect, to portray an American past ridden by violence and injustice, which Jefferson sees as extending into the twentieth century. But earlier we are given a rendering of the American past focused on a noble river-scape peopled by heroic boatmen, whose description echoes their celebration in American folklore; it is all conveyed in a nostalgic vein. We have also been told of Smithland, a small town R.P.W. had visited on his way to see the remains of the Lewis home, and which he presents as a relic of the American past. While there is a grudging recognition of it as a place of bitterness and frustration, the quality of the town is rendered primarily with affection and related to Odysseus's Ithaca (though it reminds one of Anderson's Winesburg, Ohio). As R.P.W. considers the records of Smithland, the dry documents of the past are transformed by the verse, touched with an aura of the archaic, the beautiful, and the pathetic:

> . . .I thought of the kitchen-midden
> Of a lost clan feasting while their single fire
> Flared red and green with sea-salt, and the night fell—
> Shellfish and artifact, blacked bone and shard,
> Left on the sea-lapped shore, and the sea was Time.
>
> (P. 21)

The image of the violent, unjust past that R.P.W. and Jefferson present is part of the poem's moralistic, judgmental, "religious" strain, if you will, while other of its portrayals of our history focus more on "the glory of the human effort." The two strains seem to exist in the poem insufficiently conscious of each other, not brought into significant relationship.[10]

The poem may be trying to acknowledge and join its divergent images of the past in the section where R.P.W. views a river in Kentucky (this occurs shortly before the lines about glory and virtue and burden):

> . . . I thought how men had moved on that broad flood,
> The good, the bad, the strong, the weak, all men
> . . . .
> . . . [and I] was impelled to apostrophize:
> "O you who have on your broad bosom borne
> Man and man's movement, and endured the oar,
> Keel-pole and paddle, sweep and the paddle-wheel,
> And suffered the disturbance of the screw's bronze blade,
> And tissued over that perpetual scarification
> With instant sweetness and the confident flow—

You who have suffered filth and the waste of the
                              human establishment,
Ordure of Louisville and the slick of oil,
The drowned cow, swollen, from the mountain cove,
And junk jammed on the sand bar in the sun—
I take you now as image and confirmation
Of that deep flood that is our history,
Of that deep flood that makes each new day possible
And bears us westward to the new land.
I take you as the image and confirmation
Of some faith past our consistent failure, and the
                              filth we strew."

                                        (Pp. 209–10)

Here, our "history" is made to take on an aura of both the
repellent and the exalted, one that presumably acknowledges the evil of the past along with some movement toward
the good. But if this is an attempt at a unitary image of
American history, and one that takes account of the poem's
materials, it fails badly. The evil of the past seems more a
matter of pollution than the absence of virtue in human
relationships, and the good is not rooted in historical instances of virtue or glory but consists simply of a vague
promise that the future is supposed to hold.

Other gaps confront us as we contemplate the poem,
trying to see the relationships among its parts (the religious
conceptions of Warren, or of the critics, do not join those
parts successfully). As has already been indicated, Lucy,
Jefferson's sister, plays a crucial role in the story; in her
conversation with her brother, instructing him in the error of
his ways, she seems to be speaking for Warren himself. But
even if her diagnosis of Jefferson as vain is granted, one is
still troubled by her formulation of her own failing, which she
sees as contributing to Lilburn's butchery of the slave. Her
love for her son was infected, she says, by her "dark fear of
the dark, and the dark land" (p. 188—earlier in the work
Lucy had made reference to "the dark land"). She conceives

of Lilburn as imbibing this fear with his mother's milk, and goes on to say he felt "the dark from all the woods creep in," and saw the slave "as but his darkest self/ And all the possibility of the dark that he feared"; in striking the slave he was striking down "that darkest self. . ." (p. 189). Accepting the slide here from the dark of the woods to the dark of the self so far as Lilburn is concerned, we are still left to ponder why Lucy regards *her* fear of the dark *land* as a moral failure. For much in *Brother to Dragons* works to establish nature as an oppressive, threatening presence, and fear in the face of it seems only natural. R.P.W. himself speaks of "The forest [that] reaches/ A thousand miles in darkness beyond the frail human project" (p. 45), as well as of "the unredeemed dark of the wild land" (p. 152). One frail human project, the Lewis house, is conceived of as set "against/ The disorder of the wild land" (p. 151). This last notion is assigned to Lilburn, but while he is criticized for defending the letter of civilization rather than its spirit, his conception of the opposition of house and land is left intact. (Contrast such characterizations of the land with the celebrations of the American earth in Williams's *In the American Grain*.) Why, in light of all this, should Lucy be so hard on herself for fearing the land? It would appear that Warren is straining to establish her complicity in Lilburn's act. The notion the book puts forth about universal human guilt is being demonstrated with respect to Lucy at the cost of the poem's ignoring its own case against nature. Even when it explicitly turns to nature as offering relief from the terrible drama of Lilburn, providing "an image to free us from the human trauma" (p. 96), we find ourselves in an icy, dark immensity of frozen river and forest, with nothing comforting in it. Human affairs are made oppressively minuscule by the poem's sense of the nature that surrounds them.

An important exception to this might be claimed in the picture we get of nature gone awry in the year of the murder, a time of flood, earthquakes, and strange animal behavior.

Interestingly enough, such were the actual events of the year 1811, and this *Annus Mirabilis,*[11] along with the accompanying folklore that made of nature's upheavals a response to the murder, clearly struck Warren with its literary possibilities. Here was, in the given materials of the case, the opportunity for that kind of correlation between human action and natural phenomena that Shakespeare made use of in such plays as *Macbeth* or *King Lear.* Lilburn's deed of murder can be thought of as acquiring magnitude and resonance through its placememt in the context of a tumultuous earth. Nature, at least here, would seem to enhance the human event rather than dwarf it, giving it significance. Victor Strandberg asserts that "Although Warren makes it clear that he is not speaking literally when he uses nature to dramatize God's wrath, he does draw boldly upon natural calamity as an image of some spiritual reality. In describing the *Annus Mirabilis,* Warren shows how nature is out of joint in the Shakespearean manner. . . ."[12] But there is a significant difference between the Shakespearean manner and Warren's. In Shakespeare the parallel between the human and the natural is simply presented, with the assumption being that a meaningful connection exists between the two. No such assumption is unqualifiedly available to Warren, though he undoubtedly *plays* with the idea. Its dramatic possibilities were undoubtedly too great to be resisted entirely, and after all, history made a virtual gift of them to the poet. Also, the idea *per se* has an intrinsic hold on him. But he has too much of the twentieth-century skeptic in him to assert without hedging the existence of some "spiritual reality" inhering in natural disorder.

After an originally solemn and impressive evoking of the *Annus Mirabilis,* R.P.W. focuses on the earthquake and its purported connection with Lilburn's slaying of George:

> if God shook the country like a rug,
> And sloshed the Mississippi, for a kind of warning—
> Yes, that's the folk-say too, like Lilburn's caper.

> Well, if God did it, why should God just pick out
> Poor George as His excuse? There's been God's plenty
> Of such excuses, and they multiply
> Right now in Old Kaintuck, but no earthquakes
> In quite a spell, and no other Year of Wonders
> To scare the home folks with the omens dread . . .
> . . . .
> No, what great moral order we may posit
> For old Kentucky, or the world at large,
> Will scarcely account for geodetic shifts.
>
> (P. 145)

Strandberg contends that Warren's first saying that God shook the country as a warning, and then questioning this view, provides an effect equivalent to that of "the lawyer who makes an improper appeal to the jury and smiles blandly as the judge orders it stricken from the record."[13] This is highly questionable. For one thing, the domestic metaphor describing God's purported action, along with the word *sloshed*, does not make for a particularly serious image of divine intervention to begin with (the tone here is somewhat reminiscent of Hardy's irreverent treatment of God in "Channel Firing"). Moreover, the conception of God as acting to warn is described as "folk-say . . . like Lilburn's caper." This refers to the bit of folklore which claims that Lilburn danced while the earth shook, calling on the Devil. That assertion was firmly dismissed earlier by the poem as it went on to make a quite different point about Lilburn's attitude toward the murder. Also, the poem treats lightly the traditional belief that God sent the earthquake to uncover the buried bones of the murdered slave:

> . . .dogs like bones, even fine Virginia hounds,
> And dogs have dug a bone up, now and then,
> Without involving Seraphim or earthquakes. . . .
>
> (P. 154)

Taking all these materials into consideration, we have, at

most, not an assertion of "spiritual reality," but a tension between a religious view and a sardonic skepticism, or better, a self-consciousness about entertaining a religious conception.

Another example of this occurs in R.P.W.'s response to a statement that after the day of the murder there was another earthquake, and people spoke of "the End of Time. . . ." R.P.W. says:

It takes something more to bring the End of Time
Than what came there that night in your meat-house
    [scene of the murder].
For that, as a matter of fact, was no end and no beginning,
Just an episode in the long drift of the human
Narrative, and impressive chiefly for
Its senselessness. And there's always and forever
Enough of guilt to rise and coil like miasma
From the fat sump and cess of common consciousness
To make any particular hour seem most appropriate
For Gabriel's big tootle. For instance, the folks fell down
Right in the road and prayed, but couldn't have any idea
Of what had happened in the meat-house. It was other
Quite different things, and for each man a different
Set of peculiar and well-fondled reasons,
That made that hour seem perfectly made to order
For the world's end, as this present hour would seem
To any of us if the earth shook now and the sun darkened—
To any of us, that is, if we weren't so advanced
Beyond the superstitious fear of God's Wrath.

(P. 64)

Taking, for the moment, the "advanced" and "superstitious" of the concluding lines as ironic, the passage would seem to be endorsing a religious view of man's sinfulness and the divine anger it elicits. But if this is the intention of the passage, surely the phrase "Gabriel's big tootle" is most inappropriate. If anything, it expresses a distinct bit of irreverence, mocking a traditional image. This is not to say that Warren wants the whole passage to be subverted by this expression, but his use of it does indicate a certain unease on the poet's part, generating the impression that he does not feel fully at home with the notion of God's wrath. Viewed this way, the passage does not support a reading of "advanced" and "superstitious" as wholly ironic. The poet himself can be seen as sufficiently involved with the "advanced" to make the concession of the "tootle" phrase.

Warren's self-consciousness about religious formulations is part of a larger pattern of self-consciousness in the poem, one that has been ignored or minimized. We find an instance of this pattern in the presentation of the huge Black Snake that had emerged from the ruins of the Lewis house when R.P.W. was making a visit there. One finds it difficult to fix precisely what the snake represents in its forgiving awareness of human inadequacy and its asking that *it* be forgiven. But the creature is clearly a symbol of great significance for Warren.[14] He lavishes too much poetic energy upon it for us to doubt that. However, after a rendering which, despite superficial disclaimers, builds the snake up into a magnificent presence, partly through a Miltonic incorporation of mythical allusion and exotic nomenclature, there is a distinct attempt at deflating it, through regular-guy obscenity and inane observation:

> This really happened, the big black son-of-a-bitch
> Reared from the stones, and scared me, for a fact.
> There's no harm in them, though. And they kill rats.
>
> (P. 35)

Once again, Warren is unable to present some large conception, without self-consciously standing back from it, diminishing its potency, its claim to validity.

Such is the case, too, in the notion R. P. W. puts forth that the murdered slave was himself responsible for the axe-killing, craving the murder, loving the injustice being done to him, anxious "to wreak his merciless frailty on Lilburn."

Jefferson sharply resists this view of George, and R. P. W. says:

> I only nag the question. And if Lilburn
> Is George's victim, it's only a manner of speaking,
> A way to say we're all each other's victim.
> Potentially, at least.
>
> (P.140)

This is wishy-washy, and when Jefferson goes on to ask what it proves "in the face of [George's] naked scream," R.P.W. says "Nothing" (p. 140), thereby discarding a theory of the victim as victimizer that he had developed eloquently and at some length. Does he want *us* to so discard it after experiencing its forceful formulation? It is hard to believe that he does, and yet he himself cannot be its wholehearted advocate.

A few pages later, R.P.W. argues for the existence of good by saying that even Lilburn had a deep need to see his act as a virtuous one. Jefferson is testy and impatient with this contention, and R.P.W. replies:

> I think I know how trivial you find
> My present argument, for I remember
> How trivial I've found it now and then
> In the face of brute facts.
>
> (P. 144)

Again we have had an important statement put forth, then self-consciously questioned, and we are left with neither the original contention nor its clear-cut refutation. Warren is clearly unable, in the instances cited, to assert himself against a disbelieving character (Jefferson) or, perhaps more important, against his readers, an audience conceived of by him as "modern," i.e., skeptical and a-religious, and one that he seems to feel peering over his shoulder as he writes.

We find instances of self-consciousness not only about his

beliefs but about his manner or procedures. He evokes a Mr.
Boyle, owner of the land R.P.W. had to traverse to reach the
Lewis homesite, in a style strongly reminiscent of Robert
Frost (the situation is Frostian as well). But then, as though
wishing us to know that he realizes this, R.P.W. turns on his
own presentation and says "Oh, he was quaint, or cute, was
Mr. Boyle,/ Or could be made to seem so." He goes on to
think of the possibility of Boyle's being dead by now, having

>   caught the flu,
> Fallen off his tractor in the sun, or had
> A coronary hit him on the street. . . .
>
>   (Pp. 25, 26)

The last line here is most un-Frostian, as is the verse that
follows. Is there an implicit criticism of the older poet here,
or a criticism of Warren himself for having adopted another's
mode, or irritation with his readers because of their presumed condescension to country people? The answer to this
is not clear but Warren's self-consciousness is.

Later, he tells us why the story of Lilburn and his brother
Isham could not be told in ballad form. He is then reminded
of the bone of the murdered slave that came to light, and
speaks of the dog responsible for unearthing it. The facts
apparently do not establish just what dog it was, and R.P.W.
says:

>   We have to invent our dog.
> Then make it Lilburn's hound that in effect
> Will set the hot lead in the belly of the master
> Who'd thought to name the loved animal in even
> His one last hour, and will it to his father,
> Across the mountains, in Virginia, oh, so far.
> So make it Lilburn's hound, for irony.
>
>   (P. 45)

Warren thus calls explicit attention to an invention and its
intended effect instead of simply employing it.

A somewhat different instance of self-consciousness about his means or manner can be found when Laetitia, Lilburn's wife, describes at length the death-bed scene of Lilburn's mother, and speaks finally, in seventeen lines, of her own inability to reach out to Lilburn at that terrible moment. R.P.W. says, "In other words, you couldn't/ To put the matter succinctly, forgive Lilburn" (p. 89). Does this not suggest that Laetitia has been a bit tedious, though there is every indication that Warren meant her evocation of the scene to be a moving one? Does he feel he has allowed her to go on for too long? So it would appear.

There occurs a similarly curious but more significant subversion of a character much later in the work. Jefferson, who has been made to give up his misanthropy, and to acquire hope along with humility, a transformation central to the book, delivers as his final utterance the statement: "In joy, I would end." R.P.W. answers "We must consider those who could not end in joy," and proceeds to do so (p. 196). The apparently sardonic quality of this response does not at first seem called for. Is it an expression of a continuing hostility to Jefferson despite his change of heart? This is possible, but does not appear to be the whole of the matter. What we might have here is a guilty recognition on Warren's part that the drama of Jefferson's change, and his final affirmation, do not sufficiently engage the suffering of the other characters: George, Aunt Cat, Lilburn, Meriwether Lewis, etc. That suffering has a separate, irreducible reality of its own. Jefferson's final speech, which ends with the desire for joy, gives the initial appearance of being a conclusion to the work, but its last line is turned back against his utterance as the poem disengages itself from the excited vision of a hopeful future which Jefferson's speech contains (though the poem will eventually come up with its own hopeful view later on, in the river passage quoted above). In that speech he talks of the creation of "The whole wide world and gleaming West anew" (p. 195), and goes on to invoke an Indian Ghost Dance which, a note to the poem informs us, envisioned the coming of a blessed, shining land, a "New Earth" (pp. 227-29). In its reminder after such a passage of those who did not end in joy, the poem would appear once again to have made an initial commitment and employed a mode that it cannot remain comfortable with, and that it undermines at least partially.

In *Brother to Dragons* Warren has brought together historical characters and himself to produce something that goes outside the formulations of history as that is usually undertaken, not only in the employment of his very special form, but in his passing beyond the limits of his materials. He not only makes a great deal of a piece of negative evidence—Jefferson's silence on Lilburn—but causes Jefferson to undergo a transformation in the poem that Warren does not believe he ever underwent in life itself. In a sense, then, Warren may be said to improve history, telling not only its hidden content but pointing to the way it should have gone.

In the matter of the way it actually *was,* Warren's own remarks on the relation of his poem to the historical evidence are somewhat ambiguous. In his Foreword, he subordinates the question of whether Jefferson's actual response on hearing of the murder took the form depicted in the book, to the consideration that "subsequent events in the history of America" (p. xi) might well have made him the disillusioned, misanthropic creature we see during almost the whole of the poem. At the same time, the Foreword states that "a poem dealing with history is no more at liberty to violate what the writer takes to be the spirit of his history than it is at liberty to violate what the writer takes to be the nature of the human heart" (p. xii). Did Warren mean us to apply this to his portrait of Jefferson, or to the question of the great gap between Jefferson's original view of America's glorious potentiality and the disheartening facts of the American actuality since his time? Very little of the work addresses itself to this gap, the bulk of the poem being concerned with providing a context for Lilburn's act and demonstrating Jefferson's response to it.

The book acquires or fails to acquire an extra dimension insofar as one is persuaded or not that Warren has rightly interpreted Jefferson's silence on Lilburn. It cannot be denied that Warren has created a fascinating possibility here, but one wishes he had displayed less of an animus against Jefferson, a lust to debunk him, a single-minded reduction of the man to a creature of vanity. If it was Warren's intention to dramatize the distance between the theory of America as postulated by Jefferson and the reality of America, he has carried it out almost entirely by an argument.

There is another kind of reduction, or attempted reduction, in the poem. As it draws to a close, it offers us what one critic has called, in a statement cited earlier, a "series of Christian paradoxes that form the thematic resolution of the work":

> In so far as man has the simplest vanity of self,
> There is no escape from the movement toward fulfillment.
> And since all kind but fulfills its own kind,
> Fulfillment is only in the degree of recognition
> Of the common lot of our kind. And that is the death of
>   vanity,
> And that is the beginning of virtue.
>
> The recognition of complicity is the beginning of inno-
>   cence.
> The recognition of necessity is the beginning of freedom.
> The recognition of the direction of fulfillment is the death
>   of the self,
> And the death of the self is the beginning of selfhood.
>   (Pp. 214–15)

Such statements do not take adequate account of the book's divergent values and conceptions, nor, in their assertiveness, do they acknowledge the work's self-consciousness about its ideas and procedures. There is, in these paradoxes, a denial or mere pseudo-smoothing away of the ambiguities and doubts the book has displayed as it unfolds its considerations of nature, history, and the human condition. The manifestations of Warren's struggles with his beliefs and materials, evidenced in the work's self-consciousness, are unsuccessfully denied by the sense of peace, hope, and resolution that the poem attempts to generate in its closing pages. Hard as it is on Jeffersonian optimism, *Brother to Dragons* comes up with an unearned optimism of its own.

NOTES

1. Robert Penn Warren, "The Way It Was Written," *New York Times Book Review*, 23 August 1953, p. 6.

2. *Brother to Dragons: A Tale in Verse and Voices* (New York: Random House, 1953), p. 21. Subsequent quotations from this work will be followed in the text of the chapter by the relevant page numbers.

3. John L. Stewart has noted the formal similarity of Warren's book to *Job*, although he puts it differently than I have here. See his "Robert Penn Warren and the Knot of History," *ELH* 26 (March 1959): 128.

4. For a fuller exposition of the psychology of Jefferson and Lilburn than will be attempted here, see Frederick P. W. McDowell, "Psychology and Theme in *Brother to Dragons*," in *Robert Penn Warren: A Collection of Critical Essays*, ed. John Lewis Longley, Jr. (New York: New York University Press, 1965), pp. 197–222. The essay appeared originally in *PMLA* 70 (September 1955): pp. 565–86.

5. The reader is advised to consult Boynton Merrill, Jr.'s reconstruction of the murder and its context in his *Jefferson's Nephews: A Frontier Tragedy* (Princeton, N.J.: Princeton University Press, 1976). Merrill sees Lilburn as a man beset by the loss of his mother, his elder brother, and his wife within a space of two years, by financial worries, and by marital unhappiness with his second wife. Merrill does not posit anything like the relationship to Aunt Cat, which is featured by Warren.

6. See McDowell, "Psychology and Theme"; also, Randall Jarrell, "On the Underside of the Stone," *New York Times Book Review*, 23 August 1953, p. 6; also, Victor Strandberg's chapter on the poem in his *A Colder Fire: The Poetry of Robert Penn Warren* (Lexington, University of Kentucky Press, 1965).

7. There is a letter which indicates that this is what Isham did, but there is another document which denies this. Boynton Merrill, Jr., doubts that Isham ever joined the army, and says that the only thing certain about him after he escaped from jail is that he disappeared. See *Jefferson's Nephews*, pp. 316–18.

8. Strandberg, *A Colder Fire*, p. 164.

9. This is apparently not McDowell's view. He states: "Closely allied to

Warren's reverence for . . . glory is that for virtue and its concomitant, humility."
But he does not demonstrate a connection between glory and virtue. "Psychology
and Theme," p. 218.

10. There is a split in the image of Smithland itself. For while its past can be
rendered as in the quoted "lost clan" passage, its records are cited later on in the
poem as furnishing the case of an Indian who was kicked to death "for sport."

11. See Merrill, *Jefferson's Nephews*, pp. 248–55.

12. Strandberg, *A Colder Fire*, p. 163.

13. Ibid., p. 164.

14. Strandberg invests the snake with a good deal of religious and psychological
meaning.

7

Styron's Slave:
The Confessions of Nat Turner

In his book on slavery, published in 1959, Stanley Elkins wrote: "There is a painful touchiness in all aspects of the subject. . . . How a person thinks about Negro slavery historically makes a great deal of difference here and now; it tends to locate him morally in relation to a whole range of very immediate political, social, and philosophical issues which in some way refer back to slavery."[1] The "painful touchiness" Elkins spoke of prevails as strongly as ever. It was strikingly evident in the responses to William Styron's best-selling novel, *The Confessions of Nat Turner* (1967), which takes as its subject a slave revolt in Virginia in 1831, led by Turner. Appearing at a time of unprecedented black militancy, and dealing as it does with the most notable slave uprising in our history, with such stuff as legends are made of, Styron's book attracted widespread attention, as well as a critical scrutiny not usually accorded to historical novels.

The accuracy of its portrayal of the past figured as a prominent issue in articles and reviews about it. Historians' opinions of this accuracy ranged from C. Van Woodward's contention that the book "is informed by a respect for history, a sure feeling for the period, and a deep and precise sense of place and time,"[2] to Herbert Aptheker's accusing it of major distortions and omissions.[3] Some would argue, as I noted in my introductory chapter, that the standard of

172

historical accuracy is irrelevant to the judgment of a novel, that it intrudes on the autonomy of a fictional work, on the prerogatives of the literary imagination. Richard Gilman, for example, has said that "literature, as literature, has nothing to do with history other than being able to draw upon it as it is free to draw upon anything."[4] But draw upon it for what? Surely the book *is* connected with history in Styron's own mind (he calls it "a meditation on history")[5] and, inevitably, in the reader's; such a connection cannot be ruled out by fiat. Gilman himself, finding fault with a particular aspect of Nat's characterization, notes that Styron is not supposed to be writing about a Negro "who *could be anything*, but about Nat Turner, a slave, a man whose only reality in our imagination is as a slave and the leader of a slave revolt."[6] Precisely—and this reality has not been created from nothing by Styron; it is a datum of history. By choosing to work with such a figure, Styron, in effect, placed limits on his options. True, he said that "the beauty" of Turner's revolt is that so little is known about it, and that a high degree of existing documentation about an historical event reduces "its validity as a subject for fiction. . . ."[7] But he also spoke about the use of "responsible imagination,"[8] and of inferences he drew from a primary historical document, the published confessions Turner supposedly made to a lawyer, T.R. Gray, while awaiting trial. In the prefatory note to the novel itself, Styron writes of his intention "to re-create a man and his era," and portions of Turner's original confessions are used in the text of the novel. Clearly, there is an historical impulse at work here, and it is perverse to regard the question of historical validity as irrelevant, separating it from one's response to and judgment of the book. (This is not to say that there never exists a conflict between the requirements of historical accuracy and the requirements of the novel as a work of art.)

A number of black critics objected to Styron's treatment of history (several of their essays were gathered in *William*

Styron's Nat Turner: Ten Black Writers Respond). One of the most thoughtful and articulate of these, Mike Thelwell, finds Styron guilty of purveying a *Gone with the Wind* image of the antebellum South. The home of Nat's first master, he says, "rivals Tara in its gentility, charm and benevolence. This is the Golden Age of Southern Chivalry, and what is being reconstructed for us is the enlightened benevolence of the 'Old Dominion' version of slavery. . . ."[9] Such an evaluation is highly unfair to Styron, as can be quickly seen if we compare his novel with one of its principal sources, William S. Drewry's *The Southampton Insurrection* (1900). Drewry is an unabashed racist and apologist for Southern slavery, calling the slaves "the happiest laboring class in the world. . . ."[10] Styron's novel, while presenting Nat's first master as benevolent, suggests that his kindness takes the form of an *experiment* with another human being, namely, seeing if a Negro can be given a white education. In addition, *The Confessions* does try to dramatize at least some of the indignities and cruelties of slavery, and to demonstrate how the system, together with contemporary economic circumstances, could result in the slaves of even kindly masters being sold to traders interested only in a profit. Styron's intention, quite plainly, is to show how both cruelty and considerateness could operate within the system, producing a *variety* of master-slave relationships (the book might even be said to be overly schematic in carrying out this intention). That there was such variety, that slavery did not consist of an unbroken vista of Simon Legrees and beaten blacks, has much support in the historical evidence, including the testimony of ex-slaves.

But more controversial than its portrait of any white master is the book's treatment of the slaves, of their failure to turn out in great numbers in support of Turner's uprising. Lawyer Gray, taking down Nat's confessions in the novel, estimates that out of a thousand potential rebels, only seventy-five at the most joined with Turner. He taunts Nat not only with this figure but with instances of slaves actively aiding their masters to help put down the uprising. " '. . . I have no doubt,' " he says, " 'that it was your own race that contributed more to your fiasco than anything else' " (p. 397). While Nat's reaction to this is mixed, his basic response is one of raging acquiescence, and this appears to be the book's response as well. Styron, for example, has Nat recall his fallen friend and follower, Hark, being kicked in his wounded shoulder by other Negroes. In an interview Styron said that the role of the Negroes in defending their masters was "what really crushed [Nat]. . . ."[11] While this is not explicitly stated in the original confessions, he believes it is "*hinted* at. . . ."[12] Styron could have been influenced in this matter by Drewry, who makes a great point of the role Negroes played in helping the whites subdue the rebels. At any rate, Styron said that slaves fighting against the rebels seemed to him "logically and eminently *conceivable*."[13] Herbert Aptheker, on the other hand, was quoted as declaring that it was "false and inconceivable" that the revolt would be put down by blacks armed by their masters,[14] and Henry Irving Tragle claimed "there is no evidence which indicates that slaves, collected from various homes or estates, fought as an organized body against Nat's men, as Styron described."[15]

Whether or not slave did indeed fight slave in the Turner Rebellion appears to be a moot point—as well as a secondary one. For what is really being argued here is the question of the basic slave consciousness and character created by the Southern system of servitude. *The Confessions* has been attacked (notably by Thelwell) for helping keep alive a favorite Southern stereotype, that of the slave as "Sambo"—docile, submissive, childlike, basically dependent on and affectionate toward his master. But Stanley Elkins's book on slavery has made it difficult to dismiss Sambo as simply and wholly a self-delusory image invented by the South, having no basis in reality. Elkins found a striking lack of rebelliousness among American slaves, and argued, certainly not from racist assumptions but from theories of social psychologists, that the conditions of slavery could indeed have produced a Sambo sensibility. The white man's notion of the slave as a dependent child, he believes, might well have become the Negro's image of himself. Arrayed against this view are such historians as Aptheker and Kenneth Stampp, who conceive of the slaves as being characteristically in a state of smouldering resentment. In *The Peculiar Institution* (1956), Stampp focuses on habitual, implicit slave resistance, which could take such forms as slovenly labor or stealing. Aptheker works hard, in his *American Negro Slave Revolts* (1943), to produce a picture of Negro energies as frequently directed toward open rebellion throughout the history of American slavery. Writing many years after the appearance of that book, he continued to see Turner's Rebellion as "the culminating blow of a particular period of rising slave unrest."[16] Elkins regards it as a relatively isolated incident. That Styron was drawn to Elkins's sophisticated reappraisal of the Sambo image is indicated by his having referred to that historian's study as a "brilliant analysis."[17] It is understandable that at a time when many Negroes are striving to find in their "blackness" a source of pride, they should be hostile to a novel that in great measure subscribes to Elkins's view. (Their desire to find a strain of rebellion in the slaves is analogous to the desire of American Jews to locate signs of resistance among those European Jews who were sent to concentration camps, and it is interesting to note that Elkins believes there was a similarity between the personality pattern of the slaves and that of the camp inmates.)

Styron's finding substance in the Sambo image and employing it in his novel hardly makes him a racist. He could appeal to at least a portion of the historical record to support his presentation. Interviews with ex-slaves contain some expressions of loyalty to and affection for their one-time masters.[18] Aptheker himself notes instances of slave conspiracies being betrayed by Negroes. On the other hand, it could be argued that Elkins is making too much of the lack of *successful* Negro rebellions and too little of the covert resistance Stampp cites, as well as of the machinery set up to keep the slaves in line. The point is that Styron's acceptance of Sambo as at least *a* type produced by slavery does not automatically discredit his image of the Southern past. The relative prevalence of Sambo is likely to remain a matter of historical controversy, with serious and informed minds to be found on both sides. Moreover, Styron's protagonist, together with other Negro characters treated in some detail, are violent rebels—no Sambos they.

And yet, there *is* something very disturbing in Styron's treatment of Nat and the Negro that one can feel without being a black militant. This is his portrayal of Nat's attitude toward his fellow slaves. Styron has made Nat a house servant (there is no basis in the record for this) because assigning him such a position seemed to the novelist the only way "to justify the fact that Nat *had* been educated, *could* read the Bible and knew it by heart."[19] As such a servant, Nat is brought up by his mother to despise the slaves who labor in the field (" 'Us house folks,' " she says, " 'is *quality!*' "—p. 136; italics in original), and he himself can refer to "the most squalid type of cornfield coon" (p. 66). Nat comes to recognize how his relatively privileged status has produced his attitude, but even with this recognition his feelings of contempt and disgust persist to the end (and expand to include house servants as well). Indeed, some of his most forceful utterances are expressions of such feelings. He speaks of "childishly loud" Negro laughter (p. 33), of "loutish nigger cheer" (p. 174), of "galloping eyeballs" (p. 358). He cannot stand slave speech, its "thick gluey cornfield accent" (p. 132), its "stunted [quality] unbearably halting and cumbersome with a wet gulping sound of Africa in it" (p. 262). He pictures Negroes who were sold as going to their fate like "animals," talking of trivia, nodding off to sleep with "pink lips wet and apart . . ." (p. 224). He is appalled by the odor of Negro cabins—which exists, he says, in spite of the master's attempt to teach cleanliness—"the stink of sweat and grease and piss and nigger offal, of rancid pork and crotch and armpit and black toil and straw ticks stained with babies' vomit. . . ." This makes him feel disgusted at "being a nigger . . ." (p. 184). Meditating on the fact that he had never known a Negro to commit suicide, he thinks that "my black shit-eating people were surely like flies, God's mindless outcasts, lacking even that will to destroy by their own hand their unending anguish . . ." (p. 27; ellipsis in original). He agrees, as noted before, with lawyer Gray's contention that his fellow Negroes played a decisive role in his defeat, and that a substantial number of even his followers had been forced to join the rebellion. He believes he might have succeeded in his objective of reaching the town of Jerusalem *"if it wasn't for those bootlickin' black scum of white men's ass-suckin' niggers!"* (p. 401, italics in original). On one occasion Nat thinks of "redeeming" the Negroes from the status that provokes his revulsion, but the brief articulation of that impulse is virtually buried in the book beneath expressions of that revulsion.

In this matter both historical and literary objections arise and converge. How could a Nat Turner who felt so alienated from his people have functioned as their leader, particularly in a dangerous enterprise? (Raymond, the one Negro he meets in the novel who is something of an authority figure, and whom he regards as typical, enjoys his position, in Nat's contemptuous view, on the basis of the slaves' superstitiousness and gullibility.) Styron's characterization of Nat would lead us to expect him to become insulated in his disgust, undesirous and incapable of joining with his fellow slaves in a common undertaking and commanding their trust. (The followers of the historical Nat, according to Drewry, "invariably referred to the confidence and belief the leader had inspired in them.'')[20] It might be argued that Styron's having Nat fall from his position as a relatively pampered house servant and perceive that he is ultimately only a slave, as vulnerable as any other Negro to the cruel possibilities of the system, prepares us to accept him as making common cause with the other slaves. But the recognition of a bond with them, if such there is supposed to be, does not jibe with the intense disgust for them he shows throughout, right up to the very end.

Aside from this (which is, admittedly, a debatable point), one notices that Nat's sensory impressions of the Negro often seem to be all that a white racist could ask for. Looking at the descriptions already cited, along with others, we find that the slaves, as portrayed by him, are creatures of bulging eyeballs, open wet lips, and that they stink. But, we should hasten to add, there is little for the white race to cheer about on the basis of such of its members as come within Nat's purview. *Their* sensory impact on him is, in general, quite as unpleasant as that made by the blacks. Lawyer Gray, Nat tells us, sports a grease stained waistcoat and soiled pink gloves. In the course of his interviews with Nat, he scratches his crotch, breaks wind, and leaks tobacco juice. His odor is a kind of sweet stench that almost makes Nat vomit. Judge Cobb, a white man whom Nat actually feels drawn to, emits hiccups and froglike croaks, has a face "pale as lard . . ." (p. 65). The son of one of Nat's owners has "blotches on his pale white face . . ." (p. 62). An Irish overseer is "yeasty-faced" (p. 147), a traveling salesman's countenance is "evilly cratered . . ." (p. 121). Nat Francis, a cruel master, has a "swinish squint . . ." (p. 299). His wife is "a slab-faced brute of a person with a huge goiter . . ." (p. 299)[21] Reverend Eppes, Nat's worst master, is "redly wattled in the neck" (p. 234)—and a homosexual to boot. Homosexual, too (though Drewry refers to his historical prototype as "a respectable overseer"),[22] is Ethelred Brantley, a white man baptized by Nat. It is instructive to compare Styron's

Brantley with his original, as found in the actual confessions of Turner. There, Nat speaks of having given Brantley religious instruction. It "had a wonderful effect [on him], and he ceased from wickedness, and was attacked immediately with a cutaneous eruption, and blood oozed from the pores of his skin, and after praying and fasting nine days he was healed."[23] In Styron's book, Brantley arrives on the scene with his face already broken out—"tiny sores and pustules congregated like berries amid a downy fringe of red hair" (p. 313)—and exits from the novel with, so far as we know, virtually the same complexion (although his diarrheic bowels have been brought under control). Whereas the skin of the historical Brantley figured as part of a religious experience, it is, in Styron's book, just one more repellent property ascribed to his characters.

The physical descriptions of the people in the novel, taken as a whole, do not add up to a white or black bigot's view. Rather, they operate without prejudice to establish a democracy of repulsiveness in which men, white and black, are created equally ugly. Conceivably, Nat's focusing on this ugliness could be taken as an element of characterization, Styron's rendering of a jaundiced eye. But the descriptions appear to proceed from something in Styron himself rather than from his protagonist. How else explain the ascription, in passing, to an infant two months old, of "a purple blemish spreading across the center of his tiny face like the single shriveling petal of a blighted gentian" (p. 46)? Or the use of a name like "Ashpenaz Groover" for an unseen character who figures only momentarily in the plot? This last is just one more grotesquerie, and exists objectively, outside of Nat's psyche. The world of the book is aesthetically fallen, stained with Original Ugliness. This aspect of it does not seem to be a relevant part of any historical vision, but only an extension backward of the domain of Erskine Caldwell.

Nat, to be sure, exists as something more than one who simply registers spasms of disgust in viewing the people around him. Styron has tried, at length, to reconstruct him and give us a sense of what made him act as he did in planning and executing the rebellion. But the results are diffuse and, to a large extent, unpersuasive.

One putative source of Nat's behavior, according to the novel, is the kind treatment and promise of freedom given to him by his first master, who tells him that if he works out satisfactorily in a proposed scheme of employment he will be freed at the age of twenty-five. As events turn out, his master is forced to give him over to Reverend Eppes (the wattled homosexual) under a fuzzy arrangement that will supposedly culminate in Nat's liberation. Eppes works Nat mercilessly hard and ends up selling him. Nat eventually finds himself the property of a decent man, one who respects his considerable skills as a craftsman and who behaves "like every slave's ideal master" (p. 343). It is while under this owner that Nat formulates the plan for his uprising (though he had conceived of it earlier). He asks: "Does it seem a hopeless paradox that the less toilsome became the circumstances of my life the more I ached to escape it? That the more tolerable and human white people became in their dealings with me the keener was my passion to destroy them?" (p. 342). Earlier in the book, he had made a related statement: ". . . I will say this, without which you cannot understand the central madness of nigger existence: beat a nigger, starve him, leave him wallowing in his own shit, and he will be yours for life. Awe him by some unforeseen hint of philanthropy, tickle him with the idea of hope, and he will want to slice your throat" (pp. 69–70). We would do well to compare Nat's statement about hope with one that might have been its source. Frederick Douglass wrote:

> Beat and cuff your slave, keep him hungry and spiritless, and he will follow the chain of his master like a dog; but feed and clothe him well,—work him moderately— surround him with physical comfort,—and dreams of

freedom intrude. Give him a *bad* master, and he aspires to
a *good* master; give him a good master, and he wishes to
become his *own* master.[24]

The novel's statement contains a distinct escalation of
Douglass's; it speaks of violence where Douglass spoke of
freedom and independence. What Styron appears to have
done is to have taken a frequently heard explanation of
present-day black unrest (that it is the result of a frustrating
glimpse of white mobility and affluence), greatly intensified
it, and projected it onto the past. In an interview, he stressed
Nat's having been promised freedom and then denied it:
"The seeds of the revolt are in the *promise*. This—of course
without belaboring the thing—is what's going on right now;
it's the smell of grandeur that causes the hatred and the
apocalyptic acts."[25] But there is still a large gap between
much current black militancy and Turner's desire to slit
white throats *en masse*. Styron's explanation of Nat's
behavior is strained, appears to involve a reading into, rather
than out of history, and makes a too easy appeal to human
perversity (kindness breeds a desire to kill) as a way of
explaining Nat's actions. (An opposite explanation is used to
account for those followers of Nat treated in detail, all of
whom have suffered at the hands of whites.)

Another "explanation" of Nat's behavior that emerges
from the book is a psychosexual one. Styron has claimed that
Nat's impulses "were, historically speaking, those of the
traditional revolutionary—that is to say puritanical, repressive and sublimated."[26] He has also spoken of the conflict
between "the incredibly puritanical religious feelings he had
about life in general, and his strong physical desires."[27] Not
very convincingly, Styron makes Nat's house-servant status
function to cut him off from the free and easy sexual life
ascribed to the young men working in the fields. In the course
of the story Nat's sexual experiences, with one exception,
are masturbatory and solitary—he never sleeps with a

woman, though he feels intense lust. Styron has him think, apparently to drive home the "connection" between his rebellion and his unsatisfied sexuality, that once the uprising is over he will have to take a wife. Styron has high-handedly dismissed the possibility that the historical Nat did have a wife (Drewry speaks of one), saying that there is no contemporary evidence for her existence, and that, in any case, " 'marriage during slavery was of course a travesty.' "[28] This last, ironically, is precisely the reasoning that Hark's master uses to sell away his slave's wife and children. In addition to this, the presentation of Nat's sexuality is somewhat unclear. Why, for example, does he fantasize about white girls when masturbating if, as he tells us, they "seemed to float" for him "in an immaculate effulgence of purity and perfection" (p. 177)? Precisely how do his religious feelings come to operate as the repressive force we are asked to take for granted?

The question of Nat's sexuality is linked to his relationship with Margaret Whitehead, which is central to the book as a whole. According to the original confessions, Margaret was the only person that Nat himself killed, though he attempted the murder of others. Styron was fascinated by this fact, which forms the core of his "meditation on history." He concluded that there must have been a "love-hate" relationship between them,[29] by which he appears to mean, judging from the novel, that Nat felt love and hate, Margaret only an unconscious love. An element of perversity operates in Nat's feelings toward Margaret as in his response to his master's kindness. He apparently hates her because of her concern for him, and also because she (unwittingly) arouses him.

Styron does not rest here but makes Nat's relationship with Margaret the focus of a crucial development in his protagonist, the playing out of a religious drama. In brief, Nat, planning and carrying out his bloody revolt, is seen as incarnating an Old Testament spirit of harsh condemnation

and vengefulness. He views himself as the "devastating
instrument of God's wrath" (p. 52), scourge of the sinful
white race. This conception dominates him for the bulk of
the book (he makes several comparisons between his situation, together with that of the other slaves, and Old Testament personages and events). Opposed to this conception is
a "New Testament" spirit of love, that which he feels for
Margaret and she for him, that which he sees in her just
before he kills her. It is the recognition of this spirit that,
Styron has said, "is his revelation. This is, of course, the
final message of the Bible. Not all of that old, you know,
let-us-slay-women-and-children; but it's this, it's this other
message, and this is his redemption."[30] After murdering
Margaret Nat lets a girl escape who gives the alarm that
could be considered as having led to the putting down of his
rebellion. He wonders if he had vouchsafed her life for the
life he had taken.

This portrayal of Nat's development goes beyond anything that the historical record furnishes or suggests (though
Styron claims to have found a falling off of the rebellion's
momentum after Margaret's murder); indeed, Styron may be
said to have gone counter to the record in having Nat show a
last-minute remorse for his deed and recognize the spirit of
love that Margaret embodied. The New Testament appears
to have served the historical Nat as a text for self-
justification rather than for transformation. For, according
to lawyer Gray who took down his confessions, when asked
whether he found himself mistaken about his rebellion, Nat
replied " 'Was not Christ crucified?' "[31] Gray went on to tell
of

> The calm, deliberate composure with which he spoke of
> his late deeds and intentions; the expression of his fiend-
> like face when excited by enthusiasm, still bearing the
> stains of the blood of helpless innocence about him;
> clothed with rags and covered with chains, yet daring to

raise his manacled hands to heaven, with a spirit soaring above the attributes of man.[32]

Styron has not only gone against this part of the historical record (which might be written off, though not easily, as unreliable), but against the drift of his own book. For Margaret, as she has been presented to us, is a collection of clichés, hopelessly fatuous in her girlish enthusiasms and religiosity (her death made one critic weep[33]—it is hard to see why). Nat describes her as prattling, "love-obsessed, Christ-crazed, babbling away in an echo of all the self-serving platitudes and stale insipid unfelt blather uttered by every pious capon and priestly spinster she had listened to since she was able to sit upright . . ." (p. 368). Having built such a case against her, the book is asking too much of us to accept Margaret as an incarnation of Christly love and the agent of Nat's redemption. We are given a spiritual happy ending that is decidedly forced.

Indeed, the whole religious dimension of the book has not been satisfactorily worked out. Like the Nat of the original confessions, Styron's protagonist conceives of himself as an Old Testament prophet. But just how and why he does this in the novel is not clear—it comes as a development presented rather sketchily. How does Nat go from his sense of God as simply an abiding presence to one who is directing him to serve as an instrument of divine punishment? Then, too, just what is the significance of the white temple that Nat repeatedly envisions? It appears as an excrescence in the narrative, and having Nat attach a "profound mystery" to it (p. 4) appears to be an attempt to give the story a spurious "depth." Moreover, the book's stance in relation to its religious theme is murky. Is Nat's redemption through Margaret's "New Testament" spirit of love not only his but the book's "answer," as Styron has said it is?[34] Do the two quotations at the end of the book function to suggest this? The first is a dreaful excerpt from Drewry telling how Nat's corpse was skinned and a purse made from his hide, the second a passage from the Bible in which God says "He that overcometh shall inherit all things; and I will be his God and he shall be my son." The juxtaposition of the two would seem to leave us with a terrible irony rather than an answer, especially when we consider the awful human toll taken by the rebellion, which is counterbalanced only by the celebration of that straw creation, Margaret. Finally, there is the question of Styron's basic conception of Nat's being, his drives and motives. Within the course of a single interview, Styron said that Nat's "relationship with God seemed to be the central thing in my own conception of the man," and that "obviously the religious fanaticism must have disguised a profounder reason."[35] Such as what—Nat's supposedly repressed sexuality? Styron's novel appears to be poised between taking Nat's religious sensibility seriously, working out his rebellion in religious terms, and reducing Nat's behavior to a psychosexual formulation which functions to explain *away* his religious notions. The book wants to be inside Nat's religious frame of reference, and at the same time to view it with a cold, secular gaze. The two impulses pull the novel apart.[36]

That Styron conceived of his book largely as an attempt to get inside Nat's consciousness, to view the world through his eyes, is evidenced by the book's narrative form. Asked about his choice here, Styron said:

> I think that one of the central mysteries of the writer of novels is that you don't take the easy way, you take the hardest way in order to see if you can surmount the problems. . . . in this case I realized that inevitably one of the profoundly difficult things I would have to set up for myself would be the telling of this story from the point of view of Nat himself—a first-person narrative which would somehow allow you to enter into the consciousness of a Negro of the early decades of the 19th century.[37]

Styron indicated that he had met this challenge successfully. But is this true? Didn't he (along with some of the commentators on the book) equate the mere *choosing* of the first-person form, the daring involved in that decision, with the *achievement* of a convincing narrative voice? Speaking of the book's style, Styron said that he is telling the story in his "own literary style."[38] If that is the case, and it seems to be, has Styron really taken "the hardest way" and created the illusion of a world seen through the eyes of a Negro slave? This is not to suggest simply that Styron should *a priori* have disallowed Nat the rich vocabulary he has given to him, on the grounds that it would not have been available to even a literate Negro of that era. It is to say, as Stanley Kauffmann and Richard Gilman have done,[39] that Styron should not have made Nat sound so much like a *novelist* instead of the person he was—a slave, a Negro, a religious fanatic. As such he should have been given a style that would appear to be his particular possession rather than his creator's, and one that could assimilate (as the present style cannot) the profanities and colloquialisms of the dialogue and bits of the narrative. The way it stands, the novel provides us with a curious repetition of history. T. R. Gray's version of Nat's original confessions appears to be more Gray than Turner in its style. Styron's narrative style is more his than his protagonist's. We might overlook even this if the prose had more distinction than it does—but the book offers only widely scattered examples of memorable expression.

In *Moby Dick,* Ishmael declares that to produce a mighty book, one needs a mighty theme. Styron had the ambition to choose a mighty theme, but has not given us a book commensurate with it. Though he has evoked a sense of place, he has not achieved his main task, the creation of a protagonist who compels our belief in him as a probable or even a possible Nat Turner. The book moves waveringly among its personal, social, and religious planes, uncertain itself where Turner's reality is located. It succumbs to imposing the present on the past, and the author on his character, instead of creating the sense that it has penetrated an *other,* a being of a different time. Thus, despite its ambition, it fails us both as history and as literature.

NOTES

1. Stanley Elkins, *Slavery: A Problem in American Institutional and Intellectual Life* (Chicago: University of Chicago Press, 1959), p. 1.

2. C. Vann Woodward, "Confessions of a Rebel: 1831," *New Republic,* 7 October 1967, p. 25.

3. See Herbert Aptheker, "A Note on the History," *Nation,* 16 October 1967, pp. 375–76.

4. Richard Gilman, "Nat Turner Revisited," *New Republic,* 27 April 1968, p. 24.

5. William Styron, *The Confessions of Nat Turner* (New York: Random House, 1967). This quotation is taken from the "Author's Note" to the book, which is part of the front matter and has no page number. Subsequent quotations from the novel will be followed in the text of the chapter itself by the relevant page numbers.

6. Gilman, "Nat Turner Revisited," p. 26. Italics in original.

7. Quoted in Robert Canzoneri and Page Stegner, "An Interview with William Styron," *Per/Se* 1 (Summer 1966): 39.

8. Ibid.

9. Mike Thelwell, "Back With the Wind: Mr. Styron and the Reverend Turner," in *William Styron's Nat Turner: Ten Black Writers Respond,* ed. John Henrik Clarke (Boston: Beacon Press, 1968), p. 84.

10. William S. Drewry, *The Southampton Insurrection* (Washington, D.C.: Neale Co., 1900), p. 110.

11. Canzoneri and Stegner, "An Interview with William Styron," p. 43.

12. Quoted in George Plimpton, "William Styron: A Shared Ordeal" (interview), *New York Times Book Review,* 8 October 1967, p. 30. Italics in original.

13. See "Truth & Nat Turner: An Exchange," *Nation,* 22 April 1968, p. 547. Italics in original.

14. See John Leo, "Some Negroes Accuse Styron of Distorting Nat Turner's Life," *New York Times,* 1 February 1968, p. 31.

15. Henry Irving Tragle, "Styron and His Sources," *Massachusetts Review* 11 (Winter 1970): 152.

16. Aptheker, "A Note on the History," pp. 375–76.

17. William Styron, "Overcome," *New York Review of Books,* 26 September 1963, p. 19.

18. See B. A. Botkin, *Lay My Burden Down: A Folk History of Slavery* (Chicago: University of Chicago Press, 1945); *Voices From Slavery,* ed. Norman R. Yetman (New York: Holt, Rinehart & Winston, 1970); *Blacks in Bondage: Letters of American Slaves,* ed. Robert J. Starobin (New York: New Viewpoints, 1974).

19. "An Interview with William Styron," p. 41. Italics in original.

20. Drewry, *The Southampton Insurrection*, p. 101.

21. Henry Irving Tragle points out that a photograph of the actual Mrs. Francis exists, but that it bears no resemblance to this description. Tragle, "Styron and His Sources," 149. He reproduces the photograph in his book *The Southampton Slave Revolt of 1831: A Compilation of Source Material* (Amherst, Mass.: University of Massachusetts Press, 1971).

22. Drewry, *The Southampton Insurrection*, p. 33.

23. *The Confessions of Nat Turner* (Miami, Fla.: Mnemosyne Publishing, 1969), p. 5. This is a facsimile reprint of the 1861 edition.

24. Quoted in Kenneth Stampp, *The Peculiar Institution: Slavery in the Ante-Bellum South* (New York: Alfred A. Knopf, 1956), p. 89. Italics in original.

25. "An Interview with William Styron," p. 41. Italics in original. See also Plimpton, "William Styron" (interview), p. 34.

26. Plimpton, p. 3.

27. "An Interview with William Styron," p. 42.

28. See Frank Bailinson, "Styron Answers 'Turner' Critics," *New York Times,* 11 February 1968, p. 59.

29. See "An Interview with William Styron," p. 42; also John Leo, "Some Negroes Accuse Styron of Distorting Nat Turner's Life," p. 31.

30. "An Interview with William Styron," p. 43.

31. *The Confessions of Nat Turner,* p. 5.

32. Ibid., p. 11.

33. See Martin Duberman, "Books," *The Village Voice,* 14 December 1967, p. 9. Duberman is aware of the weaknesses in Margaret's characterization but is still able to respond to her in this way.

34. "An Interview with William Styron," p. 43.

35. Ibid., pp. 40, 41.

36. Here I take essentially the same view as that put forth by Stanley Kauffmann in his "Styron's Unwritten Novel," *Hudson Review* 20 (Winter 1967–68): 675–80.

37. "An Interview with William Styron," p. 39.

38. Ibid., p. 40.

39. See Kauffmann, "Styron's Unwritten Novel," and Gilman, "Nat Turner Revisited."

8

"What Marvelous Plot . . . Was Afoot?": John Barth's *The Sot-Weed Factor*

John Barth has said that his starting point in composing *The Sot-Weed Factor* was the poem of the same name, written by Ebenezer Cooke and published in 1708, a work of interest to students of early American literature.[1] But going far beyond that satirical account, and drawing heavily on the raw historical record as preserved in the *Archives of Maryland,* Barth produced a massive novel about Cooke's adventures in England and America which dwarfs the seven-hundred-odd lines of the poem. Combining the suggestions of a number of these lines, facts gathered from the *Archives,* and characters, events, and documents of his own invention, Barth has attempted to put colonial Maryland on the map of the American literary imagination, to work with a region that has been for the most part, like the territory originally granted to Lord Baltimore, *"hactenus inculta"*—hitherto uncultivated. Leslie Fiedler noted in his review of *The Sot-Weed Factor* that Maryland "has less ready-made mythic import for other Americans than almost any region to which [Barth] might have been born."[2]

Early in the novel, Ebenezer proclaims that his virginity is part of his essence and must be preserved. That virginity, which Eben and the book identify with innocence, will in turn preserve him from time, death, and history, or so he absurdly thinks. (It is no surprise to have a character tell him

" ' 'tis not simply love ye know naught of, 'tis the *entire great real world!'* ")[3] Eben's preoccupation with his virginity gives particular weight to his declaration that, as a subject for poetry, the accomplishments in Maryland of " 'the noble house of Calvert, the Barons Baltimore' " is " 'virgin territory!' " (p. 87). He proposes writing a *Marylandiad.*

> An epic to out-epic epics. . . . The courage and persever-
> ance of her settlers in battling barb'rous nature and
> fearsome salvage to wrest a territory from the wild and
> transform it to an earthly paradise! The majesty and
> enlightenment of her proprietors, who like kingly garden-
> ers fostered the tender seeds of civilization in their rude
> soil, and so husbanded and cultivated them as to bring to
> fruit a Maryland beauteous beyond description; verdant,
> fertile, prosperous, and cultured; peopled with brave men
> and virtuous women, healthy, handsome, and refined: a
> Maryland, in short, splendid in her past, majestic in her
> present, and glorious in her future, the brightest jewel in
> the fair crown of England. . . . (Pp. 87–88)

Lord Baltimore (actually Eben's friend Henry Burlingame in disguise) tells the would-be epic writer that he is " 'all innocent of Maryland's history' " (p. 89), and fills him in on Maryland's past (Eben is about to embark for that colony). In listening to "Baltimore," Eben, together with the reader, is confronted by a bewildering proliferation of names and a profusion of events. Later, giving a supplementary history lesson to Eben, Burlingame—not in disguise this time—says " 'Tis not so deadly long a story, but I must own 'tis a passing tangled one, with much running hither and thither and an army of names to bear in mind' " (p. 152). For early as the novel's events are—the 1690s—America seems to have acquired a considerable history by the time Eben sets foot on the Maryland shore. There is virtually no primeval forest, no virgin land to be contemplated; such a domain is not within the book's sensibility. Indeed, much of the comedy of the story, as well as its serious developments, comes from the collisions between Eben, the self-proclaimed virgin, and a territory that is something less than intact. It is significant that when he lands on what he assumes is an uncharted island, it turns out to be, in the words of a planter settled there, " 'but poor shitten Maryland . . .' " (p. 312).

This phrase, which does not dampen Eben's enthusiasm for the place (it takes much to dent his innocence), serves as a capsule characterization of much of the world of the book (and one particularly appropriate to a story which has a good deal of fecal humor). For *The Sot-Weed Factor* displays a strong tendency to debunk the past, not finding in colonial America a spirit of courage, admirable endurance, and daring, but seeing our early history as made up of selfish motives and unheroic behavior, conceiving of its participants as a collection of scoundrels and perverts together with their victims. (This debunking tendency is already present in the English setting where the novel begins, as we find Sir Isaac Newton and Sir Henry More characterized as homosexuals, the quarrel between them, originating in philosophical disagreement, coming to a head because of their competition for the favor of Burlingame.) Two of the first people Eben encounters are a slave who was thrown off a ship to drown, and a displaced Indian king. The Maryland landscape is strewn with hovels and brothels. Its courts are a travesty of justice, the standard of honesty being that nobody gets a verdict he has not paid for.[4] Its indentured servants are the victims of a "redemption" racket. (All this is consistent with the spirit of Cooke's original poem.)[5] The estate of his father that Eben has come to America to manage operates as a combination "gambling house, tavern, brothel, and opium den . . ." (p. 485).

The unglorious can be traced back to the very early appearance of the white man in America, according to a pair of "documents" that Barth introduces, which purport to give the real story behind Captain John Smith's self-celebratory descriptions of his Virginia ventures, particularly his encounter with Pocahontas. One of them, *A Secret Historie*, was supposedly written by Smith himself, while the other, *The Privie Journall of Sir Henry Burlingame* (a pun on "privy" being undoubtedly intended by Barth), was allegedly kept by one of Smith's company. The first of these presents, among other things, a hilarious picture of Smith's crew seized by diarrhea and consequently unable to make much progress in sailing their boat because they " '*must continuallie hang there bummes abeame . . .*' " (p. 391). The *Journall* portrays Smith as carrying a pack of pornographic cards, gorging himself in swinish fashion, satisfying a sexually voracious Indian queen, and meeting successfully a challenge to pierce Pocahontas's hitherto impenetrable vaginal membrane. These documents would seem to confirm one of the many proverbs appearing in the book, namely, *"More history's made in the bedchamber than in the throne room"* (p. 261). All in all, Barth's descriptions of Captain Smith and of early Maryland may be said to serve as the antithesis to the romantic, chivalric self-portrait emerging from Smith's own writings, and to the picture of a colonial South embodying these qualities found in such American historical novelists as John Esten Cooke and Mary Johnston. (Though obviously very different from him, Barth displays something akin to Washington Irving's humorous, irreverent approach to the past.)

It is not only the white man who is made to look ridiculous in Barth's rendering of early America. While the first Indian we encounter is a dignified chieftain, a victim of the English, the Indians in general do not figure as nature's noblemen in the novel.[6] Smith's secret history tells of Sir Henry Burlingame being made to enter into an eating contest with an Indian, a ritual based on the tribe's assumption that the heavier a king the more secure will his followers be against enemies. One of the tribe's former kings was called *"Kekataughtassapooekskunoughmass, for that he did eate ninetie fish on the daye he became there King."* Ahatch-

whoop, the tribe's name, signifies *"a belch of gass . . ."* (p. 594). The description of the eating contest between Burlingame and the Indian Attonce is in keeping with the tone of these etymological tidbits. *". . . Attonce, sitting cross-legged, did bump his buttocks up & down upon the earthe, farther to appetyze him selfe; Burlingame also, that he give his foe no quarter, and the verie grownd shudder'd beneath there awful bummes."* After consuming an enormous amount of food, Attonce was struck upon the gut as an aid toward getting down some last morsels, whereupon he *"did let flie a tooling fart and dy'd upon the instant where he sat"* (pp. 597,598).

Not only is history, the red man's as well as the white man's, rendered in comic, reductive terms by Barth's narrative, but so, too, is myth, or what might potentially serve as myth. Compare the reverence and awe surrounding the encounter of man and animal in Faulkner's *The Bear* with Barth's account of the Indian Billy Rumbly killing a bear by thrusting a stick deep into its anus.

There is not much new about Barth's New World in relation to the Old, except for the intensity of its dubious activities. Maryland is a place much trampled by the busy feet of European settlers, and embroiled in conflicts having their source in Europe. Eben's friend Burlingame (a descendant of the keeper of the *Journall*) describes it as " 'just a piece o' the great world like England—with the difference, haply, that the soil is vast and new where the sot-weed [tobacco] hath not drained it and oft will sprout wild seeds of energy in men that had lain fallow [in England]' " (p. 180). Eben, reacting to summaries of Maryland's history, thinks of the "strange and terrible energy" of the men he has been told about, "figures awful in their energy and purpose . . ." (pp. 114, 162). William Claiborne, holding sway over the Isle of Kent, is prominent among these persons, and he is no sooner dead in the account Eben hears than John Coode is on the scene, stirring up strife. (Both of these men are based on actual, historical personages.) It is as though there had been an implicit legacy of disruptive force passed on from the one man to the other, the transmission of an Iago-like genius for creating disorder. Eben refers to Claiborne as Coode's " 'spiritual father' " (p. 372).

What is the precise form taken by the energy of men like Claiborne and Coode? In Barth's conception of them they are deeply and continuously immersed in *plots*. Burlingame, posing as Lord Baltimore, tells Eben that Maryland's history is the tale of his family's " 'struggle to preserve her, and of the plots of countless knaves to take her from us . . .' " (p. 90). After listening to the account of this struggle, Eben is moved to exclaim: " 'Ne'er have I encountered such a string of plots, cabals, murthers, and machinations in life or literature as this history you relate me—it sets my head a-twirl, and chills my blood!' " (p. 106). (This, of course, serves as a counter-statement to his earlier assumption that the history of Maryland has been "glorious," a fit subject for a *Marylandiad*.) Plots appear again and again in the book, with, e.g., William Penn described as engaged in manipulations to have the borders of his colony extended to take in what was originally a part of Maryland, while Claiborne and Coode are seen as maneuvering tirelessly to undermine Baltimore's authority and control. Burlingame, supposedly an agent of Baltimore, plots against Coode (whose energy his own rivals). At one point he tells Eben that " 'There is a wondrous wicked plot afoot to ruin the Province with pox and opium, the better to overthrow it' " (p. 476). Later it turns out that Baltimore himself may be engaged in a plot to enervate the English in America with opium, in the hope that they will succumb to the French and Indians; the colonies are to be turned into a Catholic domain with Baltimore to be crowned Emperor of America and made a saint upon his death. (Here Barth may be drawing upon rumors of Indian-Catholic alliances that frightened Protestants in seventeenth-century Maryland.)[7] Intrigue appears to be operating in Eben's own affairs, and he wonders at one point: "What marvelous plot . . . was afoot?" (p. 287).

To heighten the effect of inexhaustible colonial energies being channeled into devious plots, Barth has taken some liberties with the historical records as these appear in the *Archives of Maryland*. He has either altered the facts or linked them together in the shape of a plot. So, for example, he has Burlingame attribute to Claiborne an accusation against a colonial official that was actually made by a woman.[8] Also, Burlingame claims that Claiborne arranged to have two commissioners lost at sea, a charge for which there is no evidence in the record. Again without a basis in the book's sources, it is indicated that William Fuller and Josias Fendall, officials who had turned against Baltimore, urged a rebellion in Maryland similar to that of Bacon's rebellion in Virginia. Fendall is accused of further conspiring against Baltimore, this time with John Coode. The latter, in turn, is arbitrarily described as the associate of several other men, and Jacob Leisler, New York's equivalent of Coode, is reported as coming south for the purpose of conniving with him. This conjoining appears to be Barth's own invention. Another apparent fabrication of Barth's is the alleged plot by Indians and escaped slaves to massacre every white man in Maryland.

What emerges from these alterations of and additions to items in the *Archives* is a reinforcing of the book's image of early American history as intrigue, an intensification of the sense of events in colonial America as the products of plots and counterplots. There is enough in the documentary record to suggest that considerable truth inheres in this view (Howard Mumford Jones has written that "if Machiavelli had known as much about the performance of Europeans in America as he knew about the performance of Italian rulers, he could have drawn his illustrations quite as richly from the one case as he did from the other."[9] But Barth has chosen to go from suggestion to assertion, supplying linkages where the record supplies only lacunae. However, one is not sure whether he is seriously offering the various plots as his conception of the actual shape of events, or whether he is simply indulging a storyteller's desire to tidy up the clutter of history and mold it into a neat narrative pattern, a plot in the literary sense of the term. The latter may well be the case. Certainly, one of the striking features of the book is Barth's ingenuity in weaving together plot developments that at first seem to have little to do with each other. But if he busily arranges his historical materials into orderly patterns, he also displays a very different tendency in his treatment of the past, one that renders history as problematical.

For Burlingame's and Ebenezer's judgments of the alleged plots modulate from condemning Coode to considering the possibility that Baltimore might be a villain, and his various antagonists—Fendall, Penn, Claiborne, Coode—heroes. The compilers of the *Archives* side unequivocally with Baltimore, but the *Archives* themselves contain materials that do not encourage such a black-and-white judgment. There is, for example, a long, vigorously written document, which sees Baltimore as a Catholic oppressing Protestants, acting imperiously and taxing excessively.[10] This the compilers arbitrarily dismiss as the "grotesque tirade of some illiterate fanatic. . . ."[11] There are also documents that give a picture of Claiborne as a constructive, helpful man.[12] We can find, too, evidence to indicate that Coode was respected by his fellow members in the House of Burgesses.[13] Barth, then, is being true to the records when he has his book indicate the difficulty, if not the impossibility, of assigning with certainty the labels of good and evil to the conflicting parties in Maryland's past. But as in his treatment of history as plot, Barth is not content to stay within the limits of his documents. He will not rest with the notion that judgments about the past are difficult, but must introduce an additional complication by having Burlingame suggest that Coode and Baltimore may not exist at all. After having heard of their activities in detail, and from Burlingame himself, this suggestion strikes one as an arbitrary turn of the screw and a piece of obscurantism, mystification rather than earned mystery. (This might be considered an example of Barth's *playing* with history, a matter that will be considered more fully a little later.)

Burlingame does not seem oppressed by the difficulty of deciding which of the two warring parties, Coode or Baltimore, represents the good and which the evil. The important thing for him is a commitment to *doing*. He characterizes Coode as loving intrigue for its own sake, and he vows to match wits with him. He proceeds to do so with such energy that Eben declares: " 'Great heavens, Henry, thou'rt a plotting Coode thyself!' " (p. 178). (It is appropriate that at times he has posed as Coode.) Burlingame wishes to avoid what he has seen occur in Eben, the paralysis of the will, the falling into a state of suspended animation. This is the condition that afflicts Jacob Horner, the protagonist of an earlier Barth novel, *End of the Road*. He is told by another character that " 'Choosing is existence: to the extent that you don't choose, you don't exist. . . . It doesn't matter whether you act constructively or even consistently, so long as you act.' "[14] Burlingame appears to subscribe to the same principle, saying: " 'one must choose his gods and devils on the run, quill his own name upon the universe. . . . One must *assert, assert, assert,* or go screaming mad. What other course remains?' " (p. 365).

Given Barth's concern with the notion of action as a good in itself, one can understand his fascination with Claiborne and Coode, who, whatever their motives, were such *busy* personages, continually in movement. The conditions of the time and place in which they lived allowed their energy and resourcefulness repeated opportunities for great impact, for causing government to totter, and it may be their displays of the potency of the individual will engaged in persistent action that commands Barth's interest in these men. We might note that the book's general spirit of debunking is replaced, in its treatment of Coode, Claiborne, and Burlingame, by a tendency to admire. Responding to Burlingame's suggestion that Baltimore and Coode may be only rumors and tales, Eben says: " 'If that . . . is so . . . Heav'n knows 'twere a potent life enough!' " (p. 753).

Burlingame believes that it is Maryland's relative lack of history that allows men like Coode and himself to subordinate goals to action, even to reverse the direction of their efforts (Barth presents Coode as a Catholic priest who has turned against his coreligionists, although the *Archives* indicate he was an Anglican cleric).[15] This lack of history, Burlingame says, confers " 'philosophic liberty' " upon a man, makes him in effect a spiritual orphan (p. 181). Burlingame *is* an orphan, a condition he is originally happy in. When Eben says that a man's father is his link with the past, Burlingame rejoins: " 'Then . . . I thank Heav'n I'm quit of mine'. . . . 'It leaves me free and unencumbered' " (p. 42). This freedom, the book seems to imply, is exercised in Burlingame's impersonations—he poses not only as Coode and as Baltimore, but also as Governor Francis Nicholson, and as Monsieur Casteene, a French intriguer. In doing so, he is displaying Coode-like behavior. Coode, says Burlingame, " 'is whate'er he chooses to call himself' . . . " (p. 161). [16] But while Burlingame at first cherishes this same freedom in his life, he later tells Eben that he envies him his father: " 'what a burden and despair to be a stranger to the world at large, and have no link with history!' " (pp. 145–46). He eventually embarks upon a quest to discover who his own father was. The connection between his orphan state (the "philosophic liberty" conferred by his severance from the past) and the metamorphoses of both Coode and himself, is suggested on his learning that events had so transpired that " 'the search for my father and the search for ways to put down Coode were now the selfsame search!' " (p. 176). Barth appears to be indicating here that to search for one's father, that is, to discover one's connection with the past, is to discover moral boundaries and limits of identity, thereby relinquishing the role-playing, changes of allegiance, and unrestricted choices that the "orphan" enjoys. Learning that he is a member of the Ahatchwhoop tribe, Burlingame goes off to join it and try to dissuade its chieftain, his father, not to carry out a planned massacre of the English. He returns garbed like an Indian to see Eben and Eben's sister, Anna, but then leaves for good. Burlingame had been sexually attracted to both siblings, and desirous of having relations with them both (and simultaneously!). His androgyneity may be seen as a particular example of the "philosophic liberty" he has enjoyed prior to his discovery of his paternity. Having Burlingame cut himself off from both Eben and Anna might be Barth's way of dramatizing the assumption of limits by a man who had earlier declared himself the " 'Suitor of Totality, Embracer of Contradictories, Husband to all Creation, the Cosmic Lover! . . . I have no parentage to give me place and aim in Nature's order: very well—I am outside Her, and shall be Her lord and spouse!' " (p. 526). At the end of the book, the Cosmic Lover has renewed his connection with his past, taken on a particular task, given up his plan to enjoy both brother and sister, and disappeared into the murk of history.

But Barth makes Burlingame's ultimate fate ambiguous, suggesting the possibility that he has assumed yet one more identity, that of Nicholas Lowe. It would not be entirely inconsistent for Burlingame to have done this, for his statement that it is " 'a burden and despair' " to be an orphan, to have " 'no link with history,' " had not been his final word on the matter. Moreover, his adoption of an Indian identity was motivated by his commitment to serving the *English* in the New World. That commitment, in turn, cannot easily be seen as constituting a final position for Burlingame. Eben thinks: "how slight and qualified were Henry's ties to the cause of Western Civilization (to say nothing of English colonialism!), than which his mind and interests were so enormously more complex that it seemed parochial by comparison!'' (p. 754). There appears to be a dialectic of emotion within Burlingame, now pulling him toward establishing a particular identity, now returning him to his status of Cosmic Lover.

The Sot-Weed Factor's own relation to the past would appear to be that of a Cosmic Lover as well, in the sense that the book refuses to commit itself to a particular conception of the past, of historical truth, but wants the freedom to embrace simultaneously a variety of possibilities—that the heroes and villains of the orthodox view were indeed such, that the application of these terms should be reversed, that the men did not exist at all. At one point, Barth talks of Eben's difficulty in realizing the ''finality'' of the real world. He feels nervous and irritable at the thought of ''the whole business of Greece and Rome'' being ''the *only* way it happened'' (p. 19), and is unable to ''acknowledge in his heart that there really *had* been a Roman Empire'' (p. 289). In his approach to history, as well as to literature and philosophy, Eben is ''dizzy with the beauty of the possible. . . '' (p. 21). He appears to possess sentiments close to those of his creator. For in an interview published in 1965, Barth is reported as saying that

> a certain kind of sensibility can be made very uncomfortable by the recognition of the *arbitrariness* of physical facts and the inability to accept their *finality*. . . . it seems to me that this emotion, which is a kind of metaphysical emotion, goes almost to the heart of what art is, at least some kinds of art, and this impulse to imagine alternatives to the world can become a driving impulse for writers. I confess that it is for me. So that really what you want to do is re-invent philosophy and the rest—make your own whole history of the world.[17]

Barth is apparently reluctant to commit himself to a final

image of history, even if the image is of his own making. This does not, I think, derive so much from a brooding skepticism about the inability to arrive at the truth of the past (the attitude present in works, say, like Ezra Pound's "Near Perigord" or Faulkner's *Absalom, Absalom!*), but from a desire to *play* with history, and with ideas about it. There is a symptomatic passage in the book in which Eben speaks of

> sundry theories of history—the retrogressive, held by Dante and Hesiod; the dramatic, held by the Hebrews and the Christian fathers; the progressive, held by Virgil; the cyclical, held by Plato and Ecclesiasticus; the undulatory, and even the vortical hypothesis entertained, according to Henry Burlingame, by a gloomy neo-Platonist of Christ's College, who believed that the cyclic periods of history were growing ever shorter and thus that at some not-unpredictable moment in the future the universe would go rigid and explode, just as the legendary bird called *Ouida* . . . was reputed to fly in ever-diminishing circles until at the end he disappeared into his own fundament (p. 728).

The comparison of the historical cycle to the path of the Ouida bird is in keeping with what has already been referred to as the fecal humor of the book. But the display of learning ending in a gag points up Barth's intellectual frivolity. Ideas in *The Sot-Weed Factor* are generally not serious or passionate attempts to give shape to experience, but things to play with, as Coode and Burlingame play with governments. There are exceptions to this, as when Eben thinks of his being in a particular predicament because of the totality of the world's history, acknowledging that "as an educated gentleman of the western world he had shared in the fruits of his culture's power and must therefore share what guilt that power incurred." At the same time he feels it was as human for the white man to exploit as it was for the red and black "to slaughter on the basis of color alone. . . . " But Barth has Eben arrive at these conclusions, which move him as few things had done, "more by insight than by casuistical speculation. . . " (p. 579). The use of "insight" is a cover-up for the abruptness with which the ideas appear in (and disappear from) the text.[18] They are just more items among many, islets of ideation in the book's narrative stream, though Barth appears to be claiming great importance for them.

The trouble is that the book's ideas, even when offered in seriousness, may be said to be inadequately felt. They are, rather, simply tossed off, giving the effect that they are merely further proof of the mastery the book is so intent on conveying, part of its character as a *tour de force*. For *The Sot-Weed Factor* is a formidable performance, one which exhibits a knowledge of minute historical detail and esoteric lore, which invents whole documents of bawdy humor, which abounds in linguistic energy, and which spins an immensely sinuous plot.[19] Barth said that one of his intentions in writing the novel "was to see if I couldn't make up a plot that was fancier than *Tom Jones*."[20] (He might also have said he wanted to make up a plot more ingenious than any John Coode ever put together in real life.) Of a story within the story, a character asks: " 'Is't more knotful or bewildered than the skein o' life itself, that a good tale tangles the better to unsnarl?' " (p. 625). The book reads too much as though it were indeed a carrying out of such complex plotting, an abstract exercise in form. Unlike somebody like Faulkner, for whom the past is a burden, and who strains to cope with it in *Absalom, Absalom!* or *The Bear,* Barth appears to stand outside history the way Burlingame, as orphan, stands outside Nature's order. Like Burlingame, Barth would be history's "Lord and Spouse," mastering its facts, trying them on, rejecting them and making up alternatives, as in his invention of Smith's *A Secret Historie*. Barth might offer, in defense of this, his narrator's observation that "we all invent our pasts, more or less, as we go along, at the dictates of Whim and Interest; the happenings of former times are a clay in the present moment that will-we, nill-we, the lot of us must sculpt'' (p. 793). But one wishes *The Sot-Weed Factor* conveyed more of a sense that Barth *had* to sculpt the past in the first place—that he did not stand outside it, but felt it impinge strongly on him. Without the sense of such a pressure, one tends to assume a stance towards *The Sot-Weed Factor* similar to that ascribed by Barth to commentators on Ebenezer's poem of the same name: ''Critics spoke of it as a fine example of the satiric extravaganza currently in vogue; they praised its rhymes and wit; they applauded the characterizations and the farcical action—and not one of them took the poem seriously!'' (p. 803).[21]

There *are* things in the story that do appear to nag at Barth's imagination—the aging of the characters, violence (particularly in the form of rape), his protagonist's betraying his beloved—but these do not become part of any deeply felt, comprehensive conception of, or response to, the past. Perhaps Barth is attempting to create such a conception in his focus on Eben's innocence (is this supposed to represent a foolish national dream?), its capacity for adding, albeit unknowingly, to the sum of human confusion and misery. Near the end of the book, Eben says: '' 'That is the crime I stand indicted for' . . . 'the crime of innocence, whereof the Knowledged must bear the burthen. There's the true Original Sin our souls are born in: not that Adam *learned,* but that he *had* to learn—in short, that he was innocent' '' (p. 788). But the solemnity of this statement is not in keeping with the dominant tone of the novel or with its self-delighting narrative ingenuities. In its mockery of Eben's innocence, *The Sot-Weed Factor* offers us history as pure selfishness, or history as bawdy. But ultimately, history exists in the book as a repository of details and plots that Barth wants to master and outdo, ending up as a literary John Coode or Henry Burlingame.

NOTES

1. See "John Barth: An Interview," *Wisconsin Studies in Contemporary Literature* 6 (Winter-Spring 1965): 7.

2. Leslie Fiedler, "John Barth: An Eccentric Genius," *New Leader,* Vol. 44 (13 February 1961), p. 22.

3. John Barth, *The Sot-Weed Factor* (New York: Grosset & Dunlap, 1964), p. 74. This is the edition of the book I have used in writing this chapter (the novel was first published in 1960). Subsequent quotations from the book will be followed in the text of the chapter by the relevant page numbers. Italics in the quotations appear in the original. Barth has brought out a revised version of *The Sot-Weed Factor* which differs only slightly from the original version.

4. Here Barth may have been deliberately debunking an image of Maryland justice put forth in George Alsop's *A Character of the Province of Maryland* (1666). Alsop claimed that lawyers had little to do in Maryland, and that "the turbulent Spirit of continued and vexatious Law, with all its quirks and evasions, is openly and most eagerly opposed. . . ." See *Narratives of Early Maryland 1633–1684,* ed. Clayton Colman Hall (New York: Charles Scribner's Sons, 1910), p. 351. This is volume ten of the *Original Narratives of Early American History.*

5. Of that poem, Lawrence C. Wroth has written that among the types it depicts "one looks in vain for an upright or a literate judge, an honest merchant, a decent woman or a sober planter." This remark is found in Wroth's introduction to a facsimile reproduction of *The Maryland Muse, Proceedings of the American Antiquarian Society,* n.s. 44 (April-October 1934): 281.

6. Moreover, late in the book, when Eben is trying to avert a massacre of the whites, he puts forth the following argument to an Indian who apparently accepts it: " ' 'tis not the English case I plead: 'tis the cause of humankind, of Civilization *versus* the Abyss of salvagery. . . . I grant the English have used you ill, but to drive them out is to drive yourself back into darkness . . .' " (pp. 707–8).

7. See Herbert L. Osgood, *The American Colonies in the 17th Century* (New York: Macmillan Co., 1926), 3:493–94.

8. See *Archives of Maryland* (Baltimore: Maryland Historical Society, 1883–), 3:166–70.

9. Howard Mumford Jones, *O Strange New World* (New York: Viking Press, 1964), p. 127.

10. *Archives of Maryland,* 5:134–49.

11. Ibid., p. vii.

12. E.g., ibid., pp. 220ff.

13. E.g., ibid., 19:476.

14. John Barth, *End of the Road* (New York: Avon Books, 1964), p. 67. The book was originally published in 1958. It might be argued that Barth questions the principle of constant choosing and acting, but it is plainly a notion that intrigues him.

15. *Archives,* 20:491.

16. Cf. Francis Nicholson, Governor of Maryland, as Eben describes him: " 'He is neither this nor that . . . he is no Papist, yet he fought for James at Hounslow

Heath; he was Edmund Andros's lieutenant, and so differed with him that the two despise each other yet; Lord Baltimore chose him to be commissioned Royal Governor, thinking Nicholson shared his sympathies, but albeit Nicholson seems concerned with prosecuting Coode, he governs as if Lord Baltimore did not exist . . ." (p. 701). Burlingame and Nicholson appear to get on very well together.

17. "John Barth: An Interview," p. 8. Italics in original.

18. The notion of a shared guilt does make an earlier appearance in the book, but it is a very brief one, and occurs about eighty pages before the passage in question. Another idea that seems to be important to Eben also makes a brief appearance and is attributed to "insight" (pp. 644–45).

19. The plot is so intricate it may have gotten away from Barth himself at one point, with Burlingame giving what look like inconsistent accounts of how he came upon *The Privie Journall of Sir Henry Burlingame*.

20. "John Barth: An Interview," p. 7.

21. In talking of not, ultimately, taking the book seriously, I speak only for myself. Some critics have taken *The Sot-Weed Factor* quite seriously. See, e.g., Leslie Fiedler's piece cited in note 2. See also Chapters 3 and 4 of David Morrell's *John Barth: An Introduction* (University Park, Pa.: Pennsylvania State University Press, 1976).

9

The Passionate Puritan:
John Berryman's *Homage to Mistress Bradstreet*

Homage to Sextus Propertius is a prominent work in the Ezra Pound canon, and John Berryman was a great admirer of Pound.[1] Considering these two facts, the title of Berryman's *Homage to Mistress Bradstreet* would appear to be a deliberate echo, by which the poet was attempting to honor not only Anne Bradstreet but one of his twentieth-century masters. Like Pound's *Propertius,* Berryman's *Bradstreet* tries to recover for us a figure who had hitherto been a mere academic property, a name in textbooks rather than part of a living tradition. Both works center on a person who is seen as being at odds with a prevailing sensibility. But there are notable differences between the two poems. Where Pound is translating a text (though taking a great many exhilarating liberties with it), Berryman is trying to construct an image of the person behind the text. Where Pound is, at least partly, trying to pull Propertius's work into the present, Berryman is trying to burrow into the past, to give us a sense of the way the New World impinged on Bradstreet. He does this in a poem which is largely a dramatic monologue spoken by her, interspersed with statements by Berryman, and with exchanges between the two, as Berryman uses the device of going back in time to have a love affair with the Puritan poet.

Anne Bradstreet's place in our history has been based, of course, on her being generally regarded as the first person in America to write noteworthy verses. Her poetic productions were considered especially remarkable, both by her contemporaries and by later generations, for her being a woman. It was not common for women among the Puritans to devote as much time as Anne apparently did to composing verses, and it was particularly unusual for a woman, in the England or America of that time, to write about the subjects she chose for much of her poetry: history, politics, and natural philosophy.[2] In a number of poems, Bradstreet calls attention to the fact that it is a woman who is writing. Her elegy on Queen Elizabeth spiritedly asserts the capabilities of women, gloriously realized in that sovereign, and the prologue to her long poem *The Four Elements* concedes that men are superior poets only after it has made a tart rejoinder to those who question woman's right to wield a pen. "The Author to Her Book," a charming piece based on the fact that the publication of her first volume of poems, *The Tenth Muse,* was arranged without her knowledge, plays skillfully with the conceit of her book as a distinctly blemished urchin, herself its mother who has tried unsuccessfully to spruce it up. Beneath the modesty of the metaphor, there is a delight and confidence in her unfolding creation of it. Clearly, Bradstreet's writing of verse was of considerable importance to her, and despite her assumptions of a humble stance, she made at least a limited claim for its worth.

One of the curious things about Berryman's *Homage* is the way in which, despite its name, it denigrates Bradstreet's achievements as a poet. She was, Berryman claims, in an indication of what his title does *not* mean, "mistress neither of fiery nor velvet verse. . . ."[3] With apparent reference to her long quaternion poems (she wrote on the four elements, the four humors, the four seasons, the four ages of men, and on four monarchies) he says he is "appalled" by her "bald/abstract didactic rime . . ." (st. 12). She herself is made to speak of her "proportioned, spiritless poems . . ." (st. 42). (Her truly valuable publications, she seems to suggest, are her children.) In a prose piece, Berryman referred to Bradstreet as "this boring high-minded Puritan woman who may have been our first American poet but is not a good one." His interest in her, he said, was "almost from the beginning, as a woman, not much as a poetess."[4] "Not much" is a hedge, and we shall have to come back to the matter of Berryman's response to Bradstreet's poetry *per se,* after we have investigated the relationship between the person that emerges from her writings and Berryman's image of her as a woman.[5]

Bradstreet left to her children, as a kind of spiritual legacy, a short autobiographical sketch in prose. (Interestingly enough, it makes no mention of her activities as a poet.) She presents little in the way of circumstantial detail. Concerning her going from comfortable surroundings in England to the rigors of an existence in early America, she says only ". . . I came into this Country, where I found a new world and new manners at which my heart rose [i.e., rebelled]. But after I was convinced it was the way of God, I submitted to it and joined to the church at Boston."[6] Brief as this is, and not amplified elsewhere in her writings, at least not explicitly, it seems to have struck Berryman as very important, for his poem makes Anne's longing for the Old World and her resistance to the New an important feature of her sensibility (though he alludes to her statement of having "submitted" to her new life, he virtually ignores it). He has her refer to "the Atlantic wound" (st. 8), apparently meaning that crossing the ocean, leaving England behind, did her psychological injury. She is troubled by seeing "distinction perishing" in America (st. 7), and characterizes herself as "Ruth/away" (an echo of Keats's "Ruth . . . sick for home,/ . . . amid the alien corn"):

vellum I palm, and dream. Their forest dies
to greensward, privets, elms & towers, whence
a nightingale is throbbing.

(st. 10)

The opening statement of these lines, with its drowsy
sensuousness (created in part by its consonance), effectively
introduces Anne's musings in which "Their forest," i.e., the
forest of the Indians and/or of her fellow colonists, is
displaced by images of an English countryside, with its
combination of appealing human artifacts and natural objects. Reinforcing this nostalgia is the succeeding stanza,
where Anne says (in what must be the poem's only instance
of a comic rhyme):

> Succumbing half, in spirit, to a salmon sash
> I prod the nerveless novel succotash—

(st. 11)

Missing the merriments of English culture, she can only feel
exacerbated by the mixture of theologizing and incessant
physical labor that the Puritan settlement offers (the following lines constitute a kind of miniature version of the
opposition between Old World pleasures and Puritan grimness depicted in Hawthorne's "The Maypole of Merrymount"):

> . . . Cantabanks & mummers, nears
> longing for you. Our chopping scores my ears,
> our costume bores my eyes.
> St. George to the good sword, rise! chop-logic's rife. . . .

(st. 22)

The poem's note on this stanza indicates that *chopping*
means both *disputing* and *axing*.

Berryman evidently sympathizes with Anne's hostility to

the Puritans' logic-chopping, particularly since it was part of
a religion that could be very severe on those who deviated
from its dogmas. We are reminded of this in the poem's
treatment of the other famous Anne of the period, Anne
Hutchinson. Considered by many of the orthodox to be a
heretic, Mrs. Hutchinson at first commanded the allegiance
of John Cotton (I take this to be Berryman's reference when
he has Anne Bradstreet say "John Cotton shines on Boston's sin" [st. 15].) But Cotton, under pressure from the
church authorities, renounced her. As Bradstreet puts it in
Homage:

> . . . John Cotton rakes [i.e., inclines]
> to the synod of Cambridge.
>
> (St. 24)

She then says that "Factioning passion" has made all the
Puritans blind to Anne Hutchinson's goodness, and she
addresses her as "Bitter sister, victim! I miss you" (sts. 24,
25). The notes to the poem refer to Mrs. Hutchinson as
Anne's closest friend. Here, Berryman is positing a relationship between the two women and a response by the Puritan
poet for which there is no substantial evidence, and which
can be taken as a wishful reconstruction on Berryman's part.
Helen Campbell's biography of Bradstreet, a work on which
Berryman drew in writing his poem, contends that she *must*
have responded intensely and with commiseration to the trial
and banishment of Mrs. Hutchinson, but acknowledges that
in the poet's writings there is no mention at all of that early
American martyr.[7] Berryman appears to have succumbed to
a desire to see the past as it *should* have been, with one Anne,
deviating from the womanly norm by the act of writing,
reaching out toward the other Anne, who deviated from the
religious norm of her time.

Thomas Dudley, Anne Bradstreet's father, played a leading role in the persecution of Mrs. Hutchinson, and it is possible to see a connection between Berryman's apparent sympathy for that victim, and the description he has Bradstreet give of her father's final illness:

> Father is not himself. He keeps his bed,
> and threw a saffron scum Thursday. God-forsaken words
> escaped him raving. . . .
>   He did scold
> his secting enemies. His stomach is cold
> while we drip. . . .   (st. 43)

Dudley himself wrote a poem in which he referred to a "Cold Stomach" as a sign of his impending dissolution.[8] The "saffron scum," a vivid and terrible detail, seems to be Berryman's own invention. But the old man's "God-forsaken words" and "raving" constitute especially interesting additions to the record. Berryman appears to be suggesting that Dudley's lack of religious tolerance culminated in a deathbed blaspheming and madness. (Berryman said it was a "pleasant moment . . . when one night, hugging myself, I decided that [Anne's] fierce dogmatic old father was going to die blaspheming, in delirium.")[9] The poem here is exhibiting, as does Williams's *In the American Grain,* a characteristic American response to the Puritan fathers, judging Dudley's intolerance harshly. In treating the discontent of the two Annes with their culture, the poem clearly sides with them.

There is undoubtedly a linkage between *Homage's* portrait of Anne Bradstreet in rebellion against her surroundings and its repeated presentation of her face as disfigured by smallpox. Early in the poem, Berryman says he sees Anne "Pockmarkt & westward staring on a haggard deck . . ."(st. 4). He has her tell of being stricken by the disease and of Simon Bradstreet falling in love with her:

> That year for my sorry face
> so-much-older Simon burned,
> so Father smiled, with love. . . .
>
> (St. 14)

Later, she re-creates the sensations of her smallpox attack, and says to the poet, her would-be lover:

> This cratered skin,
> like the crabs & shells of my Palissy ewer, touch!
>
> (St. 28)

Such focusing on Anne's scars is clearly Berryman's own doing. The historical Anne's own account simply says that after she was smitten with the disease, she was "restored" by the lord.[10] A short time afterward she was married. Helen Campbell suggests, in a genteelly circumlocutory way, that Anne's attraction for her husband-to-be was in part based on good looks.[11] Jeannine Hensley has pointed out that if Anne had indeed been disfigured by smallpox the lines her brother-in-law wrote about her "comely face" would have been cruel.[12] Berryman, in presenting his scarred protagonist, appears to have appropriated the account found in Campbell of a contemporary of Anne, a Mrs. Lucy Hutchinson, who wrote of herself (using the third person) that the smallpox she contracted

> made her the most deformed person that could be seen . . . yet he [her prospective husband] was nothing troubled at it, but married her as soon as she was able to quit the chamber, when the priest and all that saw her were affrighted to look on her. . . .[13]

Berryman could have confused this account with that of Bradstreet, but it is more likely that he simply shifted the facts of the one to the other. If this last is the case, he may have done it to brand Anne externally so as to increase our sense of the displacement she feels, and of her inner protest. That is, the smallpox might be intended as emblematic of Anne's rebellious spirit. Berryman has her speak of having been visited with smallpox "for my revolt. . ." (St. 28).

This connecting of Anne's rebelliousness to her smallpox may at first appear strained, but there is an analogy for it in the actual Anne's own writings. In her autobiographical sketch she thinks of her smallpox as an affliction sent by God to chastise her for her "Pride and Vanity" which, it would appear, are linked in her mind to the "carnall" desires she experienced when she was fourteen or fifteen[14] (stanzas 13–14 of *Homage* draw on this material). She says later on, in a remarkable statement, that she does not "dare" desire the health she has sometimes had, "least my heart should bee drawn from [God], and sett upon the world."[15]

Anne Bradstreet seems to have been plagued by repeated sickness. This is attested to not only by her autobiographical sketch but by a number of her poems: "Upon a Fit of Sickness," "Upon some distemper of body," "For Deliverance from a feaver," "From another sore Fitt," and "Deliverance from a fitt of Fainting." Berryman nicely capsulizes this aspect of her life when he has her make the unglamorous observation that

> Pioneering is not feeling well,
> not Indians, beasts.

> (St. 23)

It may have been Anne's poems about illness along with her remarks about her "carnall" desires that led Berryman to present his Bradstreet as characterized by a strong consciousness of her physical being. In *Homage* she calls attention to her pockmarks, broods on her nakedness, speaks of her silky breasts, and refers to her "Body a-drain. . ." (st. 47). (Sometimes her utterances seem more an

anticipation of Sylvia Plath than expressions consonant with
the original Bradstreet's pieties; e.g., Berryman has her say
"Winter than summer worse, that first, like a file/ on a quick,
or the poison suck of a thrilled tooth. . . ." [st. 9]) It is her
awareness of her body that constitutes much of her consciousness of being a single, separate person rather than one
who is integrated into her marriage, or into the larger society
to which she nominally belongs, or, for that matter, into the
company of God's elect. But it should be added at once that
there is an ongoing oscillation in the poem, Anne moving in
and out of her role as proper Puritan and mother. Witness the
rendering of the birth of her first child, Samuel. The historical Bradstreet said only "It pleased God to keep me a long
time without a child, which was a great greif to me, and cost
mee many prayers and tears before I obtained one. . ."[16]
Berryman's Bradstreet happily realizes she is pregnant, the
months of gestation "blessing a swelling trance" (st. 18). She
goes into labor and Berryman devotes three stanzas to her
giving birth, with Anne experiencing her flesh both as
embarrassment and glory:

> > . . . everything down
> hardens I press with horrible joy down
> my back cracks like a wrist
> shame I am voiding oh behind it is too late
> . . . .
> I can *can* no longer
> and it passes the wretched trap whelming and I am me
>
> drencht & powerful I did it with my body!
> One proud tug greens Heaven. Marvellous,
> unforbidding Majesty.
> Swell, imperious bells. I fly.
> Mountainous, woman not breaks and will bend. . . .
> > > (Sts. 19–21)

The poem moves immediately from this note of personal

triumph, the triumph of woman alone, to Anne's sense that she is a member of a family, Simon's wife, Samuel's mother. But in the very stanza where we see this (st. 22), the element of restlessness and rebelliousness returns.

Anne is defined by her body, not only in her illness and her giving birth, but in her sexual impulses as well. The historical Bradstreet alluded, in a passage already noted, to her carnal desires, and she wrote one poem—"A Letter to her Husband, absent upon Publick employment"—which showed her looking forward to the resumption of conjugal relations on his return. In *Homage,* Anne's desires are not focused on her husband Simon, whom she pictures in unflattering early morning light, but on Berryman, who comes to be her lover in the poem. Moreover, in a notable passage, Anne appears highly vulnerable to a generalized phallic force. She first says:

> . . . My breath is scented, and I throw
> hostile glances towards God.
> Crumpling plunge of a pestle, bray. . . .
>
> (St. 36)

Picking up the pestle image, she continues:

> a male great pestle smashes
> small women swarming towards the mortar's rim in vain.
>
> (St. 37)

The striking visual image here is brilliantly complemented by the contrast between the open sounds of the first line, embodying masculine power—m*a*le, gr*ea*t, p*e*stle, sm*a*shes—and the closed sounds, wonderfully sustained, of the second, embodying female futility—sm*a*ll, w*o*men, sw*a*rming, t*o*w*a*rds, m*o*rtar's, r*i*m.

Anne retreats into the minutiae of motherhood in an attempt to shake off her dangerous sexual feelings:

> Prattle of children powers me home.
> . . . .
>   . . . I pare
> an apple for my pipsqueak Mercy and
> she runs & all need naked apples, fanned
> their tinier envies.
> Vomitings, trots, rashes. . . .
>
>   (Sts. 39–40)

She continues:

> When by me in the dusk my child sits down
> I am myself.
>
>   (St. 42)

The historical Anne gave only one indication in her writings that she was threatened by the lure of illicit sexuality. The persona that she presents in her poems is almost always unexceptionable by her society's standards—it is that of an adoring wife, a loving mother, a dutiful and appreciative daughter, a pious woman. This seems to have corresponded to the way she appeared in life. She was described in the preface to the reader in *The Tenth Muse* as a person

> honoured, and esteemed where she lives, for her gracious demeanour, her eminent parts, her pious conversation, her courteous disposition, her exact diligence in her place, and discreet managing of her family occasions; and more then so, these Poems are the fruit of but some few houres, curtailed from her sleep, and other refreshments.[17]

This is not to say that Anne, as she comes over in her poetry, is a paragon, pure and simple. For example, as she herself realizes, she is capable of too great an attachment to worldly objects. In "Upon the burning of our house, July 10, 1666," she displays a housewife's consciousness of and care for *things,* whose loss so obviously pains her, a feeling she attempts to purge. On another level, there are one or two poems where she seems unable to accept God's ways when these take the form of allowing a child to die. But more than in any of her poems, the autobiographical outline she left to her children is remarkably frank in attesting to her religious doubts, the need she repeatedly felt to be corrected by God's chastising rod.

However, Berryman's Bradstreet is not the overly materialistic housewife or the sometime skeptic. She is an Old World woman repelled by the crude and arduous conditions of America, a rebel against Puritan rigidity (rather than the questioner of fundamental religious beliefs), an intensely libidinal being who, while tortured by thoughts of their sinfulness, cannot obliterate her sexual impulses (to some extent she reminds one of Hawthorne's Hester Prynne). Berryman, then, has changed the terms in which his heroine's revolt is manifested from those that would appear to pertain to the original Anne. The historical Bradstreet's fallings away seem to have been largely a matter of her restless mind or her sense of the injustice of the tribulations visited on men by God.[18] In Berryman's poem, the revolt is rooted largely in her body. Also, the historical Anne usually moved determinedly toward a resolution of her intellectual or emotional conflicts (it is significant that her poem on the four humors ends with phlegm playing a mediating role among the warring elements of man's personality). Berryman's Anne seems merely to take the self-administered antidote of immersion in her life's small duties, becoming "somehow. . ./ an old woman," calmly awaiting her end (st. 50).

It is difficult to determine precisely Berryman's conception of what his poem was attempting, how it was connected for him with the historical materials that presumably provided its basis. In an interview he seemed to be indicating that *Homage* constituted a kind of stunting, a playing with his materials (cf. my remarks, pp. 203-4, on Barth's *The Sot-Weed Factor*).

> The point of the Bradstreet poem . . . was to take a woman unbelievably conventional and give her every possible trial and possibility of error and so on, and wind her up in a crazy love affair, and then get her out of it—better, get her out of it in ways that will allow her forgetting of it after a long period of time. The affair in the whole middle part of the poem is not historical but purely imaginary. The title is a pun—homage to *Mistress* Bradstreet, namely the poet's mistress in the twentieth century; he works from himself into her through the two of them, back into her, out of her, to the end of the poem, which ends in the twentieth century.[19]

But on another occasion Berryman complained that "few critics have seen that it *is* an historical poem. . . ."[20] He said then, too:

> An American historian somewhere observes that all colonial settlements are intensely conservative, *except* in the initial break-off point. . . . Trying to do justice to both parts of this obvious truth—which I came upon only after the poem was finished—I concentrated upon the second, and the poem laid itself out in a series of rebellions.[21]

This in itself is somewhat misleading, since the rebellion in *Homage* is found almost exclusively in Anne (Anne Hutchinson is the only other rebel in the poem), with her society being particularly rigid. Also, the question arises as to why, if he chose to dramatize that rebellion through a "purely imaginary" affair, did Berryman need to begin with the historical figure at all, unless he simply wanted, as a *jeu d'esprit*, to invert the conventional picture of Anne.

A more substantial reason for his choice of subject seems to lie in her poetry, or rather, in the fact that she dared to write it, and in a particular mode. Given her cultural circumstances, her venturing to be a poet appears to have

struck Berryman as admirable, even heroic. He conceives of
the forces hostile to her writing operating as close to home as
they could get. Describing a storm, he says to Anne:

> I doubt if Simon than this blast, that sea,
> spares from his rigour for your poetry
> more. . . .
>
> (St. 2)

The poetry she wrote, poor as Berryman considers it,
represented a serious effort to enrich a threadbare civilization. Berryman has her say:

> Versing, I shroud among the dynasties;
> quaternion on quaternion, tireless I phrase
> anything past, dead, far
> sacred, for a barbarous place.
>
> (St. 12)

Even though Berryman replies by making clear how little he
thinks of her verse, she seems to have appealed to him in her
efforts. If he was interested in the woman, it was at least
partly because she wrote poetry. She is not only the first
American poet, but for Berryman she is prototypical in her
ambitious attempts to go against the grain of our culture.
Speaking of having used Bradstreet as his subject, Berryman
said: ". . . I did not choose her—somehow she chose me—
one point of connection, at any rate, being the almost
insuperable difficulty of writing high verse at all in a land
that cared and cares so little for it."[22] Right after Bradstreet
says to Anne Hutchinson "Bitter sister, victim! I miss you,"
Berryman says to Bradstreet "I miss you, Anne . . ." (st. 25).
Earlier, he had told her:

> . . .We are on each other's hands
> who care. Both of our worlds unhanded us. . . .
>
> (St. 2)

What they both care about is high verse, and *Homage* can be seen as Berryman's own attempt to write it, his love affair with Anne in the poem being a means of dramatizing their common enterprise.

In *Homage,* taken as a whole, Berryman presents us with a woman that he has not so much recovered as created—the record *per se* does not support much of the portrait of Anne that emerges from the poem, and the voice he has given her, with its difficult syntax and staccato effects, could not be more different from Bradstreet's own verse voice. This is not to say that the work fails to create any sense of the New World as it might actually have registered on Anne Bradstreet, but only to recognize that the poem goes beyond this to a depiction of her nature and responses that appears to contradict the record or that exists beyond its boundaries. Berryman has Anne break out of the bindings of the facts to stand before us as he would have her, more vivid and more moving than she usually is in her own writings. He may not have produced a portrait of the historical personage that strikes us as authentic, but he *has* given us an imposing and memorable woman, one of legendary stature.

NOTES

1. See John Berryman "The Poetry of Ezra Pound," *Partisan Review* 16 (April 1949): 377–94.

2. See Elizabeth Wade White, *Anne Bradstreet: "The Tenth Muse"* (New York: Oxford University Press, 1971), p. 256.

3. *Homage* can be found in John Berryman, *Homage to Mistress Bradstreet and Other Poems* (New York: The Noonday Press, 1968). The poem consists of fifty-seven eight-line stanzas, each of them numbered. Quotations from the poem will be followed in the text of the chapter by the numbers of the relevant stanzas. The line just quoted occurs in stanza 12.

4. John Berryman, "One Answer to a Question," *Shenandoah,* 17 (Autumn 1965): 73.

5. Whether interested in her as a woman or a poet, or both, Berryman's writing about Bradstreet may have come, in part, from a competitive desire to make his mark using a domain, the New England past, more readily identified with the man most often touted as the leading poet of Berryman's generation, Robert Lowell. But

compared to Lowell, as well as to Charles Olson, Berryman's choice of Bradstreet as subject matter has something of the arbitrary about it, though the results are quite wonderful. For unlike Berryman, Olson and Lowell possess a sense of deep rootedness in New England, though manifested in different ways.

6. *The Works of Anne Bradstreet,* ed. John Harvard Ellis (Gloucester, Mass.: Peter Smith, 1932), p. 5. The letters in quotations taken from this text have been modernized.

7. Helen Campbell, *Anne Bradstreet and Her Time* (Boston: D. Lothrop, 1891), p. 105.

8. See *Works of Anne Bradstreet,* p. lvi.

9. Berryman, "One Answer to a Question," p. 74.

10. *Works,* p. 5.

11. Campbell, *Anne Bradstreet and Her Time,* pp. 21–22.

12. *The Works of Anne Bradstreet,* ed. Jeannine Hensley, (Cambridge, Mass.: Harvard University Press, 1967), p. xxiii. The lines in question read, "There needs no pointing to that comely face, / That in its native beauty hath such grace. . . ." It should be observed that Josephine K. Piercy believes Anne's face *was* marred by smallpox. See her *Anne Bradstreet* (New York: Twayne Publishers 1965), p. 76.

13. Campbell, *Anne Bradstreet and Her Time,* pp. 27–28.

14. *Works of Anne Bradstreet,* ed. Ellis, pp. 4–5.

15. Ibid., p. 20.

16. Ibid., p. 5.

17. Ibid., p. 84.

18. Ann Stanford has focused on the strain of rebellion in the poet in "Anne Bradstreet: Dogmatist and Rebel," *New England Quarterly* 39 (September 1966): 373–89.

19. See Richard Kostelanetz, "Conversation with Berryman," *Massachusetts Review* 11 (Spring 1970): 340–47.

20. Berryman, "One Answer to a Question," p. 74.

21. Ibid., 73.

22. Ibid.

10

"fish fish fish":
Charles Olson's *Maximus Poems*

Examining a map of the Massachusetts coastline, one's eye is most likely to be caught by the bold fish-hook contour of Cape Cod. Topographically much more modest is the peninsula to the North, Cape Ann. But on the "map" that emerges from Charles Olson's *Maximus Poems,* it is Cape Anne, more specifically Gloucester, that fills one's view.[1]

Olson's work invokes a series of map-makers: Martin Behaim, who constructed a globe in 1492; Juan de la Cosa, the Spanish navigator who sailed with Columbus in that same year and again in 1498; Samuel de Champlain who made a map of Gloucester Harbor; and John Smith, who charted the New England coastline from Cape Cod to Penobscot Bay. The cover of the first volume of the *Maximus Poems* is itself a map of Gloucester Harbor. But of course the "mappemunde" (map of the world) that Olson declares himself to be making in the poems is something other and more complicated than the usual charts or globes. It includes, as he says, "my being," a being steeped not only in the topography of Gloucester, but in its history and contemporary life. Moreover, that "mappemunde" takes in more than the local materials, as is indicated by the term itself and by the representation of the hypothetical Gondwanaland that appears on the cover of *Maximus Poems IV, V, VI.*[2] This representation points up what appears to be an attempt by Olson to place Gloucester on the stage of world history.

Two passages from the poems, when brought together, help illustrate the nature of this attempt. They read as follows:

> . . .my town, my two towns
> talk, talked of Gades, talk
> of Cash's.
>
> (P. 77)

> Lane's eye-view of Gloucester
> Phoenician eye-view.
> ("Lane's eye-view of Gloucester").

"Gades" is the Spanish port of Cadiz, founded, according to tradition, by the Phoenicians, as early as 100. "Cash's" is a fishing bank frequented by Gloucester fishermen. The second passage refers to Fitz Hugh Lane (1804–65), a marine painter who resided in Gloucester. On the basis of these lines, as well as other sections of *Maximus*, we can say that Olson's "two towns" consist of Gloucester and the ancient Phoenician city of Tyre.

There are several reasons why the two may have become associated in his mind.[3] The life of each cannot be thought of apart from its dependence on the sea. The Portuguese, a prominent ethnic group in Gloucester engaged in the fishing industry and praised by Olson, are seen by him as possibly being "part Phoenician" ("View: fr the Orontes"). The Tyrians had a reputation for hard work, and Olson credits early Gloucester with a work ethic:

> the adventure
>
> of the new frontier
> (not boom, or gold,
> the lucky strike,
> but work. . . .
>
> (P. 104)

Part of Tyre's industriousness went into shipbuilding; many ships were built at Gloucester, where the schooner was invented (a fact alluded to in the poems). Tyre was situated on an island of rock. The rock of Dogtown, a section of Gloucester celebrated in *Maximus IV, V, VI,* is a prominent feature of the place. Moreover, in 1643, Cape Ann was made an island by means of a cut in the Annisquam River (referred to several times in *Maximus*). Speaking of Gloucester, Olson calls it "the island of this city. . ." (p. 11). Olson sees that island city threatened:

> 128 a mole
> to get at Tyre
>
> ("128 a mole")

These lines, baffling at first encounter, make sense when seen as part of an overall joining of Gloucester and Tyre. "128" is Route 128 that runs through the suburbs of Boston and leads into Gloucester. When Alexander the Great wished to conquer Tyre, in 233 B.C. approximately, he built a mole or jetty to it from the mainland, and sacked the city. The modern highway, then, is conceived of as a portentous presence for the American equivalent of Tyre, threatening it with a loss of identity. Indeed, the first volume of the *Maximus Poems* ends with the lines

> . . .the 128 bridge
> now brings in
>
> what,
> to Main Street?
>
> (P. 160)

The Tyre-Gloucester connections that exist in the mind of the poems possibly provide a clue to why Olson insists on presenting early Gloucester in terms of the Old West. For example, he speaks of William Bradford and John Winthrop as men who came "to top the tough/ West the Puritan coast

was was [sic] fur and fish frontier cow-towns'' (p. 109).
Gloucester of 1625–26 is called a ''cowtown,'' and a fight over
fishing rights at that time is described ''as much a Western
as/ why not. . .'' (p. 112). The increase of fishing vessels in
New England waters during the 1620s is called the ''fish
rush'' (p. 112), an obvious takeoff on ''gold rush.'' Olson
remembers a dance-hall in Gloucester ''like literally ye Olde/
West. . .'' (''Wrote my first poems''). The function of such
formulations appears to be that of displacing Gloucester
from its position in our consciousness as being in the East,
and making us remember that in its early days the settlement
of the town represented a thrust toward the West, that ''the
Continental Shelf/ was Europe's/ first West. . .'' (p. 124),
and that ''the motion (the Westward motion)/ comes here,/ to
land'' (p. 121). The initiation of that motion of civilization
Olson might well have credited to the Phoenicians. Victor
Bérard, whose work on Homer was greatly admired by
Olson,[4] spoke of the myth of Agenor and his son Kadmos
seeking Europa (a myth cited in *Maximus IV, V, VI*) as
coming out of Phoenician attempts to discover a Western
continent.[5] So that the settlement of Gloucester can be seen
as constituting for Olson a climactic result of efforts begun
by the Phoenicians. Moreover, Maximus, the persona of the
poems, associates a westward motion with his own forma-
tion, the generation of what he is by his past:

 . . . all those antecedent predecessions, the precessions

of me, the generation of those facts
which are my words, it is coming

from all that I no longer am, yet am,
the slow westward motion of

more than I am
              (''*Maximus to Gloucester, Letter 27* [withheld]'')

Thus, the development of the persona is fused with the movement of civilization from East to West, from Tyre to Gloucester.

> Maximus is a whelping mother, giving birth
> with the crunch of his own pelvis.
> He sent flowers on the waves from the mole
> of Tyre. He went to Malta. From Malta
> to Marseilles. From Marseilles to Iceland.
> From Iceland to Promontorium Vinlandiae.
> Flowers go out on the sea. On the left
> of the Promontorium. On the left of the
> Promontorium, Settlement Cove

I am making a mappemunde. It is to include my being.
            ("Peloria the dog's upper lip kept curling")

(At the annual ceremony held at Gloucester to commemorate those lost at sea, flowers are cast into the outgoing tide.) Gloucester is a product of westward motion, and Maximus-Olson is a product of his residence in Gloucester.

Among the persons celebrated in the *Maximus Poems* are those men who helped to realize the westward movement, their individual venturesomeness carrying civilization from Europe to America. One of the earliest of these is Pytheus (or Pytheas), a relatively obscure figure mentioned several times in *Maximus,* a navigator and author of a geographical treatise now lost. He has been described as the first man "apparently, to give definite information of Western Europe and especially the British Islands."[6] That is to say his travels helped extend Mediterranean man's knowledge of what lay to the North and the West. He spoke of regions which were neither land, nor sea, nor air, but made up of a substance in which all these elements were in suspension.[7] Referring to this as "Pytheus' sludge," Olson sees America as "swimming" out of it (p. 78), to be explored by such men as Verrazano and John Cabot.

It is not only the spirit of exploration that helps make men heroes for Olson, but also their openness to the newness of the New Land, the care and detail with which they registered America (the admiration of such qualities links *Maximus* to *In the American Grain*). Maximus refers favorably, for example, to John Josselyn, who published an account of the botanical species he had found in New England. The chief hero for Olson among his westward-faring men is Captain John Smith (the very same personage treated so contemptuously in Barth's *The Sot-Weed Factor*). In an essay on Smith, Olson connected him to the prototypical explorer of *Maximus,* saying it was "an ancient thing this Smith had, what men had to have before Pytheus, to move. . . ."[8] Smith apparently impressed Olson in schoolboy days because of his exotic adventures and amours. He named Cape Ann "Tragabizanda" in honor of a Turkish princess who had allegedly once rescued him,[9] and called three offshore islands "The Three Turks Heads," after the Turkish champions he slew in personal combat. Both nomenclatures and their connection with Smith are cited in the poems. The mature Olson, recalling Smith's heroics, responds also to his careful mapping of the New England coastline (literally and in words),[10] and to his embrace of what he found. He showed himself

> The Capteyne
> he was, the eye he had
> for what New England offered . . .

(P. 50)

As a student of his writings, Olson was undoubtedly aware of Smith's having called Massachusetts "the Paradice of all [these] parts," and of having said "of all the foure parts of the world I have yet seen not inhabited, could I have but means to transport a Colony, I would rather live here [Massachusetts] then any where. . . ."[11] Smith may also have endeared himself to Olson because, in the words of one historian, he "was always the champion of the actual settler. He covertly censured the merely speculative Patentee. . . ."[12] Olson quotes Smith's contention that the settlers " 'have been my wife, my hawks, my hounds,/ my cards, my dice, in totall my best content' " (p. 50).

Also honored in the *Maximus Poems* is John White, who has been called "the Founder of Massachusetts" by the historian Frances Rose-Troup. The poem's references to White, along with other of its materials, in effect put forth Gloucester's claim to being the spot where the Bay State was founded, Olson attempting to dislodge the Pilgrims at Plymouth from their preeminent place in our image of early Massachusetts. Both in her book on the Massachusetts Bay Company and in her biography of White,[13] Rose-Troup argues for White and his Dorchester Company as the true founders of Massachusetts, and in the first of these volumes she stresses the separation and antagonism between the Gloucester's claim to being the spot where the Bay State was founded, Olson attempting to dislodge the Pilgrims at Gloucester, solely gave you place in the genetic world . . ." (p. 151).[15]

Olson's focus on White and the Dorchester Company may be seen as part of his general preoccupation with beginnings or with *firsts*, a word that occurs again and again in *Maximus:* first voyagings, first sightings, first settlings, first writings. In his *Call Me Ishmael,* Olson had detected such an interest in Melville, who reached "back through time. . . . He had a pull to the origin of things, the first day, the first man, the unknown sea. . . ."[16] Reaching back in time himself, Olson, in *Maximus,* refers to the mythical figure of Ousoos, "the first man/ to carve out/ the trunk of a tree/ and go out/ on the waters/ from the shore . . ." ("from a sea").[17] It seems to be the Phoenicians Olson has in mind when he talks of the time "the sea first/ awoke to men's minds" (p. 55). Perhaps he thinks of himself reembodying that consciousness when he recalls "the first time I saw/ the sea" (p. 83).[18]

Carrying his concern with firsts westward, Olson, in a section entitled "On first Looking out through Juan de la Cosa's Eyes," mentions early European explorers of the Atlantic and wonders who was the person "Who found you, land,/ of the hard gale" (p. 79). (The place referred to here may be Newfoundland or the New England coast.) Through his poetry, Olson tells us, "Gloucester can view/ those men/ who saw her/ first" (p. 107). Champlain, generally regarded as the first man to set foot on Cape Ann, is referred to several times in *Maximus*.[19]

Contemplating Gloucester's beginnings and its subsequent history, Olson's imagination is particularly engaged by "fisherman's field," that spot in Gloucester on which the Massachusetts Colony was founded. It is the "first place Englishmen/ first felt the light and winds . . ." (p. 106; see also *"proem"*). There a fishing stage (or pier) was erected, a house built ("that first house, Roger Conant's"—p. 45), and to that place there came a ship's carpenter, sent out from the Plymouth Plantation. Characterized by Bradford as "an honest and very industrious man,"[20] he is conceived of by Olson as "the first Maximus/ . . . the first to make things,/ not just live off nature . . ." (p. 31). It may be that Olson thinks of John Smith as another spiritual ancestor, and that Smith holds his honored place in the *Maximus Poems* at least partly because he too fits into the pattern of firsts. Olson once designated Smith as "the first American writer,"[21] and in his essay on Smith called him "the man who, by 1614, *knew* the country as not only not one other did . . . he had the *first* of it. . . ."[22]

The concern with firsts in *Maximus* is extended to include mention of the first house settler after the Algonquins, the first children born in Gloucester, the first settler in Dogtown (a section of Gloucester). These last instances indicate that Olson's preoccupation with firsts can take the trivial form of antiquarianism. But that preoccupation begins to assume greater substance if we recognize its connection, in Olson's mind, with what he conceives of as the newness, freshness, attendant upon man's westerly motion. The venture of the Dorchester Company in setting up fishing on Cape Ann involved a "new frontier . . ." (p. 104). "A year that year/ was new to men . . ." (p. 108). Cape Ann became the boundary "between the old/ North Atlantic . . . and the new" (p. 120). John Smith was "one man who knew the new facts early,"[23] and his having named the region he mapped *New* England undoubtedly had a special significance for Olson. Captain Christopher Levett, who wrote *A Voyage into New England,* speaks, says Olson "of each/ new thing he saw and did/ in these new parts" (p. 134).[24]

While newness *per se* seems to hold a great attraction for Olson, the newness of early America takes on a special preciousness for him because it was, in his estimation, so quickly spoiled. (His vision here is akin to that of Fitzgerald at the end of *The Great Gatsby* with its famous invocation of the "fresh, green breast of the new world.") Precious firsts, in Olson's image of early America, were rapidly replaced by shameful ones. John Endecott, who came over in 1628 as a governor appointed by the New England Company (which had bought out the interests of the Dorchester Company) is regarded by Olson as "the first of . . . the shrinkers" (p. 46). Endecott displaced Roger Conant, an Olson hero, and one of his "first acts" was the taking over of the house used by Conant (p. 45). (This seems to parallel an earlier instance of unhappy displacement, in Olson's view, when Miles Standish rather than John Smith was chosen as a navigator by the Pilgrims.) Olson puts the matter strongly: Conant was "destroyed," while Endecott became a power in "a stooge State" (p. 47).

Olson's unfavorable image of Endecott (cf. Robert Lowell's portrait of the man in *The Old Glory,* to be considered in the next chapter) may have been shaped by his reading of

Rose-Troup's *John White,* which says that the Old Planters, settlers before Endecott's coming, were in effect treated like chattels after his arrival. "They protested against this proceeding, but they found themselves confronted by a Governor who ignored all claim to consideration for those who as pioneers, by their personal exertions, had provided a plantation for him to rule. . . ."[25] Also, Endecott comes over in Rose-Troup as an abrasive presence, contrasting with Conant, the "peace-lover," who tried to mitigate the effects of the new governor's arrival.[26] In another book which Olson appears to have read, Endecott, while defended, is cited as "the opposite of Conant; arbitrary and sometimes violent . . . bigoted. . . ."[27] Endecott is linked in *Maximus* to Francis Higginson, an early minister of Salem (who suggested that name for the place as opposed to its Indian designation of Naumkeag, which it had kept under Conant's rule). Higginson seems to serve for Olson as an example of religious intolerance.[28] The poet finds such intolerance also in John Winthrop's confrontation with Anne Hutchinson. Moreover, Winthrop did not sufficiently acknowledge the newness of America, trying to transplant to its shores notions from the Old World (though the poet's treatment of Winthrop on this score is a mixed one). Olson finds evidence in Winthrop's records that

> all was faulting,
> stiffening in the master
> founders [*sic*] wills—
>
> the things
> of this world (new
> world, Renaissance
> mind named
> what Moses men tried
>
> to twist back to Covenantal
> truth) Continental

> loci inside of which they'd
> dry, sweet souls. . . .
>
> (Pp. 130–31)

A settlement in its earliest stages, where there is barter and primary production, where there is "sowing,/ reaping, building/ houses," (p. 130; see also p. 72), where land has not yet become "merchandise"—such an economy, combined with religious tolerance and with the condition and appreciation of newness, would appear to constitute for Olson the basis of an ideal America, an ideal that enjoyed only the briefest existence:

> . . . the newness
>
> the first men knew was almost
> from the start dirtied
> by second comers.
>
> (Pp. 134–35)[29]

Neither Smith nor Levett nor Conant knew what we know—that "no one/ knew better/ than to cash in" on America (p. 135). The fall from American newness must have been a particularly bitter thing to contemplate for Olson, who conceived of us as "the last 'first' people."[30]

From Olson's picture of early America, then, two opposing patterns emerge. In the first, we find exploration, appreciation, and careful recording of the new, together with founding, building, and an attempt to ease conflict. The second pattern exhibits appropriation of what others have constructed, intolerance, exploitation, and a refusal or inability to recognize the new. (This twofold pattern is close to Williams's conception of early America in *In the American Grain*.) Olson apparently finds these patterns adumbrated in the activities of the Hawkins family of England—such at least would seem to be the relevance of their inclusion in

Maximus. William Hawkins traded *with* Negroes, achieving their trust, while his son, John Hawkins, traded *in* them:

> It was the son
> was knighted, the father
> I restore.
>
>   (P. 63)[31]

Olson links Sir John to people in Gloucester who profited from the slave trade, their white houses set in contrast to the black cargo of the slave ships that enriched them.[32]

The poet's seeing a mixed moral pattern in the Hawkins family, and his pointing to both good and bad elements in the early stages of America, would appear to preclude the kind of contrast between a noble past and a debased present that we sometimes get in the works, say, of Pound or Eliot or Lowell. But Olson, at several points, employs just such a contrast (being no more consistent in his relating of past to present than the other poets mentioned). Roger Conant, for example, is played off against James Conant, one-time president of Harvard (1933–53), who is seen as destroying the school's "local" character. Olson invokes "the old measure of care" in the unfavorable remarks he addresses to a Gloucester poet and editor, Vincent Ferrini, whom he thinks of as being "more like Gloucester now is/than I who hark back to an older polis. . ." (p. 20). In the early days of Gloucester, Olson contends, the economy involved the use of "real bucks" rather than the credit system employed today, one which he despises. The "new way" of his own era promotes "cleverness, the main chance is/ its law" (p. 21). The most striking and important example of Olson's setting past against present occurs in the statement "this epoch [is] solely/ the decline of fishes. . . " ("Kinnicum"). This assertion, taken by itself, appears bizarre, but not so in the context of the *Maximus Poems*.

Fish and fishing are, for Olson, inseparable from

Gloucester past and Gloucester present (the town is one of America's chief fishing ports). Olson calls our attention to the prominence of fish in the early records of the New World's northern waters. He notes that the northeast corner of America was designated as "Tierra de bacalaos" (land of the codfish) on early maps. Sir Walter Raleigh, Bartholomew Gosnold (who sailed along the New England coast in 1602), Martin Pring (who may have set foot on Cape Ann before Champlain) are all cited by Olson as searching for sassafras (supposedly a cure for veneral disease) but finding fish instead. Olson quotes Captain Levett's charming description of

> "the fish,
> . . . which we there saw,
>
> some with wings, others with manes,
> ears, heads, who chased
> one another with open mouths
> like stone Horses in a parcke"—
>
> (p. 135)

John Smith must own his place in Olson's affections at least partly because of his lyrical advocacy of fish as a great resource of the New World. Olson assigns to Smith the phrase "silver/ streames. . ." (p. 109). Here is the passage in Smith from which this is taken:

> never could the *Spaniard* with all his Mines of Gold and Silver, pay his debts, his friends, and Army, halfe so truly as the *Hollanders* still have done by this contemptible Trade of Fish. Divers (I know) may alleage many other assistances; but this is the chiefest Mine, and the Sea the source of those silver streames of all their vertue, which hath made them now the very miracle of industry, the onely patterne of perfection for these affaires: and the benefit of fishing is that *Primum Mobile* that turnes all their spheares to this height, of plentie, strength, honor, and exceeding great admiration.[33]

It may be the elements of praise and appreciation here that distinguish Smith's response, in Olson's mind, from a mere lust for wealth. The subject of fish elicits a lyrical strain from Olson himself. He echoes Smith's "silver streames" in this description of a stretch of ground on which fish are being cured:

> green fields
> to dry the silver wealth in steady
> sweetening sun
>
> ("Kinnicum")

Olson designates Gloucester as "Queen of the fishtowns" and says

> this coast is all it's
> made of, not soil
> not beaver
>
> fish fish fish
>
> (Pp. 103–4)

The celebration of fish wittily resists the mythological; the objects of praise are enough in themselves:

> Venus
>
> does not arise from
>
> these waters. Fish
>
> do.
>
> (Pp. 57–58)

Fish serves as a measure of value in *Maximus,* as Olson, in a passage addressed to Vincent Ferrini, tells him that his magazine "is not as good as fish is" (p. 19), that Ferrini lacks the will to be

                as fine as fins are
                            as firm as

                as firm as a mackerel is
                (fresh out of water)

                                            (P. 20)

    Fish take on a further value for Olson when he looks back
to the early days of America and finds a moral struggle. In his
formulation, America

                . . . was two things, first: the Banks
                        [i.e., the fishing banks]
                . . . .
                2nd, it was treasure. . . .

                                            (P. 62)

As the passage continues it becomes clear that the "trea-
sure" of the New World came to include not only jewels and
pearls, but Negro slaves as well. Olson appears to be making
a distinction between wealth that was based on nature's
abundance, and the riches that accrued from exploitation of
the blacks. The relation of this distinction to the twofold
pattern in Olson's image of early America, spoken of above,
is obvious. Fish provided the economic base for the potentially good society.
    As might be expected, the men who go out to catch the fish
are also celebrated by Olson, their deeds occupying a
substantial portion of *Maximus*. (On the level of popular
literature, Gloucester fishermen had been given heroic
treatment in the nineteenth-century novel *Captains
Courageous*.) It may be as a prototypical instance of the
fisherman as hero that the battle at Stage Head so appeals to
Olson and is featured in *Maximus*. The fight concerned a
stage or fishing pier that had been constructed in 1624 by men
from the Plymouth Plantation. In 1625, three vessels, two
representing the Dorchester Company, and one under the

command of a Captain Hewes, appeared at Cape Ann. Hewes's crew seized the fishing stage and, employing hogsheads as barricades, defied the men sent out from Plymouth under the leadership of Miles Standish. Olson uses the historical sources telling of the event in two very different ways. On the one hand, he seems desirous of contrasting the peacemaking efforts of Conant, who succeeded in avoiding bloodshed, with the belligerence of Standish, a belligerence made to seem comic. Olson cites the plaque set up to honor Conant, which finds in the event "A Notable Exemplification of/Arbitration" (p. 48), and he draws on a historian's comparison of Standish to a "little chimney" which Olson renders both as "Short Chimney" and "small chimney" (pp. 48, 112).[34] But he swings away from the contrast between the two men, with its apparent valuing of Conant's pacifying role, to a glorification of Hewes's militant energy:

> They should raise a monument
> to a fisherman crouched down
> behind a hogshead, protecting
> his dried fish
>
> (P. 114)[35]

(Olson apparently does not like the actual monument to fishermen that Gloucester has put up and that serves as a kind of trademark for the town.)

It is not such militant postures that Olson's other Gloucester fishermen characteristically assume, but they *are* made to seem heroic in their defiance of the elements, in their racing exploits, and in the rescues they perform. The perils of the fishery are brought before us by the inclusion of a considerable amount of documentary material,[36] and by Olson's citing the annual memorial services marking the deaths of thousands of Gloucester fishermen over the period of the town's history (p. 80).[37] With his affection and respect for them, it is no wonder that Olson comments harshly on an historical document that appears to criticize the fishermen of

Gloucester. After quoting from it, he says of its author, Stephen Higginson, "the son of a bitch" (p. 75). Olson's anger was undoubtedly fueled by Higginson's being a descendant of Francis Higginson, one of the villains in Olson's image of Massachusetts's early days.

Fishermen, as well as fish, serve as a standard of the good in *Maximus*. Seeing them as such, Olson at one point fuses the fisherman and his catch, saying that a magazine should be "as knowing as a halibut knows its grounds (as Olsen [a fisherman] knows/ those grounds)" (p. 19). For Olson, the fisherman is uncursed by worldly success:

> A fisherman is not a successful man
> he is not a famous man he is not a man
> of power, these are the damned by God
>
> (P. 153)

Maximus suggests that he tried fishing as a trade but that it was not, finally, for him. However, he apparently retains a connection with that occupation in his own mind for he characterizes himself as "a wind/ and water man. . ." (p. 53). (Olson himself once worked on a fishing boat and was reported to have turned up for a class he was teaching at Harvard in a fisherman's cape.)

Fish and fishermen provide in *Maximus* the most important link between present-day Gloucester and its past, where (and how charged this simple statement must have been for Olson) "fishing was first" (p. 45). It is a treasured continuity. Gloucester's involvement with the sea "still is . . ./. . . still goes on, still is/ what counts. . ." (p. 7). One passage connects the men originally set down on Cape Ann to carry on fishing, with Maximus, residing in contemporary Gloucester,

> where fishing continues
> and my heart lies
>
> (P. 108)

But all is not as well with the fishery in *Maximus* as such lines would suggest. It was noted earlier that Olson describes the contemporary period as marked by "the decline of fishes. . . ." There are a number of places in the poems where the contrast he sometimes sees between past and present extends to Gloucester's fishing industry as well. Relatively early in *Maximus,* Olson, after mentioning John White, wonders how he himself is to serve as a founder in his own time "now that even fishing . . ." (p. 45). The ellipsis is in the original, so that the statement merely dangles the implication that fishing has gone bad. Commenting on the line, Olson supplied the missing word: *stinks.*[38] Still, the bulk of the first volume of *Maximus* celebrates fish and fishing. But as we near the end of that book, we get a cluster of statements that point to Olson's alienation from fishing and from the sea. He calls fishermen "killers," and refers to the bad smell of the sea, the sea which is now associated for him with the East rather than the West. Instead of identifying Gloucester with America's Old West, he now says that some people he sees there "don't look like cowboys and English. . ." (p. 151). He finds that "it's earth which/ now is strange. . ." (p. 149).

Such statements anticipate the opening lines of one of the early sections of *Maximus* IV, V, VI:

> the Sea—turn yr Back on
> the Sea, go inland, to
> Dogtown: the Harbor
>
> the shore the City
> are now
> shitty, as the Nation
>
> is. . .
> ("MAXIMUS, FROM DOGTOWN—II")

We might note, too, that the stench of the sea in Gloucester

Harbor, handled either lightly or fleetingly in the first volume of *Maximus,* is given a page to itself in the second (see *"Part of the flower of Gloucester"*). In the first volume, Olson had urged the citizens of Gloucester not to allow themselves to be made "as the nation is. . ." (p. 11). The lines in *Maximus IV, V, VI* about turning one's back on the sea, with their syntactic and aural joining of *shore, City,* and *shitty,* indicate that that process has already taken place.[39]

The choice of Dogtown as an alternative to the sea may be explained in part by the history of this section of Gloucester. Once the place where the best families lived, it was gradually abandoned when their business interests turned from logging and farming to fishing and shipping.[40] Olson, then, is shifting his focus to a place which, in the history of Gloucester, is disassociated from fishing. So, even though they continue to make their appearance in *Maximus IV, V, VI,* and are celebrated there, the sea and its Gloucester fishermen of past and present undergo a certain displacement by the featuring of the Dogtown materials.

Dogtown figures in several ways in *Maximus IV, V, VI.* The area has a particularly interesting topography (its rock formations are tourist attractions), and this aspect of it is stressed by Olson. Thus, part of the strangeness and fascination that "earth" has for him lies in the domain of geology.[41] But the poet is only a part-time geologist, and a section incorporating technical topographical details somehow ends with a lyrical description of the Egyptian goddess Nut (see "The Cow/of Dogtown.").

Yet another curious combining of materials occurs in the following passage where technical details of earth science are juxtaposed with a personified seascape and elements drawn from the history of Dogtown:

> Into the granite this inlet
> of the sea to poke and jam the Cut and fight
> the sand off and the yelping rocks, the granite

he rolls as Dogtown throws its pebbles and Merry
lay among them, busted
                    True inclusions
of other rocks are not commonly met with,
in the granitic material, the mass of diorite
is apparently of an irregularly circular form
                                ("The River")

The reference to Merry looks back to an earlier section given over to him. James Merry was a seaman who, in the late 1880s, visited Spain and was greatly taken with the bullfighting he saw. When friends suggested that he show them how it was done, he began to wrestle with a young bull pastured at Dogtown. He was a big man (six feet seven) and had no trouble in throwing the animal. He staged several exhibitions of this manner of bullfighting. The following year, with the bull stronger and heavier, Merry became limp after a struggle with it and had to be rescued by spectators. Some weeks later he decided to wrestle the bull in private and went to where it was kept. When he did not return, his neighbors searched for him and found his lifeless body in the pasture. The bloody rocks and the trampled grass showed that the bull had thrown Merry's body against the boulders many times.[42] In Olson's telling of the tale, which is intermixed with mythological references and phraseology, the story takes on a kind of legendary or mythical flavor (and if Olson combines geology with references to Nut, he does the same with Merry). As such, the story links up with other legends that appear in *Maximus IV, V, VI,* and with Olson's retelling of the battles of the Titans and Olympians found in Hesiod's *Theogony*. It would appear to be the story of Merry that supplies a native mythological figure presented later in the book:

Dogtown's
secret

```
head
& shoulder

   bull's shoulder

lifting Portugese hill into the light
                    ("THE FRONTLET")
```

Apart from its geology and its serving as the setting for the legendary treatment of Merry, Dogtown figures as a place through which Olson re-creates the Gloucester past by a bare rendering of who lived where and at what time. Here is a sample:

> Lt James Davis 14 acres 1717 and to share 4
> more 1728/9 with his son-in-law James
> Stanwood—all on the east side of the lower
> road, defining therefore that stretch. . . .
> ("Further Completion of Plat")

The various modes in which the Dogtown material is presented in *Maximus IV, V, VI* produce an effect different from that generated by the first volume of the poems. In the earlier book, the focus on the fishery and the treatment of the historical materials seem aimed at establishing a Gloucester whose present has an important element of continuity with its past. Men in history, sometimes heroic but always human, link up with men of the present, and Olson-Maximus connects himself to both. With the concentration on the Dogtown materials, different results are produced. In the passages dealing with the geological material, the past of Gloucester is thrust back beyond the historic and human. Rock becomes protagonist. When Dogtown *is* brought into relationship with man, through Olson's tracings of one-time domiciles, history returns to the poems but in the form of a passionate antiquarianism indulged in by an isolated researcher investigating a vanished community. Neither the poet-investigator nor that community is joined to a social present. At one point Olson does acknowledge his readers (perhaps conceived of as natives of Gloucester), by saying "My problem is how to make you believe/ these persons. . ." ("Kinnicum"). His problem is to make us *care* about them, and his mere rendering of minutiae fails to accomplish this.[43] Focusing on a particular figure in history, Merry, Olson confers on him a mythical rather than historical status. Such replacement or specialization or deformation of historical materials as we get in Olson's approach to Dogtown is undoubtedly related to the large drama of the unstable relationship between Olson-Maximus and the Gloucester community he inhabits.

Once, speaking of historical study, Olson asserted that the "Best thing to do is *to dig one thing or place or man* until you yourself know more abt [*sic*] that than is possible to any other man."[44] The *Maximus Poems* are testimony to Olson's digging Gloucester (thereby becoming like the man in the work who has his "house" on his head). Olson-Maximus starts from an initial position of intimate acquaintance with the town: he has known it since he was a boy, is particularly well-versed in its streets (having traversed them as a postman), and resides in it in the present of the poems. He is able to refer repeatedly to local details, scenes, and events. In addition to this he has made a study of the history of the place, a history to which he sees his own life joined. As a young man he scratched his legs getting up rocks at the site where the original fourteen men of the Dorchester Company set up camp. The place where there was a contest over the fishing stage is "literally in my own front yard. . . ." (p. 100). Several times an action of his is immediately given an historical setting. Gloucester is where he is "founded"; it is the "land I am shod in. . ." ("which now backs down the new houses").

At times his feeling for this place is intensely loving. The very first page of *Maximus* asks for a blessing on the roofs "of my city. . ." (p. 1). Gloucester is a "rare" place which he hopes will not be made like the rest of the country. While its past is of great interest, it need not be urged to return to that past, for in its present "polis/ still thrives" (p. 22), "polis" apparently signifying for Olson a healthy community. But as we have already seen, the Gloucester present does not always hold up when measured against the past, and the polis which can be seen as thriving on one page is, on another, made up only of a few people who are not readily identifiable (see pp. 11, 18). Similarly, the capacity for perception which Olson connects with polis is first accorded to all people, but then attributed only to a minority:

> It is not true that the many,
> even in fishing, say, Gloucester,
> are the gauge
> . . . .
> so few
> have the polis
> in their eye
>
> (P. 28)

A number of the sections of *Maximus* are titled as letters addressed to Gloucester, presumably as a collective entity, but at one point Maximus addresses himself to

> Isolated persons in Gloucester . . .
> you islands
> of men and girls
>
> (P. 12)

These materials, along with the poems' inconsistent attitudes toward the state of the fishery in contemporary Gloucester, add up to a decidedly ambivalent stance on Olson's part with respect to the place which he conceives of as the root of his being and which he has attempted to take possession of through his imagination. (A similar ambivalence can be found in William Carlos Williams's *Paterson*).

Gloucester is at once the great good place for him, separate from the corruption and commercialism of the rest of the country, and not really distinguishable from contemporary America. Its history functions in some parts of *Maximus* as a heritage that the poet as citizen wishes to bring to the attention of his townsmen for a shared exploration and celebration. But it also seems to function as a means of retreating from the present into a domain occupied solely by the poet. Olson, in effect, acknowledges this when he says, near the end of the first volume:

> Go 'way and leave
> Rose-Troup and myself
>
> (P. 150)

The poet is apparently trying to wave the present out of sight and immerse himself in the story of Gloucester's beginnings, provided by the historian Francis Rose-Troup, as a drug against current exacerbations. The focus on geology and the investigation of Dogtown minutiae in *Maximus IV, V, VI* can be seen as two extensions of this action. The first removes the human and historic completely;[45] the second reintroduces them but only in the form of a kind of archaeology centered on a lost community, which the poet is pursuing as a private passion rather than as a shared heritage. The figure of Merry, given legendary status, should be thought of in connection with Olson's retelling of Hesiod's story of Typhon, imprisoned in Tartarus by Zeus. Typhon and Merry (whose great height was approximately that of Olson) are both defeated titanic figures, perhaps anticipated by the Gloucester councilman John Burke of the first volume, who is a hero for Olson, but an isolated and beaten one. These may well serve in Olson's mind, consciously or unconsciously, as representatives of himself, defeated by a Gloucester that has betrayed its past, a town from which he has become alienated even while trying to serve it. Consider Olson, in real life, soaking up news of Gloucester from the local paper, and writing outraged letters to that publication protesting the town's apparent willingness to sacrifice the visible monuments of its past to the commercial interests of its present.[46] Within *Maximus* itself Dogtown is threatened by the building of a reservoir.

It should be noted that Olson does not simply begin with an embrace of Gloucester and then retreat to a position of alienation. The *Maximus Poems* shift back and forth between these stances, but there does seem to be an overall movement from the first to the second, accompanied by a tendency to replace the historical-public rendering of the past by a mythological-private one.

Maximus IV, V, VI can be said to seek an escape from that movement, from the fracturing of the poet's fusion with Gloucester. There is an attempt to soften the effects of suffering, rejection, separation, and conflict. At least such an interpretation might be placed on a number of the elements of that volume. If Olson turns his back on the sea to go inland to Dogtown, he has first presented an image of "WATERED ROCK" which links up with his image of "Okeanos *under/* Dogtown" ("MAXIMUS FROM DOGTOWN—I"). That is to say the rock of Dogtown and water are conceived of as being in union. If Merry was broken on the rock, Olson is somehow able to think of it as "Soft soft rock" ("subterranean and celestial"). The grubs that feed on Merry's body remove its odor from the air, and later the smell of fish (remember the association of bad smells with Maximus's alienation) is similarly removed. If Typhon and Zeus are presented as clashing, Typhon is last mentioned as the product of union between Earth and Tartarus. Moreover, we get a proliferation, in a mythologized setting, of maternal and paternal images—"heavenly mother," "Ma the Morphic," "Pa the City," "Mother Dogtown," "Father Sea" (the nutritive figures of Nut and Audumala, a figure from Scandinavian mythology, can be seen as connected to the maternal images). Okeanos is "the one which all things are" ("MAXIMUS, FROM DOGTOWN—I"), and Olson may be indicating that the contradictory chronology of events in Hesiod points to the unity of things which straightforward chronology artificially separates. Earth, heaven, ocean—all connect. Such images and concepts are in sharp contrast to a Dogtown serving as alternative to a rejected ocean, to a Merry smashed by the bull, to gods in conflict, to an Olson disgusted with his town. The elements of pain and isolation in these materials are denied or significantly qualified by the sense of well-being and connection that arises from the concept of an Okeanos. ("Oceanus" appears on the cover of *Maximus IV, V, VI,* which, Olson tells us significantly, pictures the world "before Earth started to come apart at the seams. . . .")[47] But Olson has achieved mitigation of alienation, discord, and coming apart in *Maximus IV, V, VI* only by admitting into it the theomorphism and "transubstantiations" he apparently rejected in the first volume of *Maximus,* where "waters . . . are tides . . ./are not gods" (p. 25), and where fish arise from those waters, not Venus. To a large extent such metamorphoses displace the historical or make room only for a trivial form of it.

The historical materials in *Maximus IV, V, VI* that are not merely tracings of who lived where in Dogtown either tend to echo or overlap what the first volume has presented more coherently, or else consist of isolated items—an encounter with Indians, a battle against the British—which do not seem to have much point, or any role to play in a larger pattern. There is indeed a distinct diffusiveness in *Maximus IV, V, VI,* a flying apart of its subject matter, though Olson seems to be making a claim of coherence (the formal equivalent of his efforts at showing union, reconciliation) when he speaks of "putting things together/ which had not previously/ fit" ("All night long"). In his own mind something has taken shape after an original sense of aimlessness:

> now I see what was up,
> a year ago, chomping around these streets,
> measuring off distances, looking into
> records, disconsolately
> making up things to do. . . .
>
> ("any man")

But the reader too often does not see what is up, as personal anecdotes, Greek terms, bits of Scandinavian mythology, speculations about the Phoenicians, musings about ship-building in eighteenth-century Gloucester, pass before his eyes. Here is historical and literary overload. Diversity of subject matter is accompanied by diversity of form, or at least of typographical arrangement, often making for obscurity and preciousness more than anything else. A number of the pages are assigned specific dates, presumably the times at which they were composed, and the inclusion of these adds to one's sense of viewing random jottings, a diary of disparities, rather than a developing whole. The historical materials of the first volume of *Maximus* were overly preoccupied with "firsts," made too much of a single episode (the fight at the fishing pier) or of minor figures, provided only a sketchy view of ideals and evils as Olson saw them in our past. But those materials were part of an interesting, at times engaging, attempt to maximize the local and its past, to make us appreciate objects and an occupation taken for granted (fish and fishing), to establish the widest possible context for place (Gloucester) and for the self in a place. Moreover, those materials provided a kind of ballast for the work. Olson, having pretty much mined the matters of exploration and of Gloucester's beginnings, finds in *Maximus IV, V, VI* no historical subjects to take their place, with the trivial exception of the settlers and domiciles of old Dogtown. There is little pleasure or interest in the pages given over to them.

Perhaps those pages, as well as many others in *Maximus*

IV, V, VI—dull, obscure, disjointed—result from an excessive carrying out of Olson's notion that what is important in historical study is the individual's subjective use of his knowledge. Employing John Smith's statement that "history is the memory of time" as a section title in the first volume of *Maximus*, Olson rearranges it to read "my memory is/ the history of time" in the second volume. Alienated from Gloucester, he alienates the reader by his indulgence in the subjective. Meandering through history, he serves it up piecemeal and pointless, employing a combination of traditional and homebrewed mythology to obliterate the oppressive, to join himself to the world, and perhaps to overcome a sense of his own fragmentedness as poet and historian.[48]

NOTES

1. At the time this chapter was written, only two volumes of the *Maximus Poems* had appeared (the sections of which Olson sometimes calls "letters"). A third volume was issued in 1975. The first volume is entitled *The Maximus Poems* (New York: Jargon/Corinth Books, 1960); the second, *Maximus Poems IV, V, VI* (London: Cape Goliard Press, 1968, in association with Grossman Publishers, New York). The two volumes, considered as a whole, will be referred to in the text as "the *Maximus Poems*" or simply as "*Maximus*." The first volume is paginated, and quotations from it will be followed in the text by the relevant page numbers. Any quotation from the second volume, which is not paginated, will be followed in the text by the opening line of the page on which the quotation is found.

2. Gondwanaland is a great land mass that is thought to have existed at one time, and that supposedly included South America, Africa, southern Asia, and Australia.

3. Olson's linkage of Tyre and Gloucester may appear idiosyncratic, but compared with other attempts to join the Phoenicians with the Western Hemisphere it seems tame. See, e.g., George Jones, *The History of Ancient America, Anterior to the Time of Columbus; Proving the Identity of the Aborigines with the Tyrians and Israelites* (London: Longman, Brown, Green and Longmans, 1843); Thomas Cranford Johnson, *Did the Phoenicians Discover America?* (San Francisco: no publisher listed, 1892); and Joseph C. Ayoob, *Were the Phoenicians the First to Discover America?* (Aliquippa, Pa.: no publisher listed, 1951). For information on Tyre and the Phoenicians, see George Rawlinson, *The Story of Phoenicia* (New York: G. P. Putnam's Sons, 1889), and Wallace B. Fleming, *The History of Tyre* (New York: Columbia University Press, 1915).

4. See Charles Olson, *A Bibliography of America for Ed Dorn* (San Francisco, Calif.: Four Seasons Foundations, distributed by City Lights Books, 1964), p. 7.

5. Victor Bérard, *Did Homer Live?* (New York: E. P. Dutton & Co. 1931), pp. 20, 177.

6. See *The Geography of Strabo*, translated by Horace Leonard Jones, 8 vols., Loeb Classical Library (London; W. Heinemann, 1917), 1:530.

7. Ibid., 1:399.

8. Charles Olson, *Human Universe and Other Essays* (San Francisco, Calif.: Auerhahn Society, 1965), p. 133.

9. It was Prince Charles who changed this name to "Cape Ann," so it is puzzling to see Olson state that Smith "pointed/ out/ Cape Ann,/ named her/ so it's stuck . . ." (p. 124). But Smith did give New England her name.

10. "Smith sent them a map. The map. The whole middle coast. So known, so done, the states still stand their boundaries by it." Olson, *Human Universe*, p. 135. In the first volume of the *Maximus* poems Smith is called "the stater of/ quantity and/ precision . . ." (p. 122).

11. *Travels and Works of Captain John Smith*, ed. Edward Arber, 2 vols. (Edinburgh: J. Grant, 1910), 2:719, 708.

12. Charles Herbert Levermore, *Forerunners and Competitors of the Pilgrims and Puritans*, (Brooklyn, N.Y.: New England Society of Brooklyn, 1912), vol. 2, p. 644.

13. Frances Rose-Troup, *The Massachusetts Bay Company and its Predecessors* (New York: Grafton Press, 1930); idem, *John White: The Patriarch of Dorchester and the Founder of Massachusetts 1575–1648, with an Account of the Early Settlement in Massachusetts 1620–1630* (New York: G.P. Putnam's Sons, 1930).

14. See Rose-Troup, *Massachusetts Bay Company*, p. 15.

15. Actually, Gloucester's "place in the genetic world" was conferred on her at least as early as 1854 in John Wingate Thornton's *The Landing at Cape Ann* (Boston: Gould and Lincoln, 1854), a work cited by Rose-Troup and one that Olson seems to have known. It is apparently Olson's concern with establishing Gloucester as a founding settlement, independent of the plantation at Plymouth, that leads him to focus on an apparently trivial historical incident whose significance can only be ascertained by referring to Rose-Troup's book on John White. Alluded to in the first volume of *Maximus* (pp. 115–16), and given two separate pages to itself in the second volume (see "Going Right Out of the Century," and "John Watts took"), the incident in question involves the taking by John Watts, a member of the Dorchester Company, of some salt stored on an island off the Gloucester coast. Rose-Troup says: "Apparently a small affair, but resulting in providing for the historian of New England material of enormous value in the elucidation of the story of the Dorchester Company. . . . It indicates the independence of their settlement from the Plymouth Colonists, who, though charged by the accused with complicity in the use of the missing goods, were not included as defendants. . . ." *John White*, p. 103. The theft of the salt is taken up once more in the third volume of the Maximus poems.

16. Charles Olson, *Call Me Ishmael* (New York: Reynal and Hitchcock, 1947), p. 15.

17. The figure of Ousoos or Usous occurs in a work on the Phoenicians by Sanchonintho, who presumably is the Sanuncthion referred to by Olson ("Sanuncthion lived"). See *The Theology of the Phoenicians by Sanchonintho*, translated by Philo, a native of Dyblos, and from the Greek into English by I.P. Cory in *The Phenix: A Collection of Old and Rare Fragments* (New York: William Gowan, 1835).

18. In a context that appears to be related to the Phoenicians but where the subject of the verb is not spelled out, Olson refers to "the 1st to navigate/ those waters . . ." (" 'View': fr the Orontes").

19. It may be Olson's preoccupation with firsts that explains the place given by *Maximus* to one Altham, who, like John Watts (see note 15) is a decidedly minor figure in New England history but one magnified by Olson's rendering. Distorting the historical record somewhat, Olson presents an account of a shipwreck in which Altham was supposedly involved. Actually, Altham had only heard of the wreck in question. Olson may have been trying, in addition to supplying dramatic immediacy, to give Altham heroic status by making him a direct participant. His featuring of Altham could derive from the man's having been captain of a pinnace, the *Little James*, which "may have been the first of the vessels 'of good burden and extraordinary Mould,' designed to be built by the Council for New England, to lie upon the coast for the defense of merchants and fishermen employed there. . . ." See Worthington Ford's edition of William Bradford's *History of Plymouth Plantation*, 2 vols. (Massachusetts Historical Society, 1912), 1:314n. (No place of publication is specified.) Altham's account states of the wrecked ship that "halfe her plancke timbers and knes [pieces of timber used to secure parts of a ship] were broken on such sort that then she was thought impossible to hold together. . . ." 404n. This apparently is the source of Olson's saying that Altham and another swam "until/ their knees/ were smashed/ on small rocks/ as their poor pinnace likewise poorly lay . . ." ("of the Pilgrimes going").

20. William Bradford, *Of Plymouth Plantation*, ed. Samuel Eliot Morison (New York: Alfred A. Knopf, 1952), p. 146.

21. *Charles Olson Reading at Berkeley*, transcribed by Zoe Brown San Francisco, Calif.: Coyote, distributed by City Lights Bookstore, 1966, p. 40.

22. Olson, *Human Universe*, p. 132. Italics in original.

23. Ibid., p. 134.

24. In *Call Me Ishmael*, the word *new*, used in connection with American materials, is capitalized twice. See pp. 19, 65 of that book.

25. Rose-Troup, *John White*, pp. 119–20.

26. Ibid., p. 121.

27. Thornton, *Landing at Cape Ann*, pp. 66–67.

28. Olson once said that ". . . Higginson, the minister of Salem, started everything that is . . . what we protest today." *Charles Olson Reading at Berkeley*, p. 37.

29. Cf. Olson's quoting with strong approval words he attributes to Winthrop: "They don't know they spoil—and from the beginning" ("JW (from the Danelaw) says:"). Olson does not supply the context.

30. He went on to say: "We forget that. We act big, misuse our land, ourselves."
Olson, *Call Me Ishmael,* p. 14.

31. Olson says "(the family/ span [*sic*] America from the finding/ to the settling
of those fisherman [*sic*],/ Dorchester Company, Cape Ann)" (p. 64).

32. I base this observation on the assumption that we are meant to detect a
connection between a passage on p. 5 of *The Maximus Poems* and one on p. 63—see
also p. 110 of that volume, where slavery is linked to dubious practices in the
fishery.

33. *Travels and Works of Captain John Smith,* 2:709.

34. The "little chimney" comparison is cited in Rose-Troup, *John White,* p. 90.

35. In my chapter on Lowell, I note a comparable split between that poet's
pacifist stance and his attraction to war.

36. Olson was probably following the examples of Pound and Williams in
including generous portions of prose in a long poetic work.

37. See George H. Procter, *The Fisherman's Memorial and Record Book*
(Gloucester, Mass.: Procter Bros., 1873).

38. *Charles Olson Reading at Berkeley,* p. 36.

39. The reaction against fishing in *Maximus IV, V, VI* appears to extend even to
the past. In that volume a more prominent place is given to corrupt practices in the
fishery of old, whereby defective fish were marketed. Cf. p. 110 of *The Maximus
Poems* with the passage beginning "o John Josselyn you" in *Maximux IV, V, VI*
("will be necessary on the covers of the TV dinners").

40. See Roger W. Babson and Foster H. Saville, *Cape Ann: A Tourist Guide*
(Rockport, Mass.: Cape Ann Old Bookshop, 1936), p. 18.

41. A major source of *Maximus,* John J. Babson's *History of the Town of
Gloucester, Cape Ann, Including the Town of Rockport* (Gloucester, Mass.:
Procter Bros., 1860), has an opening chapter given over to the topography of
Gloucester, and this may have influenced Olson's stress on it in *Maximus.*

42. See Melvin T. Copeland and Elliot C. Rogers, *The Saga of Cape Ann*
(Freeport, Me.: Bond Wheelwright Co., 1960), pp. 36–37.

43. "Gee," says Olson at one point, "what I call the upper road was the way/
leading by Joshua Elwell's to the wood-lots/ 1727" ("Gee, what I call the upper
road was the way"). What reader can be expected to care?

44. Olson, *A Bibliography of America for Ed Dorn,* p. 13. Italics in original.

45. Although Olson would argue that the geology of a place and the human life
there are inseparable.

46. See the Olson file in the Sawyer Free Library in Gloucester.

47. This statement can be found on the back of the title page of *Maximus IV, V,
VI.*

48. For views of Olson that endorse his use of mythology and that see him not as
fragmented but as offering an authentic mode of composition, see *Boundary 2,* 2,
Nos. 1–2 (Fall 1973–Winter 1974), passim. I should add here that the appearance of
Volume 3 has done nothing to shift my view of the defects of the *Maximus Poems.*
Volume 3, published posthumously, and edited by Charles Boer and George F.
Butterick, serves up a mix of materials very similar to that found in the earlier
books: personal anecdote or reminiscence, historical minutiae (or speculations

thereon), mythological references (more often obscure than not), and geological observations (now focused not so much on the rock of Dogtown as on the shifting of earth's land masses). Familiar too is the telegraphic, broken style of much of the verse. There is a new stress on the poet's sense of connectedness with his father, and an awareness of his own aging. Also, while Olson speaks of writing "a Republic/ in gloom," and gives other evidence of his disappointment with Gloucester and the nation, I find less of this in Volume 3 than a spirit of celebration and reverence, as he renders landscapes and seascapes, observes the tides, or muses on the movements of the earth and of its peoples.

11

The Flintlocks of the Fathers: Robert Lowell's Treatment of the American Past

> *In the writing of a poem all our compulsions*
> *and biases should get in, so that finally we don't*
> *know what we mean.*
>
> *Robert Lowell*

Land of Unlikeness, Robert Lowell's first book of verse, opened with "The Park Street Cemetery." We can see, in retrospect, that that poem's graveyard setting, its roll call of "the stern surnames: Adams,/Otis, Hancock, Mather, Revere," announced Lowell's long-sustained concern with the "fathers" of our country, with our native past, mainly as it had been forged in New England.

Given Lowell's lineage, this backward gaze, incorporating local and familial elements, seems only natural. The prominence of New England Lowells, generation after generation, is well known. On his mother's side the poet could count among his ancestors Edward Winslow, a Mayflower passenger and governor of the Plymouth plantation, as well as John Stark, a hero of the American Revolution.[1]

While such credentials establish Lowell in as long and distinguished a line of native descent as any American can claim, his treatment of the past is no simple matter of piety or celebration, though such strains can be found in his work.

255

Nor does he merely rebel against his status as a "Lowell" and condemn the past. Viewed as a whole, Lowell's treatment of American history presents a tangle of tonalities, his varying attitudes sometimes jarring against each other in a single poem or in different versions of the same poem. His feelings about the past show themselves to be in a state of flux throughout much of his career, self intersecting with history in a shifting drama. That self is immersed in an anxious, violent present which is our common property, and that immersion has helped give Lowell's handling of our past its intense and protean nature as well as its public scope.

The strongest impression of Lowell's presentation of American history, at least on a first reading, is that he did not so much turn *to* the past as turn *on* it. The nodal points of our history are, in his poems as well as in his dramatic trilogy *The Old Glory*, the unjust use of collective violence against man or against nature. The earliest victims were the Indians, their plight treated or alluded to in "Children of Light," "Concord," "At the Indian Killer's Grave," *Endecott & The Red Cross* (the first part of *The Old Glory*), and "Northwest Savage." At least two and possibly three of these works are based on King Philip's War (1675–77), which takes its name from a leading sachem who organized his people against the white settlers. Philip was eventually killed, his head mounted on a pole in Plymouth. Lowell's attention might have been engaged by this particular struggle because during it his ancestor Josiah Winslow, like his father Edward a governor of Plymouth, was put in charge of a thousand men to carry out an expedition against the Narragansetts. In the course of the campaign an Indian stronghold was successfully attacked, its defenders massacred. Wigwams containing tubs of corn were put to the torch. This last may be what Lowell is referring to in the final lines of "Children of Light" which speaks of the "burning, burning [of] the unburied grain." The poem points up the callousness of the Puritans towards the Indians by showing the whites as having, so to speak, domesticated violence, made it casual: "Our fathers wrung their bread from stocks and stones/ And fenced their gardens with the Redman's bones. . . ." King Philip is named explicitly in "Concord," which may be said to turn into an anti–"Concord Hymn." Emerson's famous concluding line celebrating the Revolutionary battle at Concord—"And fired the shot heard round the world"—is transformed by Lowell into "The death-dance of King Philip and his scream/ Whose echo girdled this imperfect globe."

"At the Indian Killer's Grave" employs for its epigraph a reference to King Philip's War found in Hawthorne's story "The Gray Champion": "Here, also, are the veterans of King Philip's War, who burned villages and slaughtered young and old, with pious fierceness, while the godly souls throughout the land were helping them with prayer." The selectivity involved in the use of this excerpt points up the animus of Lowell's poem. For "The Gray Champion" is basically a tale *praising* an event of our history, the defiance by some colonists of the British authorities in Boston. The passage taken by Lowell gives no indication of this, and the spirit of a remark that is marginal in the Hawthorne story becomes central to Lowell's poem. Out of King Philip's severed head issues a voice mocking Puritan assumptions about the "election" of souls, and jeering at the one-time power of the Puritan state. The Pilgrim Fathers are threatened with a Day of Judgment that will be unfavorable, rather than a confirmation of their virtue. The only two persons named in the poem, aside from Philip, are John and Mary Winslow, ancestors of Lowell buried in the graveyard where the poem is set. Though the poet has, in effect, misrepresented a particular Hawthorne story in his choice of epigraph, he has displayed a Hawthorne-like guilt about ancestral wrongdoing.

But the earlier writer could take pride in the rebellious colonial energies that culminated in the War of Independence, whereas Lowell's references to the Revolution are

generally no more admiring of the victors there than are his
treatments of those who triumphed over the Indians. That
the two violent enterprises are connected in his mind is
suggested by an early poem, "Song of the Boston Nativity,"
with its lines

> "here all
> The Mathers, Eliots and Endicots [*sic*]
>   Brewed their own gall,
>   Here Concord's shot that rang
>   Became their boomerang."[2]

John Endecott or Endicott was a Puritan leader who headed
the first organized campaign to suppress the Indians (in
Endecott & the Red Cross Lowell has him order the shooting
of some Indian captives). In "Concord," as we have already
seen, the description of King Philip's death-scream alludes
invertedly to Emerson's laudatory characterization of the
battle of Concord. An earlier version of Lowell's poem[3] did
not refer to Philip but did cite "the fathers' flintlock guns"
used in that Revolutionary battle. Although dropped from
the revised "Concord," the flintlocks associated with the
American Revolution make dubious appearances elsewhere
in the Lowell canon. In Section I of "The First Sunday in
Lent," a flintlock is linked with a "cannister/ Preserved
from Bunker Hill" and "stolen agates. . . ." The poem is
framed by references to "the crooked family chestnut" and
"the tormented chestnut tree. . . ." These details, particularly the ambiguous syntax of "crooked family chestnut,"
would seem to suggest a family tradition tainted with guilt.
Flintlock and Bunker Hill occur together in "Rebellion," in
which the speaker describes having sent his father crashing
into the family heirlooms: "You damned/ My arm that cast
your house upon your head/ And broke the chimney flintlock
on your skull." The speaker says he had signed a pact "to
contract/ The world that spreads in pain," and concludes, in
the original version:

My bondsmen, having had their fill,
No longer line the ditch at Bunker Hill
Where the clubbed muskets broke the redcoat's brain.[4]

This poem may be thought of as dramatizing a rebellion by the speaker-son against a tradition of violence symbolized by the family heirlooms of the Revolution. (One cannot help thinking of Lowell's own lineage and life, of both his ancestor John Stark, a hero of Bunker Hill, and of the poet's serving a jail sentence as a conscientious objector in World War II.) A flintlock makes another appearance in *My Kinsman, Major Molineux* (the second part of *The Old Glory*). Like the Hawthorne story that is its source, Lowell's drama is set in the Revolutionary period. Again like the story, the play concentrates on the gay cruelty of the populace as it rises up against its British ruler. It is not a glorious revolution. Boy, younger brother of Robin (the drama's protagonist), demonstrates his mindless appetite for violence, his affinity for the play's milieu, by his intense desire for a flintlock.

Contemplating Boy, his craving for a gun, his generic name which in itself designates him a moral lightweight, one is reminded of the quotation from Melville that Lowell incorporated in "Christmas Eve Under Hooker's Statue": "All wars are boyish." In this poem, the Civil War, like King Philip's War and the American Revolution, becomes for Lowell part of a national heritage of violence, futile and destructive. The heels of General Hooker, who commanded the Union Army at Chancellorsville, are described as "Kicking at nothing in the shifting snow." He is joined thematically to Mars, the "blundering butcher. . . ."

The violence of our wars is not the only kind that Lowell treats. In "Rebellion," the son who turns away from a family tradition that, in effect, celebrates such violence, has a dream in which "Behemoth and Leviathan/ Devoured our mighty merchants. None could arm/ Or put to sea." The juxtaposition of the mighty merchants and military violence, of putting to sea and arming, may be said to be explicated by "The Quaker Graveyard in Nantucket." That work deals in part with the hunting of sperm whales, a major American business in the nineteenth century, and one viewed by the poem in terms that derive largely from Melville's *Moby-Dick*. "Quaker Graveyard" associates the whale hunt with war, and one section of the poem depicts terrific violence directed against the whale. The relation of man to Nature here is one of antagonism and brutal exploitation. One thinks of "At the Indian Killer's Grave" with its characterization of the Puritans as hurling "Anathemas at nature and the land. . . ."

Common to the violence against men and the violence against nature in the American past depicted by Lowell is the moral smugness directing the use of force. Indian killers conceive of themselves as "Children of Light," the elect of God. Quaker hunters of the whale contend that God is on their side. (A *light-night* rhyme is present in both "At the Indian Killer's Grave" and "Quaker Graveyard," the light an ironic presence in each of the two poems.) Self-righteousness, somewhat secularized, accompanies the violence of *The Old Glory,* particularly in *Benito Cereno*. In killing Babu, Captain Delano feels himself sanctioned by God and country. The play's chauvinistic references to New England link Delano's assumptions to the spirit behind the slaughter in "Children of Light" and "At the Indian Killer's Grave," the Captain proving himself a true descendant of the Puritans.

"Mr. Edwards and the Spider" and "After the Surprising Conversions," companion pieces based on the life and writings of Jonathan Edwards, offer a variation on the theme of self-righteousness in America's past. Edwards's famous sermon on the punishment of the wicked in hell, a source of the first of these poems, can be seen as incorporating a violence of the imagination directed against his listeners.

The second of the poems tells of a member of the congregation, Josiah Hawley, responding in his induced guilt with an
act of self-violence, cutting his own throat (this is based on
an actual episode). As one critic has pointed out, Edwards
does not seem at any point in "After the Surprising Conversions" to see the role he has played in bringing about
Hawley's death.[5]

The unfavorable conception of the past that I have been
tracing links up with Lowell's notion that the present is a
continuation or repetition of the past. The poet's mind is
thrust back into history by the fact of contemporary violence, accounting for the latter by locating historical pro-
totypes, which suggest that the use of force is in the
American grain. The present repeats the violent past, and in
some of Lowell's poems the temporal distinction between
the two is lost; they are collapsed into a single present. In
"Quaker Graveyard," e.g., the poet's consideration of the
nineteenth-century whalers is touched off by the death at sea
during World War II of his cousin, Warren Winslow. The
clippers and lances of the bygone era have been replaced by
the warships and guns of our time, but the voyage of the
whaleboats, the hurting of their prey, are shaped so as to be
occurring in the present, fusing with the activity of the
modern dreadnoughts. The strategy in *Benito Cereno* is
somewhat different. There, the action is kept in the past, set
about 1800, but elements of the play suggest contemporary
American attitudes and this country's current position in the
world. Perkins, the bosun, complains that the people on a
foreign ship who have been given aid "think America is
Santa Claus." And Captain Delano (who reminded people of
Lyndon Johnson) asserts: "This old world needs new blood/
and Yankee gunnery to hold it up." The play, then, retaining
an historical character, points up a continuity of dubious
national behaviour extending into our time.

Less prominent and commented upon than his pejorative
presentation of the American past, but undeniably present in

his writings, is Lowell's admiration for or attraction to certain elements of his personal or regional heritage. "For the Union Dead," which Lowell gave weight to by making it the title poem for one of his books, offers high praise to Colonel Robert Shaw, who led a New England regiment of Negroes during the Civil War. It may be that Lowell's interest in Shaw was sparked by a kind of family connection. Charles Russell Lowell, Jr., perhaps the most dashing and attractive member of the entire Lowell clan, and the ancestor the poet said he would most like to have known,[5] was a brother-in-law of Colonel Shaw. He wrote of the Colonel: ". . . I am thankful they buried him 'with his niggers.' "[7] "For the Union Dead" refers to this same fact: "Shaw's father wanted no monument/ except the ditch,/ where his son's body was thrown/ and lost with his 'niggers.' " Himself a hero of the Civil War, Charles Russell serves as the admired subject of one of Lowell's later poems, "Charles Russell Lowell: 1835–1864." (Perhaps a fusion of the two heroes had taken place years before in Lowell's mind when he wrote "Falling Asleep over the Aeneid," with its speaker's reference to "My Uncle Charles" and his "colored volunteers.") Lowell's respective poems about the brothers-in-law are of a piece in their admiring tone, their glorification of military valor. As such, they are in distinct contrast to his treatments of war examined earlier. Lowell's handling of American wars appears to have tapped very different currents of feeling in him: he combines a pacifist's hatred of violence with an armchair general's fascinated regard for combat.[8] He can treat the latter aspect of himself humorously, as when he depicts Allen Tate discussing with him the battle of Gettysburg, "both of us too much the soldier from Sourmash. . . ." But a real attraction to war emerges as "Ashtrays and icecubes deployed as Pickett's columns [become] / a sloping forest of flashing steel."

An implicit pride in his family's connection with the American Revolution shows up in Lowell's elegy "In Mem-

ory of Arthur Winslow." He depicts Winslow, his grandfather, as trying through the accumulation of a fortune to live
up to an imposing ancestral legacy which includes military
achievement. Winslow is seen as attempting to "give back
life to men who whipped or backed the King." While this
motive is attributed to his grandfather, one detects a be-
stowing of accolades on the participants in the conflict by
Lowell himself. This impression is strengthened by reading
"Salem" with its closing lines: "Where was it that New
England bred the men/ Who quartered the Leviathan's fat
flanks/ And fought the British Lion to his knees?"

In his poems celebrating the past, the present is conceived
of as degenerate, lacking the heroism or accomplishments or
moral seriousness of earlier times. (Thus, Lowell's present,
seen either as extension of the past or in contrast to it, tends
to be viewed with disdain.) An example can be found in the
"Dunbarton" section of the Arthur Winslow elegy, set in a
New Hampshire cemetery containing graves of Lowell's
maternal ancestors. (Dunbarton was founded in part by his
forebear John Stark—the place was originally called
Starkstown—and it furnishes the setting for several of
Lowell's poems.) Lowell speaks of the graveyard trees

> . . . watching for the day
> When the great year of the little yeomen come
> Bringing its landed Promise and the faith
> That made the Pilgrim Makers take a lathe
> And point their wooden steeples lest the Word be dumb.

This passage, referring to a homely, dignified faith, is played
off against the "mouthings" of the modern minister who
waves the shades of the buried "out of sight and out of
mind." It is in the next section of the Winslow elegy that
Lowell shows his grandfather (who is part of Lowell's
present) as trying *in vain* to match ancestral achievements.
The poem regards his making of a fortune as simply not in the
same class with the deeds that serve as his model. The

present in "Salem" consists only of a somnolent sailor and sewage-filled seas. It is a far cry from the New England of those who did battle against Leviathan and British Lion. (One wonders whether Lowell was influenced by the analogous "Custom House" section of *The Scarlet Letter,* with its depiction of a sleepy, contemporary Salem set against a colonial Salem of intense, dramatic occasions.) "For the Union Dead" presents the statue of Colonel Shaw and his Negro volunteers as a distinctly alien presence in modern Boston, at once exacerbating the city and threatened by it. In the striking words of the poem, "Their monument sticks like a fishbone/ in the city's throat." But it is made to shake by the construction of a characteristic object of the contemporary city, a garage. This will house the cars that are shaped by the poem, as one critic has noted,[9] into an image of servility as opposed to the ideal of service represented by the Colonel and his men. The "monument" to a modern war, World War II, is an advertisement for Mosler safes, the " 'Rock of Ages.' "

In one Lowell poem, then, the past repels; in another it attracts, putting the present to shame. So our survey thus far would indicate. But this description is misleading, for on occasion the two attitudes come together in a single work, and such poems are the most interesting of Lowell's treatments of the past, exhibiting the conflicts of a mind in which the events of history will not stay pigeonholed, put to rest with a single formula.[9a]

A nice illustration of Lowell's unstable, ambivalent presentation of these events can be found in comparing the three versions of "Concord." Taken together they constitute a kind of palimpsest of his images of the past. The earliest version of the poem, which appeared in 1943,[10] presents New England Unitarianism as ridiculously misguided in its assumptions: "The belfry of the Unitarian Church/ Clangs with preposterous torpor." The Church is equated with the modern town "Concord, where Thoreau/ and Emerson

fleeced Heaven of Christ's robe. . . ." Emerson *and* Thoreau
are here regarded in a hostile way, their Transcendentalism
seen as having in effect sponsored Unitarianism, with its
supposedly debased theology. The second version sharpens
the point but, interestingly, drops the explicit reference to
Thoreau:

> This Church is Concord, where the Emersons
> Washed out the blood-clots on my Master's robe
> And then forgot the fathers' flintlock guns
> And the renown of that embattled scream
> Whose echo girdled the imperfect globe.[11]

Here, an absurd denial or blotting out of pain and suffering is
attributed only to Emerson by name. The last version of the
poem omits the explicit reference to him while unmistakably
alluding to his "Concord Hymn" in sardonic fashion.[12] But
the most striking change to be found in the final version is the
restoration of Thoreau, now standing out in admirable relief
against a background of violence:

> This Church is Concord—Concord where Thoreau
> Named all the birds without a gun to probe
> Through darkness to the painted man and bow:
> The death-dance of King Philip and his scream
> Whose echo girdled this imperfect globe.

We have Lowell, then, as much "in search/Of a tradition"
as the tourists gathered at his Concord, moving, in the
revisions of a single poem, from a total dismissal of the
Concord past to a mixed rendering of its heritage. Preposterous Unitarianism, yes, violence, yes—but also the example
of Thoreau's pacific, inquiring nature. The past here is a
jumble of discordant elements, and Lowell seems to recognize the irony of the town's being named "Concord." But he
has not done much more here than record the jumble.

The simultaneous presence of positive and negative renderings of the past existing in uneasy union is to be found in other poems already discussed. (My remarks hitherto have been but partial representations of such works.) For example, "At the Indian Killer's Grave" points up the Puritans' capacity for violence, and mocks their belief in the election of the soul, through the sardonic voice of King Philip, but simultaneously uses that voice to define them in terms of a noble aspiration brought down:

> ". . . Your election,
> Hawking above this slime
> For souls as single as their skeletons,
> Flutters and claws in the dead hand of time."

An unresolved split in attitude can also be found in the Arthur Winslow elegy. There, a history that in one section yields up impressive ancestors is dismissed in the next section, as a Lowell turned Catholic (he converted in 1940) flicks away his Protestant past in toto. Praying to the Virgin Mary for his grandmother, Lowell says:

> Mother, for these three hundred years or more
> Neither our clippers nor our slavers reached
> The haven of your peace in this Bay State:
> Neither my father nor his father. Beached
> On these dry flats of fishy real estate,
> O Mother, I implore
> Your scorched, blue thunderbreasts of love to pour
> Buckets of blessings on my burning head
> Until I rise like Lazarus from the dead . . .

This passage will require further comment but for now we can simply note its rejecting of the past "three hundred years," and its turning to Mary as a refuge. The fact that such lines coexist in the poem with a passage apparently praising the past makes for incoherence. Also, we wonder how to respond to the lines that introduce the passage citing the achievements of the fathers:

Now from the train, at dawn
Leaving Columbus in Ohio, shell
On shell of our stark culture strikes the sun
To fill my head with all our fathers won
When Cotton Mather wrestled with the fiends from hell.

There seems to be an anticipatory pun here in the use of "stark," for one of the ancestors alluded to as the poem proceeds is General Stark, Revolutionary War hero. On the one hand, we are given the undeniable fact of contemporary bleakness, on the other the undeniable fact of family heroism. But is what "our fathers won" placed in *contrast* to the modern starkness, or is the poem suggesting that those early winnings set the pattern for the present scene? (Either relation of past to present can be found in Lowell.)

Thus, ambivalence and ambiguity in the treatment of the past are both at work in the Arthur Winslow elegy. Perhaps less evident but very much there is an ambivalent portrayal of the past in "The Quaker Graveyard in Nantucket." Approaching that poem again, we might remember the praise in "Salem" for the men "who quartered the Leviathan's fat flanks. . . ." In "Quaker Graveyard," the whale's "fat" figures in a very different way. It is depicted in a gruesome passage as being cut to bits, and is made to rhyme with "Jehoshaphat," identified by Lowell with the Last Judgment. The fat thereby turns into a damning substance, and the energy so prized in "Salem" is treated here as hideous. But is that the whole truth? Might not traces of the "Salem" attitude persist in "Quaker Graveyard," which was published two years later? This possibility may provide a clue to the meaning of the puzzling sixth section of the work, with its abrupt shift from the Atlantic that serves as setting for all the other parts of the poem (including the final, seventh section). Focused on the English shrine of Walsingham, the sixth section begins:

There once the penitents took off their shoes

> And then walked barefoot the remaining mile;
> And the small trees, a stream and hedgerows file
> Slowly along the munching English lane,
> Like cows to the old shrine, until you lose
> Track of your dragging pain.

After the tumultuous Atlantic sections that have come before, full of violence both natural and man-made, the English setting seems to exhibit a fatuous coziness. That coziness is also deceptive. It makes initially for a loss of pain. "But see," the poem continues,

> Our Lady, too small for her canopy,
> Sits near the altar. There's no comeliness
> At all or charm in that expressionless
> Face with its heavy eyelids. As before,
> This face . . .
> Expressionless, expresses God. . . .
> She knows what God knows,
> Not Calvary's Cross nor crib at Bethlehem.

No comforting refuge is to be found here. God exists in an ahuman blankness, removed from men. A somewhat different but no more comforting conception of Him is presented at the end of the poem with its reference to:

> . . . the time
> When the Lord God formed man from the sea's slime
> And breathed into his face the breath of life,
> And blue-lung'd combers lumbered to the kill.
> The Lord survives the rainbow of His will.

The parallel openings of the third and fourth lines here, and their conjunction, would suggest that death was not an interruption of God's scheme, but an original part of it, accompanying the giving of life. Life and death, joined by the syntax, are made to seem inseparable. The last line of the passage, the last line of the poem, shows God as being unbound by any agreement not to destroy man. He survives; man, by implication, does not. (Cf. Endecott's saying in *Endecott & the Red Cross,* "Only God goes on existing. We'll be over quickly.") These lines, then, can be read as depicting a cruel, ultimately uncovenanted Deity (it is hard to understand why some critics find an affirmation here).[13] So interpreted, the poem can be seen as *sharing* Captain Ahab's view of a malevolent divinity, as well as considering the possibility, in its sixth section, of a blank, unknowable God, a notion also to be found in *Moby-Dick.* The point is that the whalers, while admittedly depicted as cruel in their killing, are not conceived of only as the ruthless exploiters and violators of God's creation that they are usually taken to be. God does not figure here as benevolent Creator, and the sailors are not regarded simply as sinners but as dupes of their theology, believing that God is on their side. Given the God of the poem, and given, too, the internecine violence among the elements of Nature as presented in the work, the whalers' violence and Ahab's raging pursuit seem appropriate responses to reality, forming a continuum with it as opposed to the attempted denial of it implicit in the pastoral piety depicted in the Walsingham section. *That* section, by its end, mocks such piety. Also, at one level, the poems's own verbal violence seems to provide a covert endorsement of the actions it presents.

All this is not to dismiss completely the reading of the poem as a work appalled by the violence it describes, but it is to find in it (as in Melville's book) an implicit attraction to that violence and the daring behind it, a linkup with the more obvious admiration of past physical heroism to be found in "Salem." "The mast-lashed master of Leviathans" in "Quaker Graveyard" seems to be a description of Ahab. This mouth-filling phrase, with its suggested comparison of Ahab to Odysseus, hardly diminishes the captain in our eyes, or the Quaker whalemen associated with him. We might note, too, a remark Lowell made in 1965:

> I always think there are two great symbolic figures that
> stand behind American ambition and culture. One is
> Milton's Lucifer and the other is Captain Ahab: these two
> sublime ambitions that are doomed and ready, for their
> idealism, to face any amount of violence.[14]

Lowell is, at least to some extent, of the Devil's party.

Continuing to look at "Quaker Graveyard," we find as an
unmistakable component of its theology the notion of man as
a creature whose puny exertions of force, attempts at
dominion, are laughable when seen against the power of the
Lord (even though the poem can find nobility in those
attempts). Whaling ships or modern warships, all are "in the
hand/Of the great God. . . ." Keeping this in mind, we can
see that "Mr. Edwards and the Spider," considered earlier,
shows Lowell and Edwards sharing a common conception of
God. "What are we in the hands of the great God?" asks
Edwards in Lowell's poem (these were Edwards's actual
words almost exactly). After putting this question, he goes
on to mock man's pretensions and to show man's subjection
to the punishing will of the Lord. Thus, even in a poem that
appears to be critical of Edwards's harsh imagination, of his
apparent relish in terrifying the congregation at his feet, we
can find an implicit assent by Lowell to Edwards's theology.
Moreover, Lowell's own picture in "Quaker Graveyard" of
the sailors drowned at sea would seem to partake of an
Edwardsian satisfaction in the contemplation of sinners
properly punished. Like Edwards's portrayal of the spider
cast into the flames, Lowell's poem provides a grand spectacle of destruction. So here again, within a single poem,
Lowell is at one level rejecting the past, at another embrac-
ing it, the two attitudes in uneasy conjunction.

Lowell's divided, unstable response to various elements
of our history further manifests itself in the ambiguity of his
"Catholic" perspective in viewing the American Protestant
past. What might be called the two poles of American

Protestant theology, Calvinism and the doctrines of Unitarianism, are both condemned by that perspective, but it is Calvinism that is Lowell's principal target. Its harshness and strenuousness are associated in his mind with a predisposition to violence. The Virgin Mary stands as a merciful refuge from these qualities. At the conclusion of "At the Indian Killer's Grave," which has emphasized the violence done to the Indian, and the sternness of the Puritan fathers, the speaker prays:

> Gospel me to the Garden, let me come
> Where Mary twists the warlock with her flowers—
> Her soul a bridal chamber fresh with flowers
> And her whole body an ecstatic womb,
> As through the trellis peers the sudden Bridegroom.

But as we have already seen, Lowell's response to violence in the American past is not one of unalloyed repugnance. The power of the fathers exerts its attraction, and at a point in his poetry where he seems to be most clearly rejecting the fathers, a curious effect occurs. It is in the last section of "In Memory of Arthur Winslow," when he has said that three hundred years of Protestant-shaped history have not attained the haven of Mary's peace. He prays:

> O Mother, I implore
> Your scorched, blue thunderbreasts of love to pour
> Buckets of blessings on my burning head
> Until I rise like Lazarus from the dead. . . .

"Thunderbreasts"—the word is curiously androgynous, and compared with the Mary invoked in "Indian Killer's Grave," this one seems to posses a masculine potency. That is to say, in a moment of apparent dismissal of the fathers, a continuing connection with masculine power is desired. With a shift of speaker (the new voice possibly being that of Arthur Winslow), the poem continues:

"On Copley Square, I saw you hold the door
To Trinity, the costly Church, and saw
The painted Paradise of harps and lutes
Sink like Atlantis in the Devil's jaw
And knock the Devil's teeth out by the roots;
But when I strike for shore
I find no painted idols to adore:
Hell is burned out, heaven's harp-strings are slack."

This passage has received notable misreadings by at least two critics, who believe that the sinking "painted Paradise" signifies "a ceremony without faith," a doomed Protestantism.[15] What such critics ignore is the *effect* of the sinking, which was to "knock the Devil's teeth out by the roots," hardly an image of religious impotence. Rather, the impotence is symbolized by the *absence* of the painted Paradise. The critics have allowed a pejorative connotation of "painted," viewed in isolation, to obscure the total picture. But their error serves to point up the confusion in the last section of the Winslow elegy taken as a whole: a Protestant tradition is seen at once as a total failure and as having possessed a religious potency in the past. Invoked as an alternative to that tradition, a Catholic conception partakes of it.

Thus, an attraction to their power keeps Lowell's sensibility tied to the very fathers he is trying to reject, producing a warring of elements in his poems about the past. Ancestors, familial or spiritual, are renounced, but duplicitous assent to them somehow enters, and the ancestral tradition is continued in the self or the spirit of the poems, rather than being terminated by it.

There is at least one Lowell poem in which this process seems to be recognized. In its original version, "Rebellion," as we saw above, marked the rejection of a violent past enshrined in family heirlooms, notably a flintlock. But the poem contains a paradox, apparently undiscerned in the first version: the son, in rejecting the violent past, was commit-

ting a violent act in the present, sending his father crashing
into the heirlooms, the flintlock breaking on his head. In its
revised version, the poem's original focus on ancestral guilt
(through reference to Bunker Hill) is replaced by a recognition of the son's guilt. The final lines now read:

> . . .I have sealed
> An everlasting pact
> With Dives to contract
> The world that spreads in pain;
> But the world spread
> When the clubbed flintlock broke my father's brain.

The sense of tension generated here by the opposing processes of contraction (refutation of the past) and spreading
(incorporation and continuation of the past) epitomizes the
jarring effect of the conflicting strains found in Lowell's
treatment of American history. His different "compulsions
and biases" get into his writing so that he may be said not to
know what he means. In what might be called Lowell's early
poetry the opposing strains are not resolved. But instances
of resolution can be found in the *Life Studies* volume and
later works.

In the "Dunbarton" poem of *Life Studies,* the speaker
remembers a landscape from his childhood in which

> the clump of virgin pine still stretched patchy ostrich
>   necks
> over the disused millpond's fragrantly woodstained water,
> a reddish blur,
> like the ever-blackening wine-dark coat
> in our portrait of Edward Winslow
> once sheriff for George the Second,
> the sire of bankrupt Tories.

Here, the past exerts its charm but is viewed with humorous
detachment. One finds an attraction to the fading portrait of a
notable ancestor, fused with a sense of the dubious status of

his immediate descendants. The one-time distinction of the past was able to bestow nothing on what came right after. "Dunbarton" shows this principle operating even within a single man's life, that of Mr. Burroughs, who helped the speaker and his grandfather rake leaves from the family graves. He

> had stood with Sherman at Shiloh—
> his thermos of shockless coffee
> was milk and grounds;
> his illegal home-made claret
> was as sugary as grape jelly. . . .

The *sh* in "Sherman at Shiloh" is ironically echoed by the same sound in "shockless" and "sugary" (and the capital S's have descended to lower case) to contrast the helper's one-time heroic status with his present condition. In this poem, Time does not break up into a heroic past versus a mundane present. The past itself is a mixed affair, and the poem knows this. Moreover, distinction and the decline from distinction are seen as ongoing human possibilities. The vision of the past here is ironic, inclusive, relaxed.

"Sailing Home from Rapallo," a poem coming later in the *Life Studies* sequence, and set partly in Dunbarton, tells of Lowell's mother being buried in the family cemetery there:

The graveyard's soil was changing to stone—
so many of its deaths had been midwinter.
Dour and dark against the blinding snowdrifts,
its black brook and fir trunks were as smooth as masts.
A fence of iron spear-hafts
black-bordered its mostly Colonial grave-slates.
The only "unhistoric" soul to come here
was Father, now buried beneath his recent
unweathered pink-veined slice of marble.

After giving the cemetery a somber weight and dignity, the speaker qualifies its character by his placement of quotation marks around "unhistoric," and his noting of the "pink-veined" marble, an alien presence among the grave-slates, just as his father is alien. While a certain humor is achieved at the latter's expense, the joke is on the cemetery as well, and on the whole notion of the "historic." The sensibility operating here contains, *consciously*, a complex mixture of the pious and the irreverent. This mixture continues at work in the remaining lines of the poem which further intertwine Lowell's paternal and maternal ancestors:

> Even the Latin of his Lowell motto:
> *Occasionem cognosce,*
> seemed to businesslike and pushing here,
> where the burning cold illuminated
> the hewn inscriptions of Mother's relatives:
> twenty or thirty Winslows and Starks.
> Frost had given their names a diamond edge. . . .
>
> In the grandiloquent lettering on Mother's coffin,
> *Lowell* had been misspelled *LOVEL.*
> The corpse
> was wrapped like *panetone* in Italian tinfoil

The play of elements here is marvelous: Lowells against Starks and Winslows, diamond-edged names against grandiloquent, misspelled lettering, the Latin motto against the homely Italian word, the cold beauty of the past against both the pretentiousness of the "historic" and the sad comedy of the present. The easy bringing of all these together, the complexity of tone, is a notable achievement. What was once an unstable, confused, insufficiently recognized clashing in Lowell's handling of historical materials has evolved into a rich, controlled mixture.

Other memorable examples of his control over diverse elements in his depiction of the American past can be found in volumes coming after *Life Studies*. In *For the Union Dead,* "Jonathan Edwards in Western Massachusetts" calls to mind "Mr. Edwards and the Spider" and "After the

Surprising Conversions" of *Lord Weary's Castle,* but is very different from them. While incorporating some of the same elements as the earlier poems—Edwards's boyhood observations of spiders, his terrifying sermon that images people as spiders in the hands of God—"Jonathan Edwards" adds touches to its portrait of the man that soften and complicate our impression of him. Acknowledgement is made of Edwards's lyrical description of the girl who was to become his wife, and of his unflattering description of himself when offered the presidency of Princeton, as well as of his reluctance to leave his studies for that position. (The poem seems to be implicitly contrasting him with Francis Bacon, who, in his downfall, was intent on maintaining a show of worldly glory, while Edwards, given a chance to escape his exile to a humble ministerial station on the frontier, wished to stay there and continue his intellectual pursuits.) Lowell shows himself sardonically aware of the ironies of Edwards's life in this address to his subject:

> You gave
> her [Mrs. Edwards] Pompey, a Negro slave,
> and eleven children.
> Yet people were spiders
>
> in your moment of glory,
> at the Great Awakening. . . .

But the poem is able to view the man whole, to see both the harshness and charm of his intensity, and to move toward an expression of affection for him without having lost sight of his faults. One gets the sense of a firm perspective being established on the past, incorporating different responses to match the variety of its materials, all in a work of controlled modulation. The reader is not troubled here, as in the earlier poems on Edwards, by a sense of unacknowledged attraction to the very sensibility supposedly under attack.

In Lowell's *Notebook*[16] a kind of sonnet about Andrew

Jackson, entitled "Old Hickory," appears as one of twenty-two pieces presented under the heading of "The Powerful." At first the poem seems to lump Jackson and Stephen Decatur (hero of the Tripolitan War) in the same category of "Those awful figures of Yankee prehistory. . . ." Decatur is the target of a sardonic comment on the American habit, treated elsewhere by Lowell, of putting violence at the service of self-righteousness. Jackson seems to be subjected to the same sort of disrespectful treatment through explicit statement as well as a humorous use of internal rhyme (note the play on the *ar* endings in the following):

> he might have been the Tsar or Bolivar,
> pillar of the right or pillar of the left—

But with the last two lines of the poem (in a formal variation on the kind of reversal that usually comes earlier in a sonnet) there is a change of tone:

> Andrew Jackson, despite appearances,
> stands for the gunnery that widened suffrage.

The violence associated with Jackson, as opposed to Decatur, is seen as having yielded a valuable result. The poem, then, confronts the fact of violence in the American past, and sorts out a smug patriotism from a genuine achievement, isolating the last for our contemplation. The final effect is one of coherence, rather than the jangling irresolution we found in Lowell's earlier treatments of violence in American history.

In the works he published in the 1960s, Lowell's chief engagement with the American past was not expressed in his volumes of poems, but in his dramatic trilogy, *The Old Glory*. There, too, we can find a coherent treatment of our history. But the coherence does not come out of what we have been examining: a controlled rendering, in artful verse, of the mixed nature of the past and of the different responses it elicits from Lowell. With *The Old Glory* there seems to have been no need in Lowell to get a rounded perspective on the past, to make distinctions among its varied elements. The past in the trilogy exhibits a steady sameness—it is unattractive throughout—and *The Old Glory* views that sameness with dry detachment. Ostensibly, in the conflicts between Endecott and Sir Thomas Morton, between the Loyalist regime of Major Molineux and the rebellious colonists, between whites and blacks, there might be a basis for choosing one party above the other. But such is not the case.

Hawthorne's story "Endicott and the Red Cross" is one of the sources for Lowell's play of the same name (the play constitutes the first part of *The Old Glory*).[17] That story views Endicott as a genuine hero who acted rightly in resisting England's attempts to dictate to the colonists (the tale is based on an actual incident). "The May-pole of Merrymount," another Hawthorne story that serves as a source of the play, contrasts the hedonism and paganism of Morton's settlement with the grimness and sternness of the Puritans, led by Endicott, who wish to root out Merrymount. Morton's colony has real charm for Hawthorne, although he finally rejects its way of life. He locates his center of value in a young couple who, ultimately, belong neither to Merrymount nor to the Puritans. With Lowell, the issue of Merrymount's gaiety versus Puritan joylessness is hardly present. The young couple figure as distinctly minor characters, barely getting into the play, and they certainly are not its moral center. Moreover, Endecott's rebellion against English authority is not the unquestioned good it was for Hawthorne. The play comes down simply to a struggle for power, uninformed by genuine moral principles. Endecott, who arrives to repress Morton and Merrymount in the name of the Red Cross of England, eventually orders the Cross torn down, his allegiance shifting rapidly under the pressure of events. In the speech exhorting his men to rebel against England, Endecott speaks of

> . . . .wars. . .prettily called the Wars of the Roses—
> they were without decency or grace,
> the opposing leaders were as alike as weeds,
> men fought for no cause that is intelligible to us now.

Morton remarks "This is a history lesson, Mr. Endecott!" Lowell's play may be said to contain a history lesson in which something like Endecott's vision of the Wars of the Roses is extended by the drama to its own events. The struggle depicted, now become part of *our* past, is made to have little more meaning to us than the Wars of the Roses had to Endecott. The issue with*in* the play, of whether the "corrupt" Church of England (allegedly tainted with "Papistry") is going to be imposed on America, is seen as a false one. Church of England vs. Puritan, Catholic vs. Protestant—these are made to appear unreal oppositions. The central fact is the use of force, or the readiness to use force by both sides, the ultimate distinction being that one side wins, the other loses.

A similar effect is present in the other two parts of *The Old glory*. Early in *My Kinsman, Major Molineux,* a character remarks that "The British/ are the only Frenchmen left" in the colony. This somewhat humorous observation is an indication of the play's sensibility. What we think of as possibly significant differences—between the British and French, between the British and the colonists, between the Loyalists and the rebels—break down. There is really little to choose between when confronted, on the one hand, by the cruelty of Major Molineux, and, on the other, by the cruelty of those who have tarred and feathered him. At one point in the action, when a clergyman prays for enlightenment from God, he means he wishes to find out which side will win. Once again this is the only basis for distinguishing between the conflicting parties. In *Benito Cereno,* Captain Delano and his boatswain Perkins, one supposedly sophisticated, the other simple, are both intent on drawing distinctions between Americans and foreigners. But the play operates so as to dissolve such notions or render them trivial (e.g., the stage directions specify that the setting for the Spanish ship be "identical" with that of the American vessel, "except for litter and disorder"). Americans and Europeans become members of a single party, ranged against the blacks. Lest we think that *here* some line is being drawn, some preference expressed for the Negroes as victims turned against their oppressors, we are told that Babu, leader of the slave rebellion, was originally a *black* man's slave in Africa. Force (European) is met with force (African) which in turn is met with a third force (American)—and that is all. To some extent all this corresponds to Lowell's source, Melville's *Benito Cereno,* but that work embodies an anguished and complex sensibility, as opposed to the disdainful reductionism of Lowell's play, with Melville brooding on the achievement and high cost of a civilization (represented by Cereno's ship), being conscious both of its grandeur and the terrible means by which it has sustained itself.

The view that prevails throughout Lowell's trilogy might be fairly summed up in this way: some of the men depicted won, some lost, all were in the wrong. There is a troubling glibness in this view, a sense that a scheme has been imposed too easily on the materials by an observer who is too emotionally removed from them. The exacerbation, admiration, or confused conjunction of both, evident in the earlier Lowell's images of the past, have given way to an Olympian repugnance before the spectacle of history, a tone which is something other and lesser than the controlled presentation, discussed above, of mixed emotions and mixed materials. The relatively objective form of the drama has, in Lowell's hands, resulted in more objectivity than one wants, and a more trivial past than one believes in. Curiously enough,

Lowell claimed that *The Old Glory* "is partly a tribute to the past. . . ."[18] Would that it were. The plays might have been richer, more persuasive, and more moving than they are.

In Lowell's early poetry, his interest in the public aspects of the American past was heightened by his consciousness of the role played by his own ancestors. With *Life Studies* and *The Old Glory*, a kind of division or specialization took place in Lowell's treatment of the past. *Life Studies* retains in even more acute form his focus on members of his family, but the past for the most part has narrowed down to his own, actual relationships with persons and places of his childhood. When he takes up the historical again, in *The Old Glory*, it is history at a remove, a more purely public past than in his earlier poetry or *Life Studies*, and filtered almost entirely through the literary creations of other men (Hawthorne and Melville). The division of approach works to the benefit of *Life Studies*, but to the detriment of *The Old Glory*. In *Notebook* Lowell dropped American history as a major subject of his verse ("Old Hickory" and "Charles Russell Lowell 1835–1864" are relatively isolated items in the book.) The young Lowell magnified his poetic self, perhaps compensating for its paucity of present by connecting it with an American past conceived of as having substance and drama. The past in *The Old Glory* is much shrunken, and in later works a middle-aged Lowell finds in his own past and present the principal materials for his poetry. An incident of his life that apparently served as the basis for "Rebellion," the symbolic revolt against the fathers, is rendered in *Notebook* as a much smaller event, a family quarrel.[19] The change proved significant. Lowell went on to become less a "Lowell," more his particular self.

NOTES

1. But however inevitable his focus on New England history appears in retrospect, Lowell's turning to it could well have been initiated by his personal contact, as a young man, with two Southerners, John Crowe Ransom and Allen Tate, particularly the latter, whose own thinking in regional-cultural terms seems to have suggested to Lowell that he could be regarded as a representative of the Puritans.

2. The poem appeared in *Partisan Review* 10 (July–August 1943): 316–17. It was collected in *Land of Unlikeness* (Cummington, Mass.: Cummington Press, 1944), in revised form under the title "The Boston Nativity." The book is not paginated.

3. It appears in *Land of Unlikeness*. A still earlier version can be found in *Partisan Review* 10 (July–August 1943): 316.

4. See *Nation,* 23 February 1946, p. 228.

5. Dallas E. Wiebe, "Mr. Lowell and Mr. Edwards," *Wisconsin Studies in Contemporary Literature* 3 (Spring–Summer 1962): 26.

6. See *Life,* 19 February 1965, p. 58.

7. Quoted in Ferris Greenslet, *The Lowells and their Seven Worlds* (Boston: Houghton Mifflin, 1946), p. 289.

8. Cf. Richard Fein, "Mary and Bellona: The War Poetry of Robert Lowell," *Southern Review* 1 (Autumn 1965): 820–34.

9. Geoffrey Hartman, "The Eye of the Storm," *Partisan Review* 32 (Spring 1965): 280.

9a. While I shall go on to demonstrate how, in a given poem, rejection of the past can give way to at least a local embrace of it, I should note here how one work already treated, "For the Union Dead," inverts this pattern. The basically admiring portrait of Colonel Shaw is partly undermined by the suggestion of a death-seeking rigidity in his behavior: "when he leads his black soldiers to death,/he cannot bend his back."

10. See note 2.

11. Lowell, *Land of Unlikeness,* unpaged.

12. It appears in *Lord Weary's Castle* (New York: Harcourt, Brace & World, 1946), p. 27.

13. See Marjorie Perloff, "Death By Water: The Winslow Elegies of Robert Lowell," *ELH* 34 (March 1967): 129. Perloff finds that the affirmation is forced.

14. Quoted in Alfred Alvarez, "A Talk with Robert Lowell," *Encounter* 24 (February 1965): 42.

15. See Hugh B. Staples, *Robert Lowell: The First Twenty Years* (New York: Farrar, Straus & Cudahy, 1962), p. 30, and Perloff, "Death By Water," p. 122. The passage in Villon which is the source of the "painted Paradise" presents it without irony or negative comment, but simply as heaven.

16. Robert Lowell, *Notebook* (New York: Farrar, Straus and Giroux, 1970) is a revision and enlargement of *Notebook 1967–68* (New York: Farrar, Straus and Giroux, 1969). "Old Hickory" appears in both volumes. *Notebook* was published in 1970.

17. But Lowell spells the name as "Endecott."

18. Quoted in Stanley Kunitz, "Talk with Robert Lowell," *New York Times Book Review,* 4 October 1964, p. 39.

19. There are two poems in *Notebook* pertaining to this event, appearing in the "Charles River" section of the book. The second of these begins in the same way as "Rebellion." It indicates sympathy for and empathy with the father, as much as anything else.

Bibliography

Alvarez, Alfred. "A Talk with Robert Lowell." *Encounter* 24 (February 1965): 39–43.

American Slavery As It Is: Testimony of a Thousand Voices. New York: Arno Press and *The New York Times,* 1968.

Appel, Jr., Alfred. *A Season of Dreams: The Fiction of Eudora Welty.* Baton Rouge, La.: Louisiana State University Press, 1965.

"Applause for a Prize Poet." *Life,* 19 February 1965, p. 49.

Aptheker, Herbert. *American Negro Slave Revolts.* New York: Columbia University Press, 1943.

———. "A Note on the History." *Nation,* 16 October 1967, pp. 375–76.

Archives of Maryland. Baltimore, Md.: Maryland Historical Society, 1883–.

Arvin, Newton. *Longfellow: His Life and Work.* Boston: Little, Brown & Co., 1963

Ayoob, Joseph C., ed. *Were the Phoenicians the First to Discover America?* Aliquippa, Pa.: no publisher listed, 1951.

Babson, John J. *History of the Town of Gloucester, Cape Ann, Including the Town of Rockport.* Gloucester, Mass.: Procter Brothers, 1860.

Babson, Roger W., and Saville, Foster H. *Cape Ann: A Tourist Guide.* Rockport, Mass.: Cape Ann Old Bookshop, 1936.

Bailinson, Frank. "Styron Answers 'Turner' Critics." *New York Times,* 11 February 1968, p. 59.

Barth, John. *End of the Road.* New York: Avon Books, 1964.

———. *The Sot-Weed Factor.* New York: Grosset & Dunlap, 1964.

Bell, Michael. *Hawthorne and the Historical Romance of New England*. Princeton, N.J.: Princeton University Press, 1971.

Bérard, Victor. *Did Homer Live?* Translated by Brian Rhys. New York: E.P. Dutton and Co., 1931.

Berryman, John. *Homage to Mistress Bradstreet and Other Poems*. New York: The Noonday Press, 1968.

———. "One Answer to a Question." *Shenandoah* 17 (Autumn 1965): 67–76.

———. "The Poetry of Ezra Pound." *Partisan Review* 16 (April 1949): 377–94.

Blair, Walter, and Meine, Franklin J. *Half Horse, Half Alligator: The Growth of the Mike Fink Legend*. Chicago: University of Chicago Press, 1956.

Blotner, Joseph, compiler. *William Faulkner's Library: A Catalogue*. Charlottesville, Va.: University Press of Virginia, 1964.

Botkin, B.A. *Lay My Burden Down: A Folk History of Slavery*. Chicago: University of Chicago Press, 1945.

Bourne, Edward Gaylord, ed. *Narratives of the Career of Hernando de Soto*. In *The Conquest of Florida*. New York: A.S. Barnes & Co., 1904.

Bradford, William. *History of Plymouth Plantation*. Edited by Worthington Ford. 2 vols. N.p.: Massachusetts Historical Society, 1912.

———. *Of Plymouth Plantation*. Edited by Samuel Eliot Morison. New York: Alfred A. Knopf, 1952.

Breslin, James E. *William Carlos Williams: An American Artist*. New York: Oxford University Press, 1970.

Brooks, Cleanth. *Modern Poetry and the Tradition*. New York: Oxford University Press, 1965.

———. *William Faulkner: The Yoknapatawpha County*. New Haven, Conn.: Yale University Press, 1963.

Campbell, Helen. *Anne Bradstreet and Her Time*. Boston: D. Lothrop Co., 1891.

Canzoneri, Robert, and Stegner, Page. "An Interview with William Styron." *Per/Se* 1 (Summer 1966): 37–44.

Cash, W.J. *The Mind of the South*. Garden City, N.Y.: Doubleday & Co., 1956.

Chase, Richard. *The American Novel and its Tradition.* Garden City, N.Y.: Doubleday Anchor Books, 1957.

Clarke, John Henrik, ed. *William Styron's Nat Turner: Ten Black Writers Respond.* Boston: Beacon Press, 1968.

The Confessions of Nat Turner. Miami, Fla.: Mnemosyne Publishing, 1969.

Conquest: Dispatches of Cortes from the New World. Edited by Irwin Blacker and Harry Rosen. New York: Grosset & Dunlap, 1962.

Copeland, Melvin T., and Rogers, Elliot C. *The Saga of Cape Ann.* Freeport, Me.: Bond Wheelwright Co., 1960.

Corrigan, Matthew, ed. Charles Olson Number, *Boundary 2, 2* (Fall 1973/Winter 1974).

Cortés, Hernando. *The Despatches of Hernando Cortés.* Translated by George Folsom. New York: Wiley and Putnam, 1843.

Cowan, Louise. *The Fugitive Group: A Literary History.* Baton Rouge, La.: Louisiana State University Press, 1959.

Dickinson, A. T. *American Historical Fiction.* New York: Scarecrow Press, 1958.

Drewry, William S. *The Southampton Insurrection.* Washington, D.C.: Neale Co., 1900.

Duberman, Martin. "Books." *The Village Voice* 14 December 1967, p. 8.

Elkins, Stanley. *Slavery: A Problem in American Institutional and Intellectual Life.* Chicago: University of Chicago Press, 1959.

Ellis, John Harvard, ed. *The Works of Anne Bradstreet in Prose and Verse.* Gloucester, Mass.: Peter Smith, 1932.

Faulkner, William. *Absalom, Absalom!* New York: The Modern Library, 1951.

———. *The Unvanquished.* New York: Random House, 1938.

Fein, Richard. "Mary and Bellona: The War Poetry of Robert Lowell." *Southern Review* 1 (Autumn 1965): 820–34.

Fiedler, Leslie. "John Barth: An Eccentric Genius." *New Leader,* 13 February 1961, pp. 22–24.

Filson, John. *The Discovery, Settlement and Present State of Kentucke.* Introduction by William H. Masterson. New York: Corinth Books, 1962.

———. *Life and Adventures of Colonel Daniel Boon.* . . . Brooklyn, N.Y.: C. Wilder, 1823.

Five Slave Narratives: A Compendium. New York: Arno Press and *The New York Times,* 1968.

Fleming, Wallace B. *The History of Tyre.* New York: Columbia University Press, 1915.

Gilman, Richard. "Nat Turner Revisited." *New Republic,* 27 April 1968, p. 23.

Green, Blakey. "Jousting Tournaments in Virginia: The Age of Chivalry Lives On." *New York Times,* 22 August 1971, p. 58.

Greenslet, Ferris. *The Lowells and their Seven Worlds.* Boston: Houghton Mifflin Co., 1946.

Hall, Clayton Colman, ed. *Narratives of Early Maryland 1633–1684.* New York: Charles Scribner's Sons, 1910.

Hartman, Geoffrey. "The Eye of the Storm." *Partisan Review* 32 (Spring 1965): 277–80.

Henderson, Harry B. *Versions of the Past: The Historical Imagination in American Fiction.* New York: Oxford University Press, 1974.

Hensley, Jeannine, ed. *The Works of Anne Bradstreet.* Cambridge, Mass.: Harvard University Press, 1967.

Hoffman, Daniel. *Form and Fable in American Fiction.* New York: Oxford University Press, 1965.

Hoffman, Frederick J. and Vickery, Olga W., eds. *William Faulkner: Three Decades of Criticism* New York: Harcourt, Brace & World, 1963.

Houston, Sam. *The Autobiography of Sam Houston.* Edited by Donald Day and Harry Herbert Ullom. Norman, Okla.: University of Oklahoma Press, 1954.

Howe, Irving. *William Faulkner: A Critical Study.* New York: Random House, 1952.

"An Interview with Eudora Welty." In *Writers and Writing,* edited by Robert Van Gelder. New York: Charles Scribner's Sons, 1946.

Irwin, John T. *Doubling and Incest / Repetition and Revenge: A Speculative Reading of Faulkner.* Baltimore, Md.: John Hopkins University Press, 1975.

Jarrell, Randall. "On the Underside of the Stone." *New York Times Book Review* 23 August 1953, p. 6.

"John Barth: An Interview." *Wisconsin Studies in Contemporary Literature* 6 (Winter-Spring 1965): 3–14.

Johnson, Thomas Cranford. *Did the Phoenicians Discover America?*. . . San Francisco: no publisher listed, 1892.

Jones, George. *The History of Ancient America, Anterior to the Time of Columbus*. . . . London: Longman, Brown, Green and Longmans, 1843.

Jones, Howard Mumford. *O Strange New World*. New York: Viking Press, 1964.

Jones, John Paul. *Battle Between the "Bon Homme Richard" and the "Serapis": Commodore Jones's Report to Congress through Dr. Franklin*. Boston: Directors of the Old South Work, 1904.

Kauffman, Stanley. "Styron's Unwritten Novel." *Hudson Review* 20 (Winter 1967–68): 675–80.

Kazin, Alfred. "An Enchanted World in America." *New York Herald Tribune Books*, 25 October 1942, p. 19.

Kip, William Ingraham. *The Early Jesuit Missions in North America*. New York: Wiley and Putnam, 1846.

Kostelanetz, Richard. "Conversation with Berryman." *Massachusetts Review* 11 (Spring 1970): 340–47.

Kunitz, Stanley. "Talk with Robert Lowell." *New York Times Book Review*, 4 October 1964, p. 34.

Leavis, Q.D. "Hawthorne as Poet." *Sewanee Review* 59 (April–June 1951): 179–205 (part 1); (July–September 1951): 426–58 (part 2).

Leo, John. "Some Negroes Accuse Styron of Distorting Nat Turner's Life." *New York Times* 1 February 1968, p. 31.

Lettres édifiantes et curieuses; écrites des missions étrangères, par quelques missionnaires de la Compagnie de Jésus, 23 Paris: N. Le Clerc, 1738.

Levermore, Charles Herbert. *Forerunners and Competitors of the Pilgrims and Puritans*. 2 vols. Brooklyn, N.Y.: New England Society of Brooklyn, 1912.

Lively, Robert A. *Fiction Fights the Civil War: An Unfinished*

Chapter in the Literary History of the American People. Chapel Hill, N.C.: University of North Carolina Press, 1957.

Longley, Jr., John Lewis, ed. *Robert Penn Warren: A Collection of Critical Essays.* New York: New York University Press, 1965.

Lowell, Robert. *Land of Unlikeness.* Cummington, Mass.: Cummington Press, 1944.

————. *"Life Studies" and "For the Union Dead."* 2 vols. in 1. New York: Noonday Press, 1967.

————. *Lord Weary's Castle.* New York: Harcourt, Brace & World, 1946.

————. *"Lord Weary's Castle" and "The Mills of the Kavanaughs."* 2 vols. in 1. New York: Meridian Books, 1961.

————. *Notebook.* New York: Farrar, Straus and Giroux, 1970.

————. *Notebook 1967–68.* New York: Farrar, Straus and Giroux, 1969.

————. *The Old Glory.* New York: Noonday Press, 1965.

Lytle, Andrew. "The Son of Man: He Will Prevail." *Sewanee Review* 63 (Winter 1955): 114–37.

McDowell, Frederick P. W. "Psychology and Theme in *Brother to Dragons.*" *PMLA,* 70 (September 1955): 565–86.

Merrill, Jr., Boynton. *Jefferson's Nephew: A Frontier Tragedy.* Princeton, N.J.: Princeton University Press, 1976.

Morrell, David. *John Barth: An Introduction.* University Park, Pa.: Pennsylvania State University Press, 1976.

Morton, Thomas. *New English Canaan.* Boston: Prince Society, 1883.

Olson, Charles. *A Bibliography on America for Ed Dorn.* San Francisco, Calif.: Four Seasons Foundation, distributed by City Lights Books, 1964.

————. *Call Me Ishmael.* New York: Reynal and Hitchcock, 1947.

————. *Charles Olson Reading at Berkeley,* transcribed by Zoe Brown. San Francisco, Calif.: Coyote, distributed by City Lights Bookstore, 1966.

————. *Human Universe and Other Essays.* San Francisco, Calif.: Auerhahn Society, 1965.

————. *The Maximus Poems.* New York: Jargon/Corinth Books, 1960.

————. *Maximus Poems IV, V, VI.* London: Cape Goliard Press, in association with Grossman Publishers (New York), 1968.

————. *The Maximus Poems, Volume Three.* Edited by Charles Boer and George F. Butterick. New York: Grossman Publishers, 1975.

Olson (Charles) File. Sawyer Free Library, Gloucester, Massachusetts.

Original Narratives of Early American History. 19 vols. New York: Charles Scribner's Sons, 1906–19.

Osgood, Herbert L. *The American Colonies in the 17th Century.* 3 vols. New York: Macmillan Co., 1926.

Parkman, Francis. *The Jesuits in America in the Seventeenth Century.* 9th ed. Boston: Little, Brown and Co., 1875.

Perloff, Marjorie. "Death By Water: The Winslow Elegies of Robert Lowell." *ELH* 34 (March 1967): 116–40.

Phares, Ross. *Reverend Devil: A Biography of John A. Murrell.* New Orleans, La.: Pelican Publishing Co., 1941.

Piercy, Josephine K. *Anne Bradstreet.* New York: Twayne Publishers, 1965.

Plimpton, George. "William Styron: A Shared Ordeal," *New York Times Book Review,* 8 October 1967, p. 2.

Prescott, William H. *History of the Conquest of Mexico, with a Preliminary View of the Ancient Mexican Civilization and the Life of the Conqueror Hernando Cortes.* New York: Harper and Brothers, 1843.

Procter, George H. *The Fishermen's Memorial and Record Book, Containing a List of Vessels and their Crews Lost from the Port of Gloucester, Mass., from 1830 to 1873.* Gloucester, Mass.: Procter Bros., 1873.

Rawlinson, George. *The Story of Phoenicia.* New York: G. P. Putnam's Sons, 1889.

Ridgely, Joseph V. *William Gilmore Simms.* New York: Twayne Publishers, 1962.

Rosenthal, M. L. *The William Carlos Williams Reader.* New York: New Directions, 1966.

Rose-Troup, Frances. *John White: The Patriarch of Dorchester and the Founder of Massachusetts 1575–1648, with an Account of the Early Settlements in Massachusetts 1620–1630.* New York: G. P. Putnam's Sons, 1930.

———. *The Massachusetts Bay Company and its Predecessors.* New York: Grafton Press, 1930.

Rourke, Constance. *American Humor: A Study of the National Character.* Garden City, N.Y.: Doubleday Anchor Books, 1953.

Sanchonintho. *The Theology of the Phoenicians by Sanchonintho.* Translated by I. P. Cory. In *The Phenix: A Collection of Old and Rare Fragments.* New York: William Gowan, 1835.

Sellers, Charles Coleman. *Lorenzo Dow: The Bearer of the Word.* New York: Minton, Balch and Co., 1928.

Sir Walter Ralegh and His Colony in America, ed. Increase N. Tarbox. Boston: Prince Society, 1884.

Slafter, E. F., Reverend, ed. *Voyages of the Northmen to America.* . . . Boston: Prince Society, 1877.

Slatoff, Walter J. *Quest for Failure: A Study of William Faulkner.* Ithaca, N.Y.: Cornell University Press, 1960.

Smith, Captain John. *Travels and Works of Captain John Smith.* Edited by Edward Arber. 2 vols. Edinburgh: J. Grant, 1910.

Squires, Radcliffe. *Allen Tate: A Literary Biography.* New York: Pegasus, 1971.

Stampp, Kenneth. *The Peculiar Institution: Slavery in the Ante-Bellum South.* New York: Alfred A. Knopf, 1956.

Stanford, Ann. "Anne Bradstreet: Dogmatist and Rebel." *New England Quarterly* 39 (September 1966): 373–89.

Staples, Hugh B. *Robert Lowell: The First Twenty Years.* New York: Farrar, Straus & Cudahy, 1962.

Starobin, Robert J., ed. *Blacks in Bondage: Letters of American Slaves.* New York: New Viewpoints, 1974.

Stewart, John L. *The Burden of Time: The Fugitives and Agrarians.* Princeton, N.J.: Princeton University Press, 1965.

———. "Robert Penn Warren and the Knot of History." *ELH* 26 (March 1959): 102–36.

Strabo. *The Geography of Strabo.* Translated by Horace Leonard Jones. 8 vols. Loeb Classical Library. London: W. Heinemann, 1917.

Strandberg, Victor H. *A Colder Fire: The Poetry of Robert Penn Warren*. Lexington, Ky.: University of Kentucky Press, 1965.

Styron, William. *The Confessions of Nat Turner*. New York: Random House, 1967.

———. "Overcome." *New York Review of Books,* 26 September 1963, pp. 18–19.

Tarbox, Increase N., ed. *Sir Walter Raleigh and His Colony in America*. Boston: Prince Society, 1884.

Tate, Allen. "The Eighteenth-Century South." *Nation,* 30 March 1927, p. 346.

———. *Essays of Four Decades*. Chicago: Swallow Press, 1968.

———. *The Fathers*. Chicago: Swallow Press, 1960.

———. "*The Fugitive* 1922–1925: A Personal Recollection Twenty Years After." *Princeton University Library Chronicle* (1 April 1942): 83.

———. "The Gaze Past, the Glance Present." *Sewanee Review* 70 (Autumn 1962): 671–73.

———. *Jefferson Davis: His Rise and Fall*. New York: Minton, Balch & Co., 1929.

———. "Last Days of the Charming Lady." *Nation,* (28 October 1925), pp. 485–86.

———. "Life in the Old South." *New Republic,* 10 July 1929, p. 212.

———. "The Novel in the American South." *New Statesman,* (13 June 1959), pp. 831–32.

———. *Poems*. Denver: Alan Swallow, 1961.

———. *Stonewall Jackson: The Good Soldier*. New York: Minton, Balch & Co., 1928.

———. *The Swimmers and Other Selected Poems*. New York: Charles Scribner's Sons, 1971.

Thornton, John Wingate. *The Landing at Cape Ann*. Boston: Gould & Lincoln, 1854.

Tragle, Henry Irving. *The Southampton Slave Revolt of 1831: A Compilation of Source Material*. Amherst, Mass.: University of Massachusetts Press, 1971.

———. "Styron and His Source." *Massachusetts Review* 11 (Winter 1970): 135–53.

"Truth & Nat Turner: An Exchange." *Nation,* 22 April 1968, pp. 543–47.

Van Doren, Mark, ed. *Correspondence of Aaron Burr and His Daughter Theodesia,* New York: Covici, Friede, 1929.

Vande Kieft, Ruth M. *Eudora Welty.* New Haven, Conn.: College and University Press, 1962.

Vickery, Olga W. *The Novels of William Faulkner: A Critical Interpretation.* Baton Rouge, La.: Louisiana State University Press, 1959.

Waggoner, Hyatt H. *William Faulkner: From Jefferson to the World.* Lexington, Ky.: University of Kentucky Press, 1959.

Warren, Robert Penn. *Brother to Dragons: A Tale in Verse and Voices.* New York: Random House, 1953.

———. *How Texas Won Her Freedom: The Story of Sam Houston & the Battle of San Jacinto.* San Jacinto Monument, Tex.: San Jacinto Museum of History, 1959.

———. "The Way It Was Written." *New York Times Book Review,* 23 August 1953, p. 6.

Welty, Eudora. *The Bride of the Innisfallen.* New York: Harcourt, Brace & Co., 1955.

———. *The Robber Bridegroom.* Garden City, N.Y.: Doubleday Doran & Co., 1942.

———. *Selected Stories of Eudora Welty.* New York: The Modern Library, 1954.

White, Elizabeth Wade. *Anne Bradstreet: "The Tenth Muse."* New York: Oxford University Press, 1971.

Wiebe, Dallas E. "Mr. Lowell and Mr. Edwards." *Wisconsin Studies in Contemporary Literature* 3 (Spring-Summer 1962): 21–31.

Williams, William Carlos. *The Autobiography of William Carlos Williams.* New York: Random House, 1951.

———. *The Great American Novel.* Paris: Contact Editions, 1923.

———. *In the American Grain.* New York: New Directions, 1956.

———. *Selected Essays of William Carlos Williams.* New York: Random House, 1954.

———. *The Selected Letters of William Carlos Williams.* Edited by John C. Thirlwall. New York: McDowell, Obolensky, 1957.

Woodward, C. Vann. *The Burden of Southern History*. Baton Rouge, La.: Louisiana State University Press, 1960.

———. "Confessions of a Rebel: 1831." *New Republic* 7 October 1967, pp. 25–28.

Wroth, Lawrence C. "Introduction" to *The Maryland Muse*. *Proceedings of the American Antiquarian Society*, n.s. 44 (April-October 1934): 267–308.

Yetman, Norman R., ed. *Voices from Slavery*. New York: Holt, Rinehart, & Winston, 1970.

Index